Image Processing for Automated Diagnosis of Cardiac Diseases

Image Processing for Automated Diagnosis of Cardiac Diseases

Edited by

Kalpana Chauhan

Department of Electrical Engineering, Central University of Haryana,
Mahendragarh, India

Rajeev Kumar Chauhan

Department of Electrical Engineering, Dayalbagh Educational Institute,
Agra, India

ACADEMIC PRESS
An imprint of Elsevier

ELSEVIER

Academic Press is an imprint of Elsevier
125 London Wall, London EC2Y 5AS, United Kingdom
525 B Street, Suite 1650, San Diego, CA 92101, United States
50 Hampshire Street, 5th Floor, Cambridge, MA 02139, United States
The Boulevard, Langford Lane, Kidlington, Oxford OX5 1GB, United Kingdom

Notices
Knowledge and best practice in this field are constantly changing. As new research and experience broaden our
understanding, changes in research methods, professional practices, or medical treatment may become
necessary.

Practitioners and researchers must always rely on their own experience and knowledge in evaluating and using
any information, methods, compounds, or experiments described herein. In using such information or methods
they should be mindful of their own safety and the safety of others, including parties for whom they have a
professional responsibility.

To the fullest extent of the law, neither the Publisher nor the authors, contributors, or editors, assume any liability
for any injury and/or damage to persons or property as a matter of products liability, negligence or otherwise, or
from any use or operation of any methods, products, instructions, or ideas contained in the material herein.

Library of Congress Cataloging-in-Publication Data
A catalog record for this book is available from the Library of Congress

British Library Cataloguing-in-Publication Data
A catalogue record for this book is available from the British Library

ISBN 978-0-323-85064-3

For information on all Academic Press publications
visit our website at https://www.elsevier.com/books-and-journals

Publisher: Mara Conner
Acquisitions Editor: Tim Pitts
Editorial Project Manager: Chiara Giglio
Production Project Manager: Sojan P. Pazhayattil
Cover Designer: Miles Hitchen

Typeset by SPi Global, India

Contents

Contributors

Megha Agarwal
Department of Electronics and Communication Engineering, Jaypee Institute of Information Technology, Noida, India

Rajeev Agrawal
Department of Electronics and Communication Engineering, G.L. Bajaj Institute of Technology and Management, Greater Noida, India

V. Ajantha Devi
AP3 Solutions, Chennai, Tamil Nadu, India

M.A. Ansari
Department of Electrical Engineering, Gautam Buddha University, Greater Noida, India

Arun Balodi
Department of Electronics and Communication Engineering, Atria Institute of Technology, Bangalore, India

Kalpana Chauhan
Department of Electrical Engineering, Central University of Haryana, Mahendragarh, India

Rajeev Kumar Chauhan
Department of Electrical Engineering, Dayalbagh Educational Institute, Agra, India

I. Lakshmi
Department of Computer Science, Stella Maris College, Chennai, India

Rajat Mehrotra
Department of Electrical Engineering, Gautam Buddha University, Greater Noida, India

Amol D. Rahulkar
Department of Electrical and Electronics Engineering, National Institute of Technology, Goa, India

Anju Saini
Department of Mathematics, Graphic Era University, Dehradun, India

Aswini K. Samantaray
Department of Electrical and Electronics Engineering, National Institute of Technology, Goa, India

Amit Singhal
Department of Electronics and Communication Engineering, Bennett University, Greater Noida, India

Pragati Tripathi
Department of Electrical Engineering, Gautam Buddha University, Greater Noida, India

T. Vani
Department of Computer Science, Rajeswari Vedachalam Government Arts College [Affiliated to University of Madras], Chengalpattu, Tamil Nadu, India

Preface

The field of medical image processing is expanding daily, as is its use in industrial and medical fields. There are many challenges and opportunities in image processing methods and ongoing research is examining how to use these methods to automatically diagnose diseases. This book examines the current and emerging technologies developed for the automated diagnosis of cardiac diseases. The concepts outlined in this book can be tested for research purposes and the new advances in algorithms can be applied in practical applications. Readers will learn some of the techniques useful for obtaining images of the heart. The book presents basic as well as advanced concepts of image processing techniques.

Chapter 1 discusses different heart diseases, including irregularities that influence the normal functioning of the heart valves, the heart's electrical system, and the muscles and coronary arteries of the heart. The focus of this chapter is heart valve diseases, especially those related to the mitral valve. In particular, the chapter examines the diagnosis, causes, and symptoms of mitral regurgitation (MR). It is shown that echocardiography is the superior imaging technique in this disease.

Chapter 2 deals with machine learning (ML) procedures in cardiovascular multimodal imaging. In particular, the chapter proposes convolution neural network (CNN) models for featuring the correspondences between multimodal information. These portrayals are additionally expected to visualize the cardiovascular life structures in more detail for better understanding and investigation. In addition, the chapter examines how quantitative investigation can benefit when these scholarly image portrayals are utilized in division, movement following, and multimodal image registration.

Chapter 3 depicts the cardiac anatomy in detail for better understanding and study. In addition to anatomical study, the chapter discusses how quantitative research can benefit from the use of trained image representations in segmentation, motion tracking, and multimodal image registration. A probabilistic edge-map representation is implemented to define anatomical correspondence in multimodal cardiac images and to demonstrate its use in spatial image alignment and anatomical localization. In addition, a novel image super-resolution system is implemented to improve cardiac cinema MR images.

Chapter 4 offers a brief description of the theoretical structures and their applications for segmental cardiac imaging, image enhancement, and multimodal image alignment. These analytical methods share common goals: time efficiency, quantitative objective evaluation, and enhancement and analysis of multimodal image data. In this survey, the authors concentrate on how the learning of image representation will accomplish these goals and improve the accuracy and robustness of the techniques applied.

Chapter 5 describes fuzzy-based despeckling methods for echocardiographic images. The authors propose and analyze hybrid fuzzy filters that integrate a non-local means (NLM) filter with three different types of fuzzy filters. The authors compare the proposed methods with fifteen despeckling filters on standard test images and echocardiographic images of the mitral valve in three views. The performance of one proposed hybrid fuzzy filter, HFF3, exhibited the best performance compared to the others in terms of edge preservation and denoising of speckle noise.

Chapter 6 examines machine learning-based medical diagnosis as a fast, non-invasive, timesaving, and accurate method. As this method is non-invasive, it is preferred over existing methods. The chapter explains the concept of machine learning and its significance in the medical diagnosis of cardiac diseases.

Chapter 7 examines the use of various wavelet transforms in content-based image retrieval for diagnosis of cardiac diseases. It discusses wavelet properties and analyzes retrieval performance of various orthogonal, bi-orthogonal, and Gabor wavelet transforms. The authors evaluate the different wavelet transforms using several cardiac image databases, namely, NEMA, OASIS, and EXACT09, in terms of average retrieval precision (ARP) and average retrieval rate (ARR).

Chapter 8 illustrates broadly constructed computer-aided approaches for evaluating ECG signals. Artificial intelligence techniques give precise and mechanical classifications of heartbeats to identify arrhythmias or unexpected changes in cardiac morphology. These techniques are also used for automatic syndrome analysis, monitoring, and stratification by managing extended ECG recordings for which diagram and physical investigations can be monotonous and time consuming. AI is flexible and can be practically utilized in wearable ECG devices, assuring competent and dependable monitoring of the heart in both clinical and residential settings. The chapter also examines 3D computer simulations as influential apparatuses for understanding ECG results.

Chapter 9 proposes a new regularization model for detecting ECG image boundaries. The method helps the curve to approach the desired boundaries while maintaining smoothness for better visualization. The authors use region-based segmentation along with speckle density as the data fitting energy to determine intensity information in local regions. The proposed improved regularization and fitting-based segmentation (IRFS) technique with a new regularization model and fitting function successfully achieved the right minima and region along with improved capability of the curve to draw the desired boundaries.

Chapter 10 considers a publicly available dataset of cine-MRI (magnetic resonance imaging) images to detect heart failure cases with (or without) infarction. Local texture-based patterns are used to extract relevant information from the image. The chapter examines four different types of pattern-based features: local binary pattern (LBP), local ternary pattern (LTP), difference of Gaussian LTP (DoGLTP), and ternary co-occurrence pattern (LTCoP). Various machine learning classifiers are employed to differentiate between normal heart images and heart failure images. Performance metrics are computed for these classification strategies and a detailed comparison is provided to highlight the most accurate method for automated identification of heart failure.

Chapter 11 is about the fusion method adopted in the diagnosis of cardiac diseases. The advancements in medical image fusion research outlined in this chapter demonstrate the importance of fusion in improving cardiac diagnosis, monitoring, and visualization. The algorithms used for cardiac image fusion methods can improve image quality and can be used in different applications. The prominent approaches tested on cardiac images include discrete wavelets transform (DWT), principle component analysis (PCA), and maximum model. The performance of the methods shows that the combination of one or more methods of image fusion is effective in cardiac image analysis.

Acknowledgment

Thanks to our supporter during the editing of this book. Editing a book is harder than we thought and more rewarding than we could have ever imagined. This would have not been possible without the adjustment made by our son Shaurya Chauhan. He has cooperated a lot and gives his continuous emotional support during this journey.

We are eternally grateful to our parents, who taught us discipline, love, manners, respect, and so much more that have helped us to succeed in life. They ever encouraged us to work hard. We would like to thank all our family members and friends for their direct and indirect support. Thanks to the doctors and hospitals that have provided real images and data for the research. Thank you to all the contributors who have added their research in the form of chapters in this book.

Thanks to everyone in our publishing team.

Cardiac diseases and their diagnosis methods

1

Kalpana Chauhan[a] and Rajeev Kumar Chauhan[b]

Department of Electrical Engineering, Central University of Haryana, Mahendragarh, India[a]
Department of Electrical Engineering, Dayalbagh Educational Institute, Agra, India[b]

Chapter outline

Image Processing for Automated Diagnosis of Cardiac Diseases. https://doi.org/10.1016/B978-0-323-85064-3.00011-X

1.1 **Introduction**

The heart is a muscular structure and a central component of the vertebrate cardiovascular system. The heart functions in a closed loop manner, that is, oxygenated blood is pumped from the lungs to the whole body and deoxygenated blood is pumped back from the lungs to the body. The transfer of blood from heart to the body is carried out by the arteries and arterioles, while the returning of the blood is done through the venules and veins. Blood transport is vital to bring oxygen and nutrients to the body's tissues as well as to remove carbon dioxide and waste products/chemicals [1].

The human heart is located between the lungs. Because of slight tilting of its apex on the left side of the chest, heart rhythm or beating occurs in this location causing an illusion that the heart is located on that side. The size of a human heart is that of a tightly closed fist. It beats about 100,000 times in a day.

Although the heart pumps blood, delivering oxygen to the entire body's muscles and organs for them to function, it also needs its own oxygen-enriched blood to work properly. The heart functions as a large muscular pump with arteries, veins, and valves, and an electrical system. The electrical system triggers pulse, thereby stimulating the heart to beat. The heart muscles then squeeze the blood to push the oxygenated blood throughout the entire body in one large arterial circuital system and the deoxygenated blood through the pulmonary arteries to the lungs. The two, one-way valves create separation between the four different chambers, namely, the left ventricle (LV) and left atrium (LA), and right ventricle (RV) and right atrium (RA), for forming the dual pumps of the heart adjusting both rate and flow of the oxygenated and deoxygenated blood throughout each cardiac cycle or heartbeat. The more activity a person performs, the more the heart muscles must work to supply the necessary quantity of blood to the muscles to be utilized during the activity.

Mitral regurgitation (MR) is a mitral valve insufficiency that causes a change in the size and/or shape of the LV, affecting its functioning and resulting from ischemic heart disease [2, 3]. MR leads to myocardial infarction (MI) in about 20% of cases [4, 5]. The severity of MR increases around 30% in patients suffering from coronary artery disease (CAD) with ischemic LV dysfunction [6].

There are many approaches available to diagnose MR that are helpful in determining severity grade and dysfunction [7–13]. Diagnostic methods include assessment of regurgitation volume, orifice size, orifice, and regurgitant orifice with the help of echocardiography or catheterization. In addition, two-dimensional (2D) contrast echocardiography and Doppler echocardiography are efficient ways for assessing MR. We discuss the advantages of these techniques later in the chapter [14–20].

To begin, this chapter discusses different heart conditions by categorizing heart valves and their related diseases, with a special focus on MR. It also presents various diagnostic methods and the qualitative and quantitative parameters useful in grading MR severity. Finally, the chapter ends with a discussion of different modes and techniques of echocardiography.

1.2 **Heart valves**

The two atrioventricular (AV), one-way valves are thin structures, having connective tissues and endocardia. These valves, namely, the bicuspid/mitral and the tricuspid AV valves are located between the LA and the LV, and the RA and RV, respectively. The two semilunar, one-way valves are made up of three flaps, each composed of connective tissues and endocardium as well as fibers to prevent the valves from flapping inside out. Their shapes are like a half moon and thus they are called the semilunar

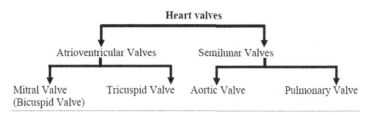

FIG. 1.1

Classification of heart valves.

(SL) aortic valve and SL pulmonary valve. These valves are located between the left ventricle and aorta and between the RV and the start of pulmonary artery. Fig. 1.1 shows these valves. The heart's one-way blood flow is maintained with the help of four heart valves, each one having a specific position on the exits of the four chambers. These four heart valves allow only the one-way flow of blood in the forward directions and restrict the backward flow of blood. Sequence of blood flow is from the atria (right and left) into the ventricles (right and left) through the open tricuspid and mitral valves, respectively, as shown in Fig. 1.1. According to pressure change in the chambers, there is an opening or closing of AV valves. They close during the ventricular systole (contraction) when the ventricle pressure increases the pressure in the two atria. This action keeps the valves snapped shut and prevents backward flow of blood. The contraction of the ventricles leads to forced opening of the pulmonary and aortic valves to pump the blood from the right and left ventricles into the pulmonary artery (through open valves) towards the lungs, and through the aortic valve to the aorta and the body. At the end of contraction, the ventricles begin to relax and the aortic and pulmonic valves remain closed during the diastole. Backward flow of blood into the ventricles is prevented by these valves. This pattern repeats again and again, causing continuous blood flow from the heart to the lungs and the body.

1.3 Mitral valve regurgitation

To visualize the mitral valve (MV), clinicians must choose a technique that enhances the image according to their visual perception and that works in accordance with the kind of image [21]. Log transformation does not give satisfactory results (subjective assessment) in the contrast enhancement of echocardiographic images due to high white pixel spreading. This white spreading overlaps the important features. The reason for this problem is that more pixels will shift in the high-intensity value when the log transformation is applied. To overcome this problem, the figure of 1 in Eq. (1.1) of log transformation is replaced by a variable, say, a. This offers a flexible way to analyze the image at different values of a. This value can be changed by clinicians in accordance with their visual perceptions for better visualization of the image. The normal MV opens when the LV relaxes (diastole) to allow blood flow from the LA and to fill the LV (decompressed).

During systole or contraction of the LV, the pressure in the LV increases. This increased pressure leads to closure of the MV and restricts blood flow from leaking into the LA. At this time, the blood flows to the aorta (passing the aortic valve) and the body. The annulus, leaflets, and subvalvular apparatuses work in a complex manner for the proper functioning of the valve. The mitral leaflet tissues

Table 1.1 The layers of valve tissues: fibrosa, spongiosa, and atrialis/ventricularis [22].

Layer	Location	Composition	Function
Fibrosa	Faces the LV	High concentration of collagen, thickest layer	Bears most of the load during coaptation
Spongiosa	Middle layer	High concentration of glycosaminoglycans (GAGs) and proteoglycans (PGs)	Provides shear between outer support layers and diffuses gasses and nutrients
Atrialis (Ventricularis for semilunar valves)	Faces the LA	High concentration of collagen and elastin thinnest layer	Elastin allows for strain when the valve is open

are organized in three layers: fibrosa, spongiosa, and ventricularis. Table 1.1 [23, 24] describes the location, composition, and functions of these layers.

1.4 Heart diseases

Heart diseases are abnormalities that affect the valves, functions, electrical system, muscles, and arteries of the heart. Some common heart diseases include:

- Coronary artery disease (CAD)
- Myocardial infarction (MI)—a severe type of heart disease
- High blood pressure or hypertension (HBP)
- Heart valve disease
- Cardiomyopathy or heart muscle disease
- Pericarditis
- Rheumatic heart disease (RHD)

1.4.1 Coronary artery disease (CAD)

CAD is a disease in which a deposit called plaque grows on the inside wells of the coronary arteries and restricts the normal oxygenated blood supply to heart muscles. It is almost often due to the progressive buildup of cholesterol and other fatty materials, known as atherosclerotic plaque or atheroma, in the walls of the coronary arteries. This process is known as atherosclerosis and can affect many arteries, not just those of the heart. As an atheroma develops, it may gush into the artery, narrowing the artery's interior (lumen) and partially blocking blood flow. Calcium accumulates inside the atheroma over time. The supply of oxygen-rich blood to the heart muscle (myocardium) becomes inadequate when an atheroma blocks more and more of a coronary artery. To encourage good health, it is recommended to reduce dietary fat intake to no more than 25–35% of daily calories. However, some doctors believe that to minimize the risk of coronary heart disease, fat must be reduced to 10% of daily calories. Another way to mitigate risk factors for CAD is to consume a low-fat diet that also tends to lower elevated total and LDL (bad) cholesterol levels.

1.4.2 **Myocardial infraction (MI)**

In severe CAD disease, the plaque deposit suddenly blocks normal flow of blood and heat to heart muscles such that they cannot get enough oxygen and thus begin to die. An MI causes permanent damage to the heart muscle due to oxygen shortage. An MI may result in impairment of diastolic and systolic function and can render the patient vulnerable to arrhythmias. An MI may also cause a variety of serious complications.

1.4.3 **High blood pressure or hypertension (HBP)**

HBP is the condition when the force of the blood flowing through blood vessels is continuously very high. There are many causes of HBP, including heart disease, smoking, stress, lack of physical activity, and so on.

1.4.4 **Heart valve disease**

Improper functioning of valves creates valve diseases. Stenosis is the restriction of blood flow due to narrowing of a valve. MR due to incomplete closing of the MV is the main type of heart valve disease.

1.4.5 **Cardiomyopathy or heart muscle disease**

Cardiomyopathy is a type of progressive disease in which there is an abnormal enlargement, thickening, and stiffing of the heart. Due to these abnormalities, the heart muscles are not able to pump blood properly.

1.4.6 **Pericarditis**

Pericarditis is a condition in which the pericardium becomes inflamed. Pericarditis is typically acute, meaning it occurs out of nowhere and can last for months. The disorder normally goes away after three months, but attacks can last for years.

1.4.7 **Rheumatic heart disease (RHD)**

RHD is a chronic heart disease that may arise due to rheumatic fever, which is a streptococcal (strep or throat) infection. Fig. 1.10 shows the RHD condition.

1.5 **Mitral valve diseases**

MV diseases broadly can be of three types: (1) Mitral stenosis: when the orifice of the MV narrows and restricts normal diastolic blood flow from the LA into the LV; (2) Mitral regurgitation (MR): backward blood flow into the LA during systole that may be acute or chronic; and (3) Mitral valve prolapse: posterior displacement or bending of the anterior, posterior, or both MV leaflets towards the left atrium. MR is the focus of this chapter as it is the second most common valvular lesion after aortic stenosis (AS). Study of MR is understood to cover all the other MV diseases.

1.5.1 Mitral regurgitation (MR)

MR or mitral insufficiency is the most common valve disorder. When the heart is affected by MR, there is leakage of backward blood flow through the MV during the contraction and a reduction in the amount of blood supplied to the body.

If MR does not progress, then the amount of MR is small and the backward leakage has no significant consequence. However, if there is significant MR, then the LV must work harder to fulfill the oxygenated blood demand of the body. To meet this increased demand, the heart muscles (i.e., myocardium) have to do more work and this creates a sequence of changes in the blood circulation system. These types of changes take a long period of time, sometimes several years or decades, and depend upon the severity of the regurgitation. The causes of MR also determine how quickly the heart begins to fail, that is, they give the information of failure in terms of weakening of heart apparatus. Weak heart apparatuses are the sources of a sudden heart attack.

1.5.2 Causes of mitral regurgitation

MR may increase from mild to moderate to severe due to various cardiac diseases or other heart valve abnormalities. Some of these include:

- *Mitral valve prolapse*: Due to deformation and elongation of valve leaflets, the normal coaptation of the leaflets is restricted. This is known as mitral valve prolapse. Due to this abnormality in valve motion, the direction of blood flow is partially reversed. The blood leaks backward from the LV to the LA. Mitral prolapse may range from mild to severe.
- *Infective endocarditis*: Sometimes heart valves are infected by bacteria, fungus, or some other organisms that affect the blood stream. This is known as infective endocarditis (IE). The organisms stick to the valves causing an abnormal structure, known as vegetation, to grow. This vegetation thickens the valve and changes its direction, thus restricting leaflets from joining during the valve's closing operation. Endocarditis develops faster on previously abnormal heart valves than on normal heart valves.
- *Rheumatic fever*: Rheumatic fever occurs due to throat infection. If this infection is not treated, it can cause inflammation of the heart valves and other valvular complications. Rheumatic fever is common in developing countries.
- *Congenital heart abnormality*: MR may also occur in patients born with abnormalities of the heart.
- *Other types of heart disease*: Heart attacks and muscle injuries and abnormalities may also lead to MR.
- *Trauma*: When the valve chords are broken, there is a sudden displacement of the leaflets and thus leaflets are not able to withstand their normal position. These flailed leaflets are not able to join, allowing severe valvular leakage.

1.5.3 Mitral regurgitation signs and symptoms

In cases of mild and moderate regurgitation, patients may never show symptoms or serious complications. Even patients with severe MR may show no signs and symptoms, although symptoms may occur if the LV becomes abnormal or if atrial fibrillation or pulmonary hypertension occurs. Pulmonary hypertension occurs when blood pressure increases in the pulmonary artery. This makes it harder on the right side of the heart to supply adequate oxygenated blood to the body.

If the LV is severely enlarged, there is risk of serious heart disease and even heart failure. These patients typically show signs of weakness, shortness of during work, and collection of fluid in the lower legs and abdomens leading to swelling in the feet.

1.5.4 Mitral regurgitation diagnosis

MR may be diagnosed by using a stethoscope to listen for a heart murmur. The change in heart sound is due to backflow of blood through the MV. There may be other reasons for a heart murmur as well. Other recommended tests for MR diagnosis include:

- Chest X-ray: A chest X-ray shows a picture of the large heart vessels to determine size and shape. It is also helpful in diagnosing lung infections or the accumulation of fluid in the lungs. If X-ray shows enlargement of the heart, this may indicate severe MR.
- Electrocardiogram (ECG): An ECG is a one-dimensional signal that shows the electrical activity of a heartbeat. An ECG may be helpful in detecting disturbed rhythms related to causes of MR like CAD. Disturbed rhythms can also be related to other abnormalities of the heart.
- Echocardiogram: An echocardiogram is a direct picture of the heart. High-frequency ultrasound waves are used take a picture of the heart's chambers and determine their size and shape. The test can capture movement of the heart valves as well as the thickness, size, and motion of the heart wall. The test is helpful for determining the volume of blood pumped by the heart per minute, also called cardiac output. Echocardiography can also detect the pressure in different chambers and major blood vessels of the heart. Most often, echocardiography is done by applying the transducer from the outside (i.e., transthoracic echocardiogram (TTE)), whereas some cases require insertion of the transducer (i.e., transesophageal echocardiogram (TEE)).

Echocardiography and color Doppler echocardiography have their own utility in the evaluation of MR severity, however, they each exhibit their own advantages/disadvantages and limitations. Quantitative parameters help clinicians to group MR into categories of mild, moderate, and severe. Doppler echocardiography is a method used to confirm MR. M-mode or 2D echocardiography is not able to determine the specific signs of MR. Continuous echocardiographic examination allows the visualization of MR progression. Changes can be seen by taking echocardiograms at different time intervals. Volume overloading in the LA or in the LV is the initial echocardiographic feature of MR. Volume overloading occurs due to the stroke volume transfer between the two chambers. However, the thickness of the wall is normal (because the wall mass increases at the time of enlargement). If the end-diastolic dimension becomes greater than 5.5 cm, and a noticeable hyperdynamic wall motion is seen on the interventricular septum, then LV volume overload is easily recognized.

1.6 Cardiac disease diagnosis methods

There are various noninvasive and invasive methods to diagnose the various cardiac diseases. Each method has advantages and limitations. Fig. 1.2 shows the classification of the different methods.

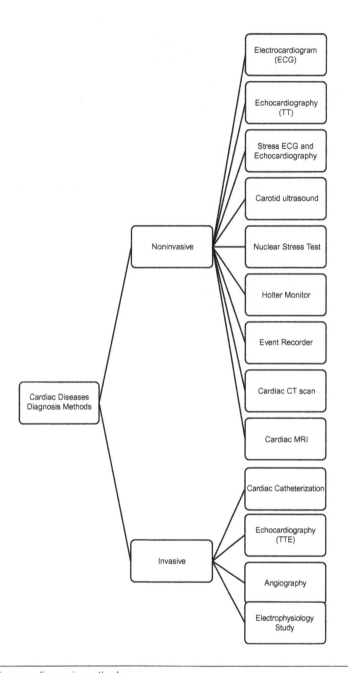

FIG. 1.2

Different cardiac diseases diagnosis methods.

Echocardiography detects the size of the cardiac chamber, wall motion, wall thickness, valve motion, and anatomy of valves, proximal great vessels, and pericardium. It presents a live picture of cardiac functionality and anatomy. Echocardiography is a sensitive tool for determining volume of pleural and pericardial fluid, to identify mass lesions that may be inside or near the heart. This modality is effective for diagnosing congenital heart diseases as well as myocardial or valvular pathology. It is a safe procedure because TTE is done without the insertion of chemicals, which may damage the myocardium.

1.6.1 Principles of echo

Ultrasound has high-frequency (>20,000 Hz), pulsed sound waves. When ultrasound waves enter the tissues, they transmit through them and are reflected back based on acoustic impedance of the tissues. The density of the tissue times the velocity at which sound waves travel through the tissues is the acoustic impedance. Ultrasound reflection depends upon the mismatching of the impedances between the two tissues. The greater the difference, the greater the reflection. Bones have high acoustic impedance, whereas air has low acoustic impedance. Therefore, bone-tissue and air-tissue interfaces exhibit great mismatch of acoustic impedance, resulting in high reflection of ultrasound waves. As such, imaging of deeper structures is restricted when the ultrasound beam inter*sec*ts the air-filled and bony structure because they reflect the beam to image their outer structure. Therefore, some suitable places have been selected to take the image of the heart. For echocardiography, intercostal spaces within the cardiac windows (where the heart is against the thorax, without intervening lungs) or from subcostal windows (depending upon the species) are ideal for imaging the heart.

The speed of an ultrasound wave varies depending upon the tissue type through which it is propagating. The speed of an ultrasound beam is approximately 1540 m/sec through soft tissues. Based on the relation with the transducer's parameters, the size, thickness, and location of the soft tissues can be calculated at any point and at any instant. The reflection, refraction, and transmission rules of the ultrasound wave are the laws of geometric optics. Reflection, refraction, and absorption of the ultrasound waves depend upon the difference of acoustic impendences at the interfaces. As the ultrasound beam is distanced from the transducer, its intensity decreases because of the scatter, divergence, absorption, and reflection of energy of the wave at the interface of the tissues. When the ultrasound beam is perpendicular to the image structures, it forms the greatest reflection to create a strong echo. The transducer receives these reflected echoes and creates an image on the ultrasound machine. The transducer acts as a receiver about 99% of the time. The images formed by the transducer can be displayed on a monitor, recorded for future use, or printed on paper. Optical CDs can be recorded to form a data bank.

1.6.2 Modes of echocardiography

Echocardiography can be classified into three modes: M-mode, two-dimensional (2D, B-mode, or real time), and Doppler. One type of echocardiographic examination creates a complementary finding from the other modes. Therefore, the different modes are performed simultaneously.

1.6.2.1 M-mode echocardiography
A high sampling rate is used in M-mode echocardiography. High-clarity images are obtained from an M-mode echocardiogram, allowing for accurate measurement of cardiac dimensions and evaluation of cardiac motion. It is difficult to place the M-mode beam at the exact location in the heart and therefore it is difficult to obtain clear echoes and carry out critical measurements. It is also difficult to obtain meaningful results from the calculations performed on the obtained measurements. The right parasternal position permits the standard view of M-mode. To avoid the disturbance generated by the papillary muscles in the LV's free wall, the M-mode cursor should be positioned within the heart (the right parasternal short-axis view). The MV, LV wall (at the level of the chordae tendineae), and aortic root (aorta/left atrial appendage) views are included through the standard M-mode view. A linear sweep is added to show motion patterns, as shown in Fig. 1.3.

1.6.2.2 Two-dimensional echocardiography
A real-time image of both depth and width of a plane of tissues is obtained in 2D echocardiography. It is possible to take unlimited number of imaging planes; however, there are some standard views, which are helpful in the evaluation of the extracardiac and intracardiac structures.

More information about the shape and size of the heart is obtained in 2D echocardiography than in M-mode. 2D echocardiography also gives the spatial relationships of the heart's structures during the cardiac cycle. Both M-mode and 2D recordings are done simultaneously for obtaining more

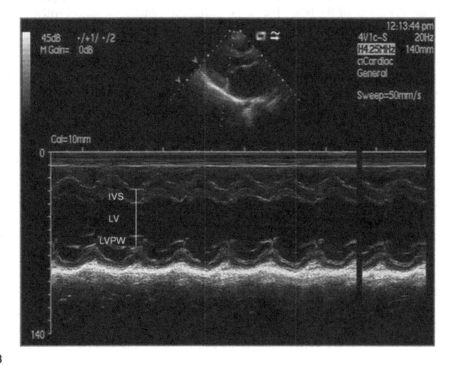

FIG. 1.3

Example of M-mode display of MV.

information about cardiac anatomy and clinical values. This makes echocardiography a major diagnostic tool. Fig. 1.4 shows an image obtained with the help of 2D echocardiography.

1.6.2.3 Doppler echocardiography

Blood flow patterns, velocity, and direction are obtained using Doppler imaging. Color Doppler works based on detecting change of frequency of reflected ultrasound waves. The phenomenon is referred to as Doppler shift. This change in frequency occurs as the ultrasound waves reflect off the moving blood cells, which are either moving towards the transducer or away from the transducer. In this way, color Doppler helps to document and quantify insufficiency of the MV, also referred to as MR. An accurate measurement of blood flow velocity is possible if the direction of blood flow is precisely parallel to the direction of the ultrasound beam. The results become increasingly inaccurate as the angle θ, shown in Fig. 1.5, deviates from the zero angle between the blood flow direction and the beam direction. Eq. (1.1) describes the relationship that determines blood flow velocity.

$$F_d = \frac{2f_o}{c} V \cos \theta \tag{1.1}$$

where F_d is the Doppler frequency, f_o is the original frequency, V is the blood flow velocity, c is the light velocity, and θ is the angle of the transducer.

Clinically, two types of Doppler echocardiography are employed in general: pulsed wave (PW) Doppler, as shown in Fig. 1.6, and continuous wave (CW) Doppler, as shown in Fig. 1.7.

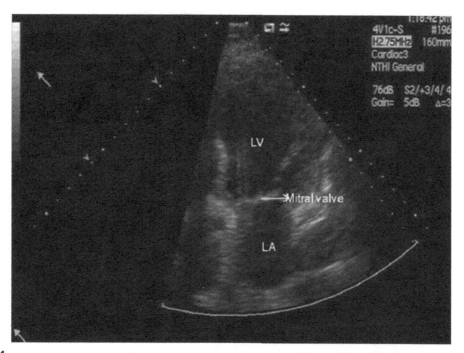

FIG. 1.4

Apical 4-chamber view of MV taken with 2D echocardiography.

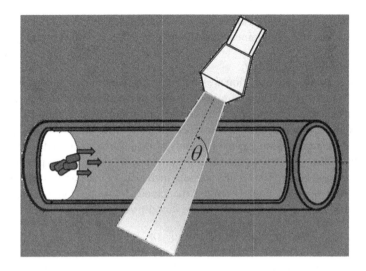

FIG. 1.5

The Doppler phenomenon.

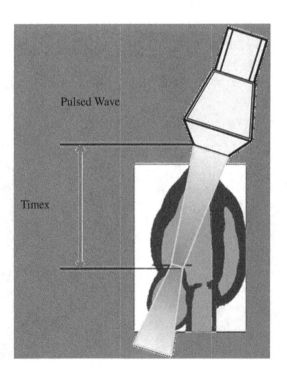

FIG. 1.6

Example of a PW Doppler.

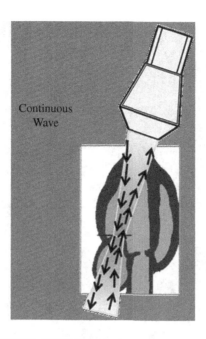

FIG. 1.7

Example of CW Doppler.

In PW Doppler, the ultrasound beam is transmitted as short bursts to a point (fixed as the "sample volume") on a distance from the transducer. The advantage of this type of Doppler is that it is easy to calculate the spectral characteristics, blood flow velocity, and direction from a specified point in the heart or blood vessel. The measured maximum velocity is limited because of the limited pulse repetition frequency and is a major disadvantage. The transducer used in PW Doppler systems alternate transmission and reception of ultrasound, as in the M-mode transducer (Fig. 1.7). One of the advantages of PW Doppler is that it can provide Doppler shift data selectively along the ultrasound beam from a small segment, also known as "sample volume."

Dual crystals are used in CW Doppler to simultaneously and continuously send and receive ultrasound waves. The flow with high velocity can also be measured with CW because there is no maximum measurable velocity (Nyquist limit). In CW Doppler, the velocity and direction of sampled blood flow is in the spread form, not in the specific area, which is a disadvantage of this modality. As its name suggests, continuous ultrasound waves are generated with continuous ultrasound reception. Fig. 1.7 shows two crystal transducers, one crystal for each function, and the dual-function accomplishment.

Color flow Doppler echocardiography is a combination of M-mode and 2D modalities with the imaging of blood flow and is a form of PW Doppler. Multiple scans can be carried out for taking multiple samples along the scan line with this technique. Color coding is assigned to the mean frequency shift that is obtained from different velocity and directions of many sample volumes. There are several types of mapping available for this purpose. The BART (blue away and red towards) system is most commonly used. The presence of multiple velocities and differences in relative flow velocity can be obtained. Different maps that depend on color and brightness are used to indicate multiple velocities.

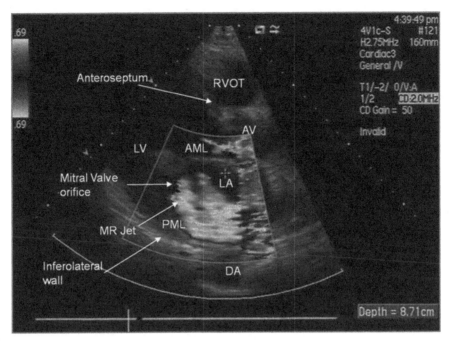

FIG. 1.8

Example of color Doppler imaging in systolic parasternal long-axis view MR.

Fig. 1.8 shows a 2D image of blood flow into the LA at the time of systole during MR [25–31]. The colors (red and blue) represent the direction of a given color jet and the different velocities, which can be represented by hues from dull to bright. A turbulent jet shows the mosaic pattern of many colors. A 2D display of flow is shown according to size, direction, and velocity.

Meaning of color There is useful information in the flow map of an image. The color red is assigned to the flow toward the transducers and the color blue is assigned to the flow away from the transducers.

1.6.3 Two-dimensional recording techniques

Techniques for both M-mode echocardiography and 2D echocardiography are similar. In 2D echocardiography a stationary ultrasound beam is used as a flashlight. It illuminates only a small area of the heart at a time. A 2D transducer is like a circular saw, which is rotated on the chest at the time of rest. It is rotated around the point using the index mark printed on the transducer. The index mark on the transducer represents the right-hand side of the machine display. A more complex maneuver is necessary during 2D examination so that an aligned scan plane is achieved with the desired anatomic axis of the heart.

In 2D echocardiography transducer manipulation, the scan plane pivots about the transducer axis when *rotating* the transducer. For example, there will be a change from the parasternal long axis to the parasternal short axis if there is a rotation through 90 degrees. *Tilting* of the transducer form a series of radial planes. The axis of the transducer is moved in the plane of the scan when *Anglin*. One example is to bring an object to the center of the field of view at an edge. Fig. 1.9 shows the location of the planes to access the heart.

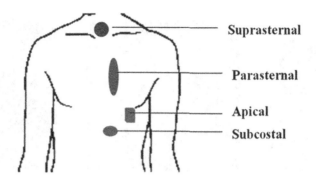

FIG. 1.9

Planes for accessing the heart to perform echocardiography.

1.6.4 Advantages and limitations of echocardiography

1.6.4.1 Advantages

- portable
- does not restrict clinician, nurse, or testing equipment access to sick patients
- can be performed in the upright position in severely orthopnoeic patients
- noninvasive, safe, and suitable for follow-up investigations
- relatively cheap
- widely available

1.6.4.2 Limitations

- Image quality is dependent on operator skill and patient anatomy and position, generally best in the left lateral position. It may be severely impaired by air between the chest wall and heart (e.g., hyperinflated lungs in obstructive airways disease, patients on mechanical ventilation, those with pneumothorax or who are supine or in the right lateral position, etc.). Narrow rib spaces and obesity may also cause technical difficulty.
- Information is often qualitative rather than quantitative. Significant intra- and inter-observer variation is observed when images are suboptimal.
- Left atrial appendage, and in adults, superior vena cava and majority of aorta and pulmonary arteries above valve/root level, cannot be imaged.
- Image quality is generally inferior to transesophageal echo.
- Offers limited capacity for differentiation between different types of tissues and fluids.

1.7 Results and analysis

Fig. 1.10 shows nine cases of MR imaged with color Doppler echocardiography. The images are taken at different views of the heart. The mosaic pattern of color shows the regurgitation.

    In the next section, we present an analysis of MR findings based on regurgitant area and vena contracta width.

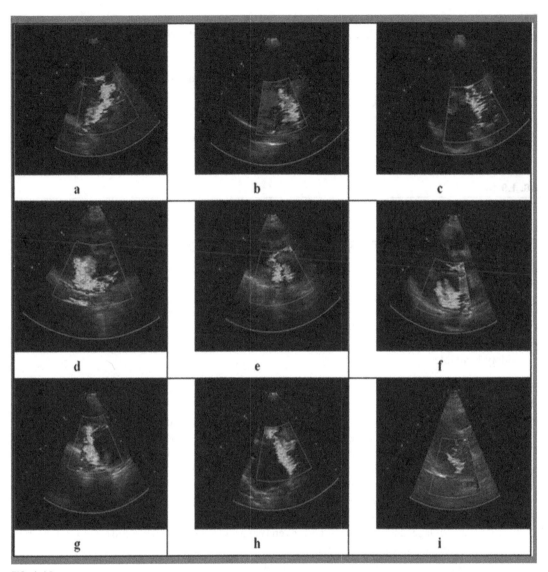

FIG. 1.10

Images from MR-affected patients taken with color Doppler echocardiography [25].

1.8 Discussion

Table 1.2 shows grades of MR severity obtained from imaging both regurgitant area and vena contracta width. Severe MR is defined as jet area greater or equal to $10\,cm^2$. In moderate MR, vena contracta width should be greater than $0.5\,cm$ when jet area is in the range of 3 to less than 10. Vena contracta

Table 1.2 Severity grade analysis of MR [25, 26].

Images	Jet area drawn by clinician (cm^2)	Vena contracta width (cm)	MR severity grade
1	15.39	0.58	Severe
2	10.86	0.61	Severe
3	9.38	0.46	Moderate
4	13.23	0.56	Severe
5	9.72	0.46	Moderate
6	12.94	0.56	Severe
7	11.29	0.54	Severe
8	11.86	0.54	Severe
9	5.59	0.39	Moderate

width of 0.3 cm to less than 0.5 cm represents moderate MR. Values less than moderate conditions indicate mild MR, which is not represented here.

1.9 Conclusions

This chapter discussed various types of heart disease, with a focus on MR. It presented the symptoms and causes of MR as well as diagnostic methods for this condition. Echocardiography was shown to be superior to other modalities, although it does suffer from some limitations.

References

[1] S.S. Mader, The Cardiovascular System in Understanding Human Anatomy and Physiology, fifth ed., The McGraw-Hill Companies, 2004, p. 227 (Ch. 12).

[2] C.L. Reid, D.T. Kawanishi, C.R. McKay, U. Elkayam, S. Rahimtoola, P.A. Chandraratna, Accuracy of evaluation of the presence and severity of aortic andmitral regurgitation by contrast 2-dimensional echocardiography, Am. J. Cardiol. 52 (5) (1983) 519–524.

[3] M.E. Goldman, V. Fuster, T. Guarino, B.P. Mindich, Intraoperative echocardiography for the evaluation of valvular regurgitation: experience in 263patients, Circulation 74 (1986) 1–143.

[4] M.M. Guerreiro, C. Abreu-Lima, M.R. Gomes, Value of intraoperative 2-dimensional contrast echocardiography (2-DCE) for assessing the presence and severity of mitral regurgitation, in: Proceedings 1st International Symposium on Echocardiography and Doppler in Cardiac Surgery, 1988, p. 69.

[5] M.M. Guerreiro, F.J. Sepulveda, M.R. Gomes, Usefulness of intraoperative epicardial 2 dimensional echocardiography in surgical decision, Int. J. Cardiac Imag. 4 (1) (1989) 71.

[6] S. Zhang, J.P. Marques de Sa, C. Abreu-Lima, M. Guerreiro, Mitral regurgitation assessment by automated analysis of intracavitary contrast 2-D echocardiograms, in: Proceedings Computers in Cardiology, 1990, pp. 671–674, https://doi.org/10.1109/CIC.1990.144309.

[7] K.S. Dujardin, M. Enriquez-Sarano, K.R. Bailey, R.A. Nishimura, J.B. Seward, A.J. Tajik, Grading of mitral regurgitation by quantitative Doppler echocardiography: calibration by left ventricular angiography in routine clinical practice, Circulation 96 (1997) 3409–3415.

[8] M. Honey, J.H. Gough, S. Katsaros, G.A. Miller, V. Thuraisingham, Left ventricular cine-angio-cardiography in the assessment of mitral regurgitation, Br. Heart J. 31 (1969) 596–602.

[9] S. Blumlein, A. Bouchard, N.B. Schiller, M. Dae, B.F. Byrd III, T. Ports, E.H. Botvinick, Quantitation of mitral regurgitation by Doppler echocardiography, Circulation 74 (2) (1986) 306–314.

[10] F. Recusani, G.S. Bargiggia, A.P. Yoganathan, A. Raisaro, L.M. Valdes-Cruz, H.W. Sung, C. Bertucci, M. Gallati, V.A. Moises, I.A. Simpson, A new method for quantification of regurgitant flow rate using color Doppler flow imaging of the flow convergence region proximal to a discrete orifice, Circulation 83 (2) (1991) 594–604.

[11] G.S. Bargiggia, L. Tronconi, D.J. Sahn, F. Recusani, A. Raisaro, S. De Servi, L.M. Valdes-Cruz, C. Montemartini, A new method for quantitation of mitral regurgitation based on color flow Doppler imaging of flow convergence proximal to regurgitant orifice, Circulation 84 (4) (1991) 1481–1489.

[12] N. Fujita, A.F. Chazouilleres, J.J. Hartiala, M.O. Sullivan, P. Heidenreich, J.D. Kaplan, H. Sakuma, E. Foster, G.R. Caputo, C.B. Higgins, Quantification of mitral regurgitation by velocity-encoded cine nuclear magnetic resonance imaging, J. Am. College Cardiol. 23 (4) (1994) 951–958.

[13] M. Enriquez-Sarano, J.B. Seward, K.R. Bailey, A.J. Tajik, Effective regurgitant orifice area: a noninvasive Doppler development of an old hemodynamic concept, J. Am. College Cardiol. 23 (2) (1994) 443–451.

[14] F. Grigioni, M. Enriquez-Sarano, K.J. Zehr, K.L. Bailey, A.J. Tajik, Ischemic mitral regurgitation. Long-term outcome and prognostic implications with quantitative Doppler assessment, Circulation 103 (13) (2001) 1759–1764.

[15] S.F. Yiu, M. Enriquez-Sarano, C. Tribouilloy, J.B. Seward, A.J. Tajik, Determinants of the degree of functional mitral regurgitation in patients with systolic left ventricular dysfunction: a quantitative clinical study, Circulation 102 (12) (2000) 1400–1406.

[16] G.A. Lamas, G.F. Mitchell, G.C. Flaker, S.C. Smith Jr., B.J. Gersh, L. Basta, L. Moyé, E. Braunwald, M.A. Pfeffer, Clinical significance of mitral regurgitation after acute myocardial infarction, Circulation 96 (3) (1997) 827–833.

[17] T. Kumanohoso, Y. Otsuji, S. Yoshifuku, Mechanism of higher incidence of ischemic mitral regurgitation in patient with myocardial infarction: quantitative analysis of left ventricular and valve geometry in 103 patients with prior myocardial infarction, J. Thoracic Cardiovasc. Surg. 125 (1) (2003) 135–143.

[18] B.H. Trichon, G.M. Felker, L.K. Shaw, C.H. Cabell, C.M. O'Connor, Relation of frequency and severity of mitral regurgitation to survival among patients with left ventricular systolic dysfunction and heart failure, Am. J. Cardiol. 91 (5) (2003) 538–543.

[19] D.S. Bach, S.F. Bolling, Improvement following correction of secondary mitral regurgitation in end-stage cardiomyopathy with mitral annuloplasty, Am. J. Cardiol. 91 (5) (1996) 66–69.

[20] F.A. Tibayan, F. Rodriguez, F. Langer, D. Liang, G.T. Daughters, N.B. Ingels Jr., D. Craig Miller, Undersized mitral annuloplasty alters left ventricular shape during acute ischemic mitral regurgitation, Circulation 110 (11 (Suppl. II)) (2004) II98–II102, https://doi.org/10.1161/01.CIR.0000138395.45145.45.

[21] D.H. Adams, R. Rosenhek, V. Falk, Degenerative mitral valve regurgitation: best practice revolution, Eur. Heart J. 31 (2010) 1958–1966.

[22] J.D. Bronzino, Biomedical Engineering Handbook, vol. 2, CRC Press, 1999.

[23] J.A. Sethian, Level Set Methods and Fast Marching Methods: Evolving Interfaces in Computational Geometry, Fluid Mechanics, Computer Vision, and Material Science, second ed., Cambridge University Press, Cambridge, UK, 1999.

[24] R. Gonzalez, R. Woods, Digital Image Processing, second ed., Prentice-Hall Inc., 2002.

[25] K. Saini, M.L. Dewal, M.K. Rohit, A fast region-based active contour model for boundary detection of echocardiographic images, J. Digital Imag. 25 (2) (2012) 271–278.

[26] K. Chauhan, R.K. Chauhan, A. Saini, Enhancement and de-speckling of echocardiographic images, in: N. Dey, A.S. Ashour, F. Shi, V.E. Balas (Eds.), Soft Computing Based Medical Image Analysis, Elsevier, 2018, pp. 61–79.

[27] K. Chauhan, R.K. Chauhan, Boundary detection of echocardiographic images during mitral regurgitation, in: M. Hassaballah, K. Hosny (Eds.), Recent Advances in Computer Vision: Theories and Applications, vol. 804, Springer, 2018, pp. 281–303.

[28] M.L. Dewal, K. Saini, M.K. Rohit, Assessment of mitral regurgitation severity with intensity based region growing, Int. J. Hybrid Inform. Technol. 8 (6) (2015) 45–56.

[29] K. Saini, M.L. Dewal, M.K. Rohit, Level set based on new signed pressure force function for echocardiographic image segmentation, Int. J. Innov. Appl. Stud. 3 (2) (2013) 560–569.

[30] K. Saini, M.L. Dewal, M.K. Rohit, Statistical analysis of speckle noise reduction techniques for echocardiographic images, in: Proceedings International Conference on Methods and Models in Science and Technology, vol. 1414, 2011, pp. 95–99.

[31] K. Saini, M.L. Dewal, M.K. Rohit, A modified hybrid filter for echocardiographic image noise removal, Int. J. Signal Process. Image Process. Pattern Recogn. 5 (2) (2012) 61–72.

Cardiac multimodal image registration using machine learning techniques

2

V. Ajantha Devi

AP3 Solutions, Chennai, Tamil Nadu, India

Chapter outline

2.1 Introduction

2.1.1 Image registration

Image registration [1, 2] is a way to map information from images with the assistance of a reference image. The objective of such mapping is to coordinate the related images based on certain highlights to aid in the image fusion process.

Image registration requires two 3D images: a reference and a floating image. To balance the images, the reference image is fixed in space while the floating image is changed numerically until it is enlisted

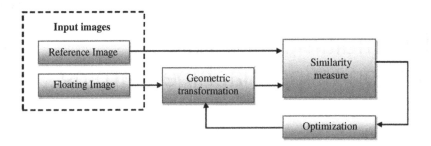

FIG. 2.1

Flowchart of the study.

to the reference image, as shown in Fig. 2.1. The mathematical transform function, or registration transfer, is assessed from a few comparative properties of the two images.

Image registration methods differ in the kind of data they extract from images and in the way they decide the registration transform. To analyze these techniques, it is important to aggregate image registration in a typical edge. Image registration comprises three steps: (1) image feature extraction, (2) registration transform calculation, and (3) quality measurement.

Images are developed to remove specific features or boundaries, for example, edges or moments. These features are then utilized in the registration algorithm. The registration algorithm determines the registration transform of the reference and floating images. The registration transform is either determined scientifically or assessed iteratively using the registration algorithm. The fundamental prerequisite [1] of any registration approach is the capacity to decide precisely and dependably the degree and nature of fit between images and in this manner the legitimacy of the registration transform.

2.1.2 Medical image registration

Medical imaging is increasingly being utilized [3] for disease diagnosis and treatment. Researchers from all fields, particularly those in neuroscience, use imaging to examine measures of illness and determine course of disease. For research purposes, it is often helpful to look at various images acquired from multiple modalities, rather than a single image from one modality obtained at different times [4].

The measure of information created by each progressive generation of imaging frameworks is more prominent than that created by the previous generation. This pattern is set to repeat with the development of the multislice helical CT scan and magnetic resonance imaging (MRI) [5, 6] frameworks with higher angle qualities. There are, accordingly, potential advantages to improving the route in which these images are analyzed and consolidated, as shown in Fig. 2.2. Modernized methodologies offer favorable circumstances, particularly by unequivocally modifying the information in different pictures and arranging the joined images to register them.

2.1.3 Cardiac image registration

Cardiovascular images obtained through various modalities can give corresponding data. In this way, the combination of at least two co-registered multimodal datasets into a solitary portrayal can help in

Type of Diagnosing	X-Ray	CT Scan	MRI	Ultrasound	PET Scan
Define	X-rays are quick, painless tests that produce images of the structures inside Patient body, especially bones.	CT scans use a series of x-rays to create cross-sections of the inside of the body, including bones, blood vessels, and soft tissues.	MRIs use magnetic fields and radio waves to create detailed images of organs and tissues in the body.	Ultrasound uses high-frequency sound waves to produce images of organs and structures within the body.	PEt scans use radioactive drugs (called tracers) and a scanning machine to show how Patient tissues and organs are functioning.
Diagnosing Method	Patient will lie, sit, or stand while the x-ray machine takes images. Patient may be asked to move into several positions.	Patient will lie on a table that slides into the scanner, which looks like a large doughnut. The x-ray tube rotates around Patient to take images.	Patient lie on a table that slides into the MRI machine, which is deeper and narrower than a CT scanner. The MRI magnets create loud tapping or thumping noises.	A technician applies gel to Patient skin, then presses a small probe against it, moving it to capture images of the inside of Patient body.	Patient swallow or have a radiotracer injected. Patient then enter a PET scanner (which looks like a CT scanner) which reads the radiation given off by the radiotracer.
Duration	10-15 minutes	10-15 minutes	45 minutes – 1 hour	30 minutes – 1 hour	1.5 – 2 hours
Imaging method	Ionizing radiation	Ionizing radiation	Magnetic waves	Sound waves	Radiotracers
Used to diagnose	• bone fractures; • arthritis; • osteoporosis; • infections; • breast cancer; • swallowed items; • digestive tract problems	• injuries from trauma; • bone fractures; • tumors and cancers; • vascular disease; • heart disease; • infections; • used to guide biopsies	• aneurysms; • Multiple Sclerosis (MS); • stoke; • spinal cord disorders; • tumors; • blood vessel issues; • joint or tendon injuries	• gallbladder disease; • breast lumps; • genital/prostate issues; • joint inflammation; • blood flow problems; • monitoring pregnancy; • used to guide biopsies	• cancer; • heart disease; • coronary artery disease; • Alzheimer's Disease; • seizures; • epilepsy; • Parkinson's Disease

FIG. 2.2

Method of diagnosing the medical image.

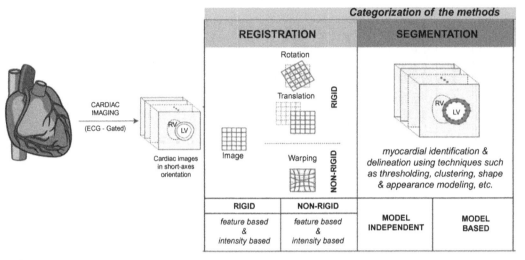

FIG. 2.3

Cardiac image registration and segmentation.

cardiovascular diagnosis, as shown in Fig. 2.3. The utilization of a multimodal imaging approach in medical practice is restricted by disadvantages in exact image registration. A few methodologies have been created to register 3D cardiovascular datasets [7]. These methodologies can be categorized by according to the following three key aspects:

- *the area where the arrangement change is characterized (search space)*: For the search space, the inflexible change strategy is the most effortless since it utilizes only six boundaries (three translational and three rotational). Elastic registration can be used as well, however, its medical application is restricted by high computational costs [8].
- *the capacity that depicts the nature of the arrangement (similarity metric or registration metric)*: The result of a similarity metric, which demonstrates decency of the match, is a major question in developing an enrollment technique. Obviously, the proximity metric must be efficient in order to merge to a global average for optimal coordination, and it must also be processed in a fair period of time. Various strategies utilize the separation between chosen mathematical highlights of the image, for example, anatomical tourist spots [9], surfaces on the chest [10, 11], or heart surfaces [12, 13], to gather information from anatomical focuses or surface divisions and compare. These strategies are not always easy to perform considering the disparate data given by various modalities, particularly when a deformity in the myocardial divider exists. Consequently, voxel-based closeness measurements, for example, using common data [14–16], don't make assumptions about the connection between pictures.
- *the optimization methodology used to determine the change that expands the characterized comparability work:* The last step of a registration cycle is optimization, which can figure the change that augments the characterized similitude metric and adjusts the heart datasets.

2.1.4 **Classification of image registration methods**

Fundamentally, the registration of input images requires the determination of the component space, a likeness measure or arrangement quality, a transformation type, and a pursuit technique. An incredible number of medical image registration strategies have been introduced, and several categories have been proposed to group them. These include registration philosophies [17] using information dimensionality (1D, 2D, 3D, 4D, etc.), wellspring of the image features used to make the registration (intrinsic or extrinsic properties of patients), transformation area (local or global), transformation flexibility (rigid, affine, projective, or curved), tightness of property coupling (interpolating or approximating), boundary assurance (direct or search situated), and cooperation (intelligent, self-loader, or programmed). Maintz and Viergever expanded this categorizing to nine principal standards [18], where every model was partitioned into at least one submeasure, as shown in Fig. 2.4.

The registration of images from a similar methodology but utilizing distinct procurement boundaries, for example, the enlistment of T1-MRI with T2-MRI or proton-thickness MRI pictures, is regularly delegated as multimodal. Registration techniques are additionally normally ordered utilizing the component space image data. This data might be the power of the crude voxels, the force slope, factual data identified with the voxel power, or structures extracted from the images to be registered, for example, sets of focuses, edges, forms, charts, surfaces, and volumes.

2.2 **Datasets**

The medical need to combine correlative data is underscored by the achievement of half-and-half scanners, which can obtain multimodal information that gives integral data from a solitary image. The most significant models of this type include positron outflow tomography (PET) [10] and computer tomography (CT) instruments [19–21], which are widely used in cardiology due to their capacity to characterize the relationship between coronary artery disease (CAD), as uncovered by CT, and myocardial perfusion, as estimated by PET.

The dataset is divided into 100 pictures for preparing and 40 pictures for model approval. Next, the learning rate for "Adam" to 0.0001, and the size of the bunch was set to 64. for preparing the quantity of ages were set as 1000 for end-diastolic volume (EDV) or end-systolic volume (ESV) expectation. After setting every one of these boundaries to manufacture a productive model, assessed at two stages. In the underlying stage, assessed under three CNN designs [22, 23]: VGG-19 (19 layers deep) [24], GoogLeNet (22 layers deep) [25], and ResNet-50 (50 layers deep) [26], with an additional single hub layer. Based on this first assessment, the structure of the designated CBB engineering is improved in the second stage.

The result of the forecast was evaluated by connecting consolidated diverse CNN models.

2.3 **Convolutional neural networks for image registration**

Deep learning neural networks (DNNs) [27] have garnered increased attention due to their extraordinary accomplishments in computer vision. One type of DNN, the convolutional neural network (CNN) [28], has played a pivotal role in this achievement. Fig. 2.5 compares and contrasts CNNs with more

Classification Criteria	Subdivision		
Dimensionality	Spatial dimension: 2D/2D, 2D/3D, 3D/3D		
	Temporal series		
Nature of the registration basis	Extrinsic		
	Invasive	Stereotactic frames	
		Fiducials (screw markers)	
	Non-invasive	Moulds, frames, dental adapters, etc.	
		Fiducials (skin markers)	
	Intrinsic		
	Landmark based	Anatomical	
		Geometrical	
	Segmentation based	Rigid models (points, curves, surfaces, volumes)	
		Deformable models (snakes, nets)	
	Voxel property based	Reduction to scalar/vectors (moments, principal axes)	
		Using full image contents	
	Non-image based (calibrated coordinate systems)		
Nature of transformation	Rigid (only rotation and translation)		
	Affine (translation, rotation, scaling and shearing)		
	Projective		
	Curved		
Interaction	Interactive	Initialization supplied	
		No initialization supplied	
	Semiautomatic	User initializing	
		User steering/correcting	
		Both	
Optimization procedure	Parameters computed directly		
	Parameters searched (the transformation paramers are computed iteratively using optimizaiton algorithms)		
Imaging modalities involved	Monomodal		
	Multimodal		
	Modality to model (register the coordinate system of the imaging equipment with a model coordinate system)		
	Patient to modality (register the patient with the coordinate system of the imaging equipment)		
Subject	Intra-subject		
	Inter-subject		
	Atlas		
Object	Head (brain, eye, dental, etc.)		
	Thorax (entire, cardiac, breast, etc.)		
	Abdomen (general, kidney, liver, etc.)		
	Limbs		
	Pelvis and perineum		
	Spine and vertebrae		

FIG. 2.4

Classification criteria of image registration.

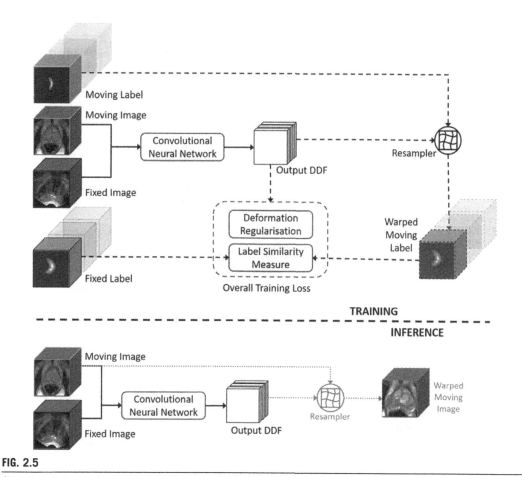

FIG. 2.5

Convolutional neural networks (CNN) on cardiac MR image registration.

conventional techniques. These models must consolidate input images with ground truths for the system to figure out how to plan these contributions to the yields.

When prepared, other images can be introduced to the CNN and the anticipated output will deliver an effective segmentation. Preparing a CNN utilizing this strategy implies that there is practically no requirement for predisposed, postprepared, and handmade highlights, which saves quite a bit of time. A number of renowned CNN structures incorporate VGGNet [24], GoogLeNet [25], and ResNet [26], all of which have been used to obtain cutting-edge image characterization results.

2.4 Cardiac image registration multimodalities

In multimodular [28, 29] image registration, the comparability metric is most significant for a couple of reasons, as shown in Fig. 2.6. First, some anatomical structures may not be obvious in two modalities

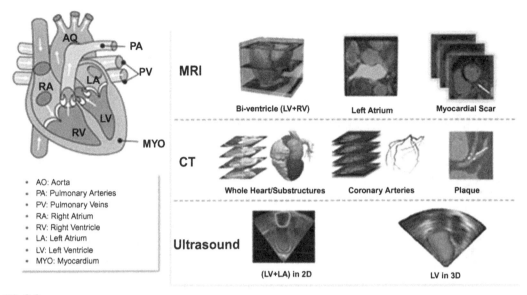

FIG. 2.6

Cardiac image registration multimodalities.

(e.g., ultrasound (US) and MRI) due to the physical properties of the imaging frameworks. Second, anatomical tissues may be pictured with categorization of picture comparability measurements that are utilized in multimodular clinical image registration issue. The focal point of this audit and theory is the advancement of dependable similarity measurements to recognize correspondences between multimodular images [30].

2.4.1 MR-based image registration

The three fundamental models used for the vast majority of learning procedures are VGGNet [24], GoodLeNet [25], and Res-Net [26] structures. VGGNet follows the standard CNN style [31]. It contains convolution layers, pooling, and completely associated layers progressively. GoogLeNet include multiscale convolution layers, whereas ResNet executes a unique planning procedure to allow fast connection between systems join quick and departure the inclination disappearing.

Left ventricular assessment is vitally important for determining cardiovascular disease. Estimating its volume, as shown in Fig. 2.7, helps in diagnosis and determining treatment. In this work, a prehandling procedure was applied to the Sunnybrook Cardiac Dataset (SCD) [32] and Cardiac Atlas Project (CAP) dataset [33]. Then, CNN systems was applied.

This assessment suggests that registration can be performed on floating images obtained from MRI. Limitations may include lack of MR-suitable catheters and the nonattendance of 3D images, as shown in Fig. 2.8.

  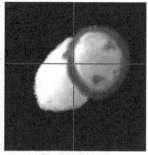

a) Source image (120x120x12)   b) Target Image (120x120x12)   c) Registered Image

FIG. 2.7

3D MR volume.

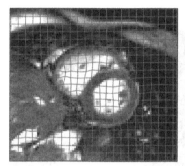  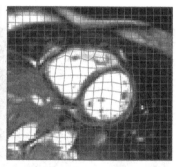

FIG. 2.8

Cardiac image registration.

2.4.2 CT X-ray-based registration

The high diagnostic value of noninvasive coronary angiography [34, 35] using cardiac CT is dependent on the identification and subsequent revision of movement antiquities. As a result, movement amendment calculations have a significant computational impact and potential failure modes, necessitating a movement relic recognition project to determine if movement remedy is needed at all.

The movement relics in the coronary corridors can be anticipated by profound learning draws near is examined. A forward model recreating heart movement by making and incorporating fake movement vector fields in the filtered back projection (FBP) [36] algorithm permits preparation of information from nine tentatively ECG-set off great clinical cases. Fig. 2.9 shows the training a CNN model [37] ordering 2D movement free and movement bothered coronary cross-area images.

2.4.3 Ultrasound-based registration

Echocardiography [38] is an imaging methodology that portrays the heart region utilizing US waves. It is equipped for creating both quantitative and subjective data dependent on a set of involved approaches. Ultrasound can be utilized in numerous applications [39–41], for example, to find tumors,

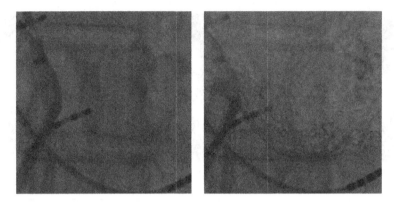

FIG. 2.9

CT Image during respiration.

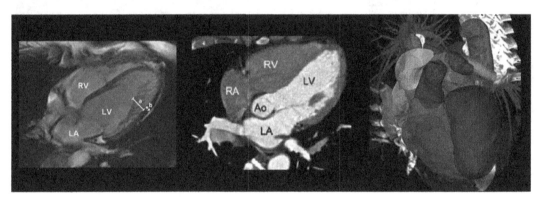

FIG. 2.10

3D ultrasound volume of cardiac.

determine malignancy, guide radiation treatment, and so on. Fig. 2.10A–C shows an ultrasound of a liver tumor and prostate biopsy.

2.5 Evaluation of multimodal imaging

Multimodal cardiovascular imaging is fundamental for obtaining combined anatomical and practical data from the heart. Exact registration of various imaging modalities provides clinicians and analysts valuable information about the heart that is inaccessible using a solitary methodology. Medical imaging is continually developing, as demonstrated by the improved precision of current imaging modalities.

Every methodology has its advantages and disadvantages, hence the introduction of multimodal imaging systems that can join the best visual perspectives from different sensors to provide clinically pertinent data. A good image registration algorithm is necessarily basic, as any mistakes can lead to negative consequences of the multimodal image combination. The calculation's handling speed should likewise be equipped for preparing ongoing information, as the output of registration will be used constantly to guide the clinician in any dynamic cycle during a medical procedure.

The cardiovascular system's characteristics are perplexing, complex and deformable in nature. The position of the heart will in general change with changes in body position, breath, and heartbeat. There are a few anatomical tourist spots in cardiovascular images, which will in general be envisioned and deciphered from various perspectives through different imaging modalities. A few milestones will be less obvious through specific modalities, for example, ischemia. As a result, the field of focus, technique, and implementation are all between subordinate and extremely critical data to collect prior to enrollment.

Cardiovascular image registration is a field open to testing since there is yet a standard system or completely programmed technique that exists to deal with the different qualities of clinical circumstances. A superior comprehension and extension of both clinical information of the organ being imaged and specialized information on image registration methods will help to improve cardiac imaging overall.

2.6 Conclusion and discussion

This chapter examined cardiovascular image registration strategies and the modalities they include. As noted, heart imaging registration assumes a conclusive function during image-guided medical procedures, in which the image serves as a guide to the medical professional for making careful choices. Registration accordingly requires a tradeoff between all perspectives including accuracy, precision, robustness, reliability, computational speed, interactivity, user-friendliness, patient comfort, and cost; that ought to likewise be effectively incorporated into a standard clinical work process and is viable with working room convention for medical procedures.

In this chapter, multimodal cardiac image registration was described using a convolution neural network (CNN) that involved three steps. In the first step, the cardiac images to be integrated were deteriorated into low- and high-recurrence segments by the CNN. In the second step, two distinctive combination rules were utilized to meld the low-recurrence and high-recurrence groups. The combined image offers more data and improved quality. The low-recurrence groups were melded using the nearby mean combination rule, while the high-recurrence groups were intertwined using the neighborhood fluctuation combination rule. In the last step, the melded image was remade by the CNN with the composite coefficients. Results [42] show that the CNN technique improves the subtleties of image registration for multimodal images.

References

[1] E.P. Ambinder, A history of the shift toward full computerization of medicine, J. Oncol. Pract. 1 (2) (2005) 54–56.

[2] T. Peters, K. Cleary, Image-Guided Interventions: Technology and Applications, Springer Science & Business Media, 2008.

[3] P. Aljabar, R. Heckemann, A. Hammers, J.V. Hajnal, D. Rueckert, Classifier selection strategies for label fusion using large atlas databases, in: Medical Image Computing and Computer Assisted Intervention (MICCAI), Part I. Vol. 4791 of Lecture Notes in Computer Science, 2007, pp. 523–531.

[4] J.V. Hajnal, D.L.G. Hill, D.J. Hawkes, Medical Image Registration, CRC Press, June 2001.

[5] A. Roche, G. Malandain, N.J. Ayache, Unifying maximum likelihood approaches in medical image registration, Int. J. Imaging Syst. Technol. 11 (1) (2000) 71–80.

[6] J. Hartiala, J. Knuuti, Imaging of heart by MRI and PET, Ann. Med. 27 (1995) 35–45.

[7] T. Mäkelä, P. Clarysse, O. Sipilä, et al., A review of cardiac image registration methods, IEEE Trans. Med. Imaging 21 (9) (2002) 1011–1021.

[8] W.R. Crum, T. Hartkens, D.L.G. Hill, Non-rigid image registration: theory and practice, Br. J. Radiol. 77 (Suppl. 2) (2004) S140–S153.

[9] M.A. Wirth, C. Choi, A. Jennings, Point-to-point registration of nonrigid medical images using local elastic transformation methods, in: Proceedings of the IEEE International Conference on Image Processing and Its Application, 2, 1997, pp. 780–784.

[10] J.N. Yu, F.H. Fahey, H.D. Gage, et al., Intermodality, retrospective image registration in the thorax, J. Nucl. Med. 36 (12) (1995) 2333–2338.

[11] T.J. Mäkelä, P. Clarysse, J. Lötjönen, et al., A new method for the registration of cardiac PET and MR images using the deformable model based on the main thorax structures, in: W. Niessen, M. Viergever (Eds.), *Proceedings of the Medical Image Computing and Computer-Assisted Intervention (MICCAI'01)*, 2001, pp. 557–564. Lecture Notes in Computer Science, 2208/2001.

[12] T.L. Faber, R.W. McColl, R.M. Opperman, J.R. Corbett, R.M. Peshock, Spatial and temporal registration of cardiac SPECT and MR images: methods and evaluation, Radiology 179 (3) (1991) 857–861.

[13] J. Declerck, J. Feldmar, M.L. Goris, F. Betting, Automatic registration and alignment on a template of cardiac stress and rest reoriented SPECT images, IEEE Trans. Med. Imaging 16 (6) (1997) 727–737.

[14] J.P.W. Pluim, J.B.A. Maintz, M.A. Viergever, Mutualinformation-based registration of medical images: a survey, IEEE Trans. Med. Imaging 22 (8) (2003) 986–1004.

[15] P. Viola, W.M. Wells, Alignment by maximization of mutual information, Int. J. Comput. Vis. 24 (2) (1997) 137–154.

[16] F. Maes, A. Collignon, D. Vandermeulen, G. Marchal, P. Suetens, Multimodality image registration by maximization of mutual information, IEEE Trans. Med. Imaging 16 (2) (1997) 187–198.

[17] P.A. Elsen, E.-J.D. Pol, M.A. Viergever, Medical image matching—a review with classification, IEEE Eng. Med. Biol. Mag. 12 (1) (1993) 26–39.

[18] J.B.A. Maintz, M.A. Viergever, A survey of medical image registration, Med. Image Anal. 2 (1) (1998) 1–36.

[19] R. Liao, S. Miao, P. de Tournemire, S. Grbic, A. Kamen, T. Mansi, D. Comaniciu, An artificial agent for robust image registration, in: AAAI, 2017, pp. 4168–4175.

[20] G. Carneiro, J.C. Nascimento, A. Freitas, The segmentation of the left ventricle of the heart from ultrasound data using deep learning architectures and derivative-based search methods, IEEE Trans. Image Process. 21 (3) (2012) 968–982.

[21] A. Madani, R. Arnaout, M. Mofrad, R. Arnaout, Fast and accurate view classification of echocardiograms using deep learning, NPJ Digit. Med. 1 (1) (2018) 6.

[22] L.V. Romaguera, M.G.F. Costa, F.P. Romero, C.F.F. Costa Filho, Left ventricle segmentation in cardiac MRI images using fully convolutional neural networks, in: Medical Imaging 2017: Computer-Aided Diagnosis, vol. 10134, International Society for Optics and Photonics, 2017, p. 101342Z.

[23] R.P. Poudel, P. Lamata, G. Montana, Recurrent fully convolutional neural networks for multi-slice MRI cardiac segmentation, in: Reconstruction, Segmentation, and Analysis of Medical Images, Springer, 2016, pp. 83–94.

[24] K. Simonyan, A. Zisserman, Very Deep Convolutional Networks for Large-Scale Image Recognition, arXiv preprint arXiv:1409.1556, 2014.

[25] C. Szegedy, W. Liu, Y. Jia, P. Sermanet, S. Reed, D. Anguelov, D. Erhan, V. Vanhoucke, A. Rabinovich, Going deeper with convolutions, in: Proceedings of the IEEE Conference on Computer Vision and Pattern Recognition, 2015, pp. 1–9.

[26] K. He, X. Zhang, S. Ren, J. Sun, Deep residual learning for image recognition, in: Proceedings of the IEEE Conference on Computer Vision and Pattern Recognition, 2016, pp. 770–778.

[27] B.D. de Vos, F.F. Berendsen, M.A. Viergever, H. Sokooti, M. Staring, I. Išgum, A deep learning framework for unsupervised affine and deformable image registration, Med. Image Anal. 52 (2019) 128–143.

[28] Y. Hu, M. Modat, E. Gibson, W. Li, N. Ghavami, E. Bonmati, G. Wang, S. Bandula, C.M. Moore, M. Emberton, S. Ourselin, J.A. Noble, D.C. Barratt, T. Vercauteren, Weakly-supervised convolutional neural networks for multimodal image registration, Med. Image Anal. 49 (2018) 1–13.

[29] W.R. Wells, P. Viola, H. Atsumi, S. Nakajima, R. Kikinis, Multimodal volume registration by maximization of mutual information, Med. Image Anal. 1 (1996) 35–51.

[30] Tavard, et al., Multimodal registration and data fusion for cardiac resynchronization therapy optimization, IEEE Trans. Med. Imaging 33 (2014) 1363–1372.

[31] L.K. Tan, Y.M. Liew, E. Lim, R.A. McLaughlin, Cardiac left ventricle segmentation using convolutional neural network regression, in: Biomedical Engineering and Sciences (IECBES), 2016 IEEE EMBS Conference on. IEEE, 2016, pp. 490–493.

[32] P. Radau, Y. Lu, K. Connelly, G. Paul, A. Dick, G. Wright, Evaluation framework for algorithms segmenting short axis cardiac MRI, in: The MIDAS Journal—Cardiac MR Left Ventricle Segmentation Challenge, 2009. Available: http://www.cardiacatlas.org/studies/sunnybrook-cardiac-data/.

[33] C.G. Fonseca, M. Backhaus, D.A. Bluemke, R.D. Britten, J.D. Chung, B.R. Cowan, I.D. Dinov, J.P. Finn, P.J. Hunter, A.H. Kadish, et al., The cardiac atlas project - an imaging database for computational modeling and statistical atlases of the heart, Bioinformatics 27 (16) (2011) 2288–2295. Available: http://www.cardiacatlas. org/challenges/lv-segmentation-challenge/.

[34] D. Pyke, C. Symons, Calcification of the aortic valve and of the coronary arteries, Br. Heart J. 13 (1951) 355–363.

[35] R.D. Rifkin, A.F. Parisi, E. Folland, Coronary calcification in the diagnosis of coronary artery disease, Am. J. Cardiol. 44 (1979) 141–147.

[36] J. Cammin, P. Khurd, A. Kamen, Q. Tang, K. Kirchberg, C. Chefd Hotel, H. Bruder, K. Taguchi, Combined motion estimation and motion compensated FBP for cardiac CT, in: M. Kachelriess, M. Rafecas (Eds.), 11th International Meeting on Fully Three-Dimensional Image Reconstruction in Radiology and Nuclear Medicine (Fully3D), 2011, pp. 136–139.

[37] T. Würfl, F.C. Ghesu, V. Christlein, A. Maier, Deep learning computed tomography, in: S. Ourselin, L. Joskowicz, M.R. Sabuncu, G. Unal, W. Wells (Eds.), *Medical Image Computing and Computer-Assisted Intervention–MICCAI* 2016, vol. 9902, Springer International Publishing, 2016, pp. 432–440.

[38] M. Döring, F. Braunschweig, C. Eitel, T. Gaspar, U. Wetzel, B. Nitsche, G. Hindricks, C. Piorkowski, Individually tailored left ventricular lead placement: lessons from multimodality integration between three-dimensional echocardiography and coronary sinus angiogram, Europace 15 (5) (2013) 718–727.

[39] A.M. Pouch, P.A. Yushkevich, B.M. Jackson, J.H. Gorman, R.C. Gorman, C.M. Sehgal, Dynamic shape modeling of the mitral valve from real-time 3D ultrasound images using continuous medial representation, in: J.G. Bosch, M.M. Doyley (Eds.), *Proceedings of Medical Imaging 2012: Ultrasonic Imaging, Tomography, and Therapy*, vol. 8320, International Society for Optical Engineering (SPIE), San Diego, CA, February 2012.

[40] K.Y.E. Leung, M. van Stralen, M.M. Voormolen, et al., Registration of 2D cardiac images to real-time 3D ultrasound volumes for 3D stress echocardiography, in: J.M. Reinhardt, J.P.W. Pluim (Eds.), *Proceedings of Medical Imaging 2006: Image Processing*, vol. 6144, International Society for Optical Engineering (SPIE), Graz, Austria, May 2006.

[41] G. Gao, G. Penney, Y. Ma, et al., Registration of 3D trans-esophageal echocardiography to X-ray fluoroscopy using image-based probe tracking, Med. Image Anal. 16 (1) (2012) 38–49. in English.

[42] O. Russakovsky, J. Deng, H. Su, J. Krause, S. Satheesh, S. Ma, Z. Huang, A. Karpathy, A. Khosla, M. Bernstein, A.C. Berg, L. Fei-Fei, ImageNet large scale visual recognition challenge, Int. J. Comput. Vis. 115 (3) (Apr. 2015) 211–252.

Anatomical photo representations for cardiac imaging training

3

I. Lakshmi

Department of Computer Science, Stella Maris College, Chennai, India

Chapter outline

3.1 Clinical background and motivation

In this section, we give a brief introduction to human heart anatomy and physiology, with particular attention to electromechanical events that occur during the cardiac cycle. MR imaging is addressed later, and we illustrate the different techniques used particularly in cardiac MR imaging, such as

Image Processing for Automated Diagnosis of Cardiac Diseases. https://doi.org/10.1016/B978-0-323-85064-3.00005-4

ECG gating, respiratory motion correction, and cine imaging. Similarly, we give a brief overview of the ultrasound imaging and its clinical function in cardiovascular disease (CVD) diagnosis. The section ends with a summary of the quantitative measures used in CVD evaluation and study of cardiac function.

3.1.1 The anatomy and function of the heart

The human heart [1] pumps blood through the circulatory system that supplies the body's cells with oxygen and nutrients while eliminating carbon dioxide and other waste. It has four chambers as shown in Fig. 3.1: the atria (upper) and the ventricles (lower). The two sides of the heart are separated by the antrioventricular septum. When a septal defect exists, the two sides of the heart do not directly interact with each other, but they function together.

Blood circulates through two different channels through the heart [2]: the coronary circuit and the systemic circuit. De-oxygenated blood returns to the right side of the heart in the former, which is pumped into the right ventricle (RV) and then into the lungs where oxygen is absorbed. At the end oxygenated blood returns through the pulmonary vein to the left atrium (LA). The left ventricle (LV) pumps the oxygenated blood into the aorta and the arterial circulation in the systemic circuit. The atrioventricular (AV) bicuspid (mitral) and tricuspid valves distinguish the left and right atria,

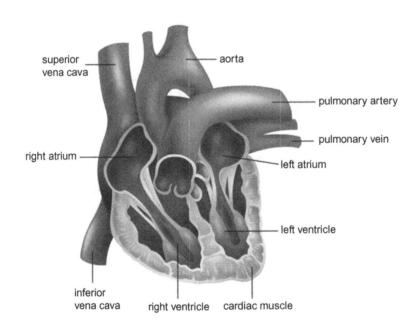

FIG. 3.1

The anatomy of the human heart: coronary blood vessels, ventricles, and atria. The arrows show the flow of blood through the heart.

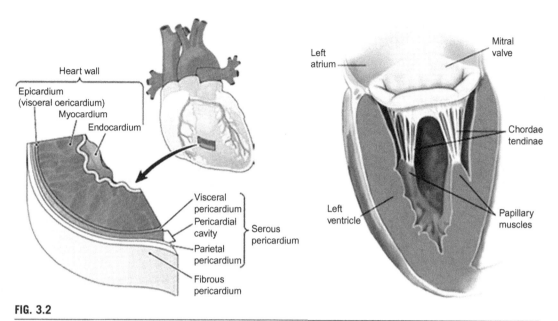

FIG. 3.2

Layers of the heart wall *(left)* and mitral valve of the left ventricle *(right)* [2].

and ventricles, respectively. The papillary muscles are ventricular muscle projections, which connect to the AV valve cusps (Fig. 3.2). The papillary muscles in both ventricles tense during ventricular contraction and prevent backward flow of ventricular blood to the atrial cavities. The ventricular wall consists of three layers: epicardium (the outermost layer of the wall), myocardium (the middle layer) containing the contraction muscle, and endocardium (the inner layer) having contact with the blood stream. Fig. 3.2 indicates that the muscle cells make up the majority of the ventricular wall, and the LV wall is thicker than the RV wall because there is a need for more blood pressure to transport the oxygenated blood to various areas of the body.

3.1.2 The cardiac cycle and electrical activation

The cardiac cycle is a series of electrical and mechanical events that occur during the phases of heart relaxation (diastole) and contraction (systole). The ventricular diastolic stage involves blood flow from the atria to the ventricles, and the ventricular systole includes blood flow from the ventricles to the pulmonary artery and the aorta. Cardiac systole is the myocardial cells' mechanical response to an electrochemical stimulus originating from the sinoatrial (SA) node. By acting as a pacemaker it controls the cardiac cycle. The electrical activity originating from the SA node propagates through the heart's fibrous skeleton (first the atrial mass, then the AV node) and the subsequent depolarization wave from top to bottom of the heart triggers the mechanical activation (cf. Refs. [2, 3]). The conduction of the electrical activity through the fibrous skeleton can be seen on an electrocardiogram (ECG), as shown in Fig. 3.3.

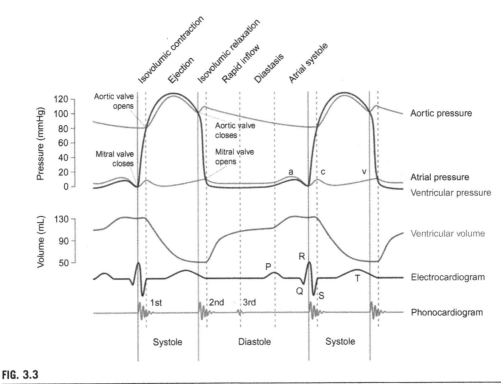

FIG. 3.3

Wiggers diagram showing the electromechanical activity of the heart in a cardiac cycle.

The figure has been adapted from https://en.wikipedia.org/wiki/Wiggers_diagram.

During each heartbeat, the ECG recording represents the electrophysiological activity and is obtained using electrodes mounted on the skin. In the same figure the conduction at the atria is shown as the P-wave and the PR interval corresponding to the delay in the AV node follows. The propagation of electrical activity across the ventricular myocardium creates the QRS complex, and the T-wave is known as ventricular repolarization (relaxation of the muscles). In imaging devices, the ECG signal is often widely used as a gating signal to capture heart images at different phases of the heart cycle.

3.1.3 Cardiac magnetic resonance (CMR)

Imaging magnetic resonance imaging (MRI) is a noninvasive and nonionizing imaging technique that can produce tomographic images with an unprecedented contrast between soft tissues. It does not use ionizing radiation, as opposed to X-ray computed tomography (CT) but is based on the absorption and emission of energy in the electromagnetic spectrum range of radio frequency (RF) [4]. MR images are generated based on spatial differences in the phase and frequency of the absorbed and released RF energy from the anatomical tissues. The magnetically aligned hydrogen nuclei produce transverse magnetization under the influence of a strong magnetic field as a response to applied RF pulse sequences, captured by the scanner and then reconstructed as an image. The tissue's magnetic response over time is formed by atomic properties, which vary depending on the form of tissue [5]. Cardiac MR (CMR) has been commonly used in the form of cardiac imaging to examine the structure and function of the cardiac chambers, valves, and main vessels. Assessment of infarct segments, myocardial wall abnormalities, and calculation of LV volume are some examples of this clinical use [6]. In the past, the technology was limited due to imaging difficulties associated with cardiac and respiratory motion, as well as long processing time. CMR imaging has seen further applications in cardiovascular disease [7] in recent years, with improvements in spatial and temporal resolution and shortened scanning times. Parallel imaging is, in particular, a widely used method for reducing imaging time [8], and ECG gating is also required to minimize artifacts of cardiac motion.

3.1.4 Electrocardiogram gating

Sampling of the magnetic pulse must be performed within tens of milliseconds to obtain an image of the heart that is unaffected by the cardiac motion. This situation restricts the number of phase encodings (spatial resolution) and often requires a limited period for relaxation (image quality). While such acquisition can be accomplished in practice, it will come at the cost of poor quality and resolution of the images. Of this purpose, k-space data sampling for each slice is performed over several cardiac cycles in standard CMR imaging protocols by synchronizing the RF pulse sequence with respect to a defined collection of cardiac reference phases. To synchronize the MR data acquisition, an MR-compatible ECG device is used, which detects the R-wave and triggers the sequence controller as shown in Fig. 3.4.

3.1.5 Respiratory motion

In traditional CMR imaging techniques, the encoding process of each 2D image slice involves data processing over several cardiac cycles, which may result in many minute imaging periods. This means that respiratory motion can introduce data artifacts and inconsistencies between the data acquired at

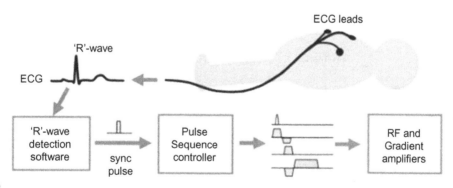

FIG. 3.4

ECG synchronization of the pulse sequences. ECG recording is used to detect the QRS complex, which triggers the pulse sequence generator to produce RF and gradient pulse waveforms. This is repeated for each cardiac cycle.

Image Courtesy: J.P. Ridgway, Cardiovascular magnetic resonance physics for clinicians: part I, J. Cardiovasc. Magn. Reson. 12(1) (2010) 71.

various cardiac cycles in k-space. There are three approaches [9] as a solution to this problem: (I) retrorespective gating of images with a signal gathered from a respiratory belt, (II) single-shot rapid imaging techniques, and (III) repeated breath-holding.

3.1.6 Cine cardiac MR imaging

Cine MR imaging visualizes the temporal heart chamber dynamics and can be used for functional assessment. Data points are acquired at multiple time points for each cardiac phase by filling separate k-space lines over many cardiac cycles, which result in image reconstruction for all cardiac phases. The pictures are later considered a series of films. The procedure for the acquisition of cine images is shown in Fig. 3.5. Breath-hold cine MR imagery allows for the acquisition of k-space data for each heart process in segments. In this way, at the cost of a decreased temporal resolution, which can be circumvented by echo-sharing, acquisition times can be shortened even further [10]. Spoiled gradient echo (GE) was chosen as a pulse sequence for practical visualization because it requires very short repetition times. The blood-pool (BP) appears bright with the GE series, and the contrast between the

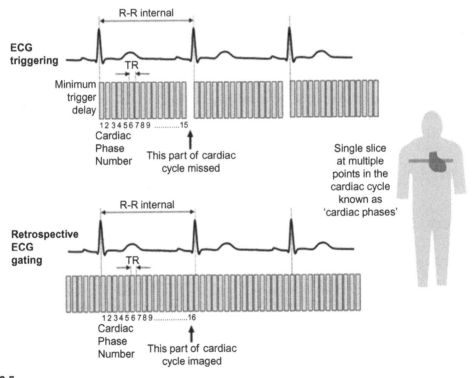

FIG. 3.5

Cine MR images for all cardiac phases (N=16) are acquired over multiple cardiac cycles in segments of k-space data during breath-hold. ECG gating is used to synchronize the RF pulse sequences.

endocardium and BP makes it ideal for assessment of ventricular function and flow analysis [9]. On the other hand, the spin echo (SE) series is more suited to anatomical imaging. This uses relatively small metal artifacts, which takes longer processing times. It more plays a secondary role in CMR imaging, but it still proves useful for purposes such as structural evaluation of ventricular abnormalities [10]. Steady state free-precession (SSFP) [11] is an alternative to the GE method, allowing for greater independence of blood-flow contrast and fast acquisition speed, which was a constraint for very short RF repeat times [12].

3.1.7 Cardiac MR imaging planes

High-resolution 3D cine imaging of the heart is difficult because of long processing times, heart movement, and repetitive breath-holding. For this purpose, stacks of thick 2D slices for multiple cardiac phases are acquired from different imaging planes. To classify these planes during the acquisition, first scout imagery is performed with a simple single-shot sequence, and then the long-axis (LAX) planes are administered along a line stretching from the cardiac apex to the mitral valve core. Finally, the SAX plane is defined, which extends at the level of the mid left-ventricle perpendicular to the hearts LAX. Ventricular volumetric measurements are often performed on SAX stacks since it yields cross-sectional slices almost perpendicular to the myocardium boundaries. This way partial volume effects can be reduced and ventricular measurement accuracy can be improved [13]. Typically the in-plane and through-plane resolutions of the SAX stacks are in between 1–2.5 and 8–10 mm, respectively.

3.1.8 Indices of cardiac function

Quantitative analysis of the cardiac ventricles using imaging data starts with delineation of the endocardial and epicardial boundaries of the myocardium. Once the contours are defined for each slice in the stack of images, local and global volumetric measurements can be performed for the assessment of ventricular function and mass [13]. These measurements have clinical importance in diagnosis of cardiac-related pathologies such as hypertrophy and dilated cardiomyopathy [14]. Myocardial mass (M) is a particular example. It corresponds to the weight of the heart muscle and is computed by multiplying the ventricular volume (V) calculated from the contours, with the density of the myocardium ($\rho_m = 1.05\,\text{g/cm}^3$) [15]. Left-ventricular (LV) myocardial mass is computed as $M_{LV} = V_{LV} \cdots \rho_m$. Global functional indices indicate the overall performance of cardiac ventricles in their ability to supply blood to the rest of the body [16]. They require myocardial contouring in at least two points in the cardiac cycle: end-diastole (ED) and end-systole (ES). As a global functional index, the stroke volume (SV) corresponds to the volume of oxygenated blood pumped from the LV in each cardiac cycle, which is equal to the difference between the LV volumetric measurements at ED and ES phases: $SV = V_{ED} - V_{ES}$. Ejection fraction (EF) is the fraction of stroke volume (ejected blood) with respect to the volume of the filled heart (V_{ED}) and is defined as $EF = SV/V_{ED}$. Another functional index is the cardiac output, which is defined as the amount of blood ejected from the LV per minute and is equal to the SV multiplied by the heart rate. Although global indices are good indicators of functional abnormalities, they do not convey specific information about which parts of the ventricle have reduced or altered contractile function. Additionally, there could be instances where global measurements fall within the healthy range while the wall motion be abnormal. For these reasons, local functional analysis of the ventricular wall is performed including wall thickening and strain analysis, which can precisely identify reversibly injured yet viable parts of the myocardium [7]. A recent survey study [16] on local cardiac wall motion provides more detailed information for interested readers.

3.1.9 Cardiac ultrasound imaging

Generic ultrasonic imaging (US) includes a piezoelectric transducer and a visualization processing unit. Ultrasonic pulses produced by the transducer pass through body tissues and encounter echo-generating interfaces and scatterers. Such reflections arise when an interface of specific acoustic impedance meets with the US wave. The reflected waves are later detected and converted to signal readings by the same transducer. The US beam's travel time and direction are used to reconstruct the depth picture along one axis, as shown in Fig. 3.6. You can create a cross-sectional 2D image by transmitting pulses from an array in multiple directions using beam forming [17], and the visualized intensity values correspond to the energy of the attenuated echo signal (B-mode imaging) [18]. 2D-phased and 3D-matrix array transducers are composed of multiple piezoelectric elements, and they can automatically collect a series of 3D volumes by steering the ultrasound beam electronically [19]. It is particularly suitable for cardiac applications and usually collects 10–20 volumes per second [18]. In terms of accurate visualization of soft-tissues and bony structures, the US cannot compete with tomographic imaging systems (e.g., MR, CT). Nevertheless, it is capable of imaging tissue deformations in real time for surgical guidance and is invaluable for evaluating cardiac function because of its portability, large availability, and low cost [20]. It can provide a wealth of information [21], including heart size and shape (internal chamber size quantification), LV volume estimate, pumping power, regional wall movement, and location and duration of any damage to tissues. Such tests are used in particular for the diagnosis and assessment of ischemic heart disease. Three typical transducer locations are used in cardiac US imagery (echocardiography) for data acquisition: parasternal, subcostal, and apical views. Fig. 3.7 displays views from regular transthoracic photographic windows. The quality of US data is always operator-dependent, and thus automated analysis challenges differ depending on view and objects such as shadows and reverberations [21]. In comparison to B-mode imaging, the US Doppler imaging method offers information on the rate and direction of blood flow in the heart and is used in cardiac valve area and function assessments [22].

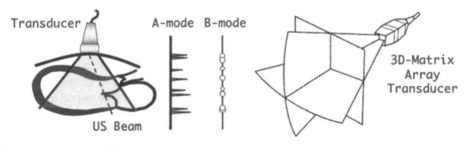

FIG. 3.6

The reflected ultrasound (US) beam is captured by the transducer and the area highlighted in blue scanned the same way using multiple beams, which corresponds to B-mode. A-mode shows the amplitude of the received echo for a single beam. 3D-US imaging is done with a matrix array that is composed of many piezoelectric crystals.

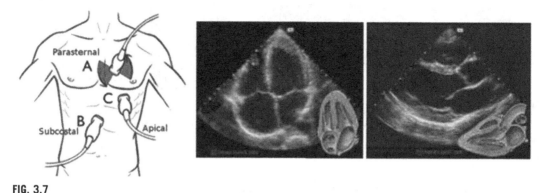

FIG. 3.7

Standard transthoracic cardiac US imaging windows. Apical 4-CH and parasternal long-axis views are shown in the middle and right, respectively.

3.2 Technical challenges in multimodal cardiac image analysis and objectives

Quantification of ventricular volume and mass is essential to cardiovascular pathology evaluation, and CMR is the main reference imaging technique for quantitative analysis [2, 10]. Nevertheless, there are many drawbacks of cine CMR, such as restricted by plane image resolution and respiratory motion artifacts that occur because of the need to obtain cine images over many cardiac cycles. Similarly, imaging artifacts found in 3D-US images will hamper computer-aided heart function research. The technological limitations faced by the imaging systems involve the design for quantitative evaluation of reliable and accurate frameworks for the image analysis. In addition to predictive accuracy, ease of use and interpretability are important for the application of these frameworks in clinical diagnosis

3.2.1 Limited through-plane resolution and imaging artifacts in CMR

Cine CMR images are acquired to capture spatial and temporal information from the heart, and due to repeated breath-holds and acquisitions at different heart phases, long scanning times are needed. Slices in the SAX direction are acquired as a compromise between SNR and acquisition time, with fairly broad slice thickness as shown in Fig. 3.8. This may reduce the precision of the volumetric measurements (e.g., EF, SV) obtained with automated (contouring) segmentation devices. For this reason, most segmentation algorithms perform myocardium delineations independently for each slice without taking the information through plane much into consideration [23].

There may be some drawbacks associated with this form of 2D analysis approach: (I) partial volume effect due to low resolution (LR) can result in measurement error, (II) respiratory motion artifacts found between adjacent slices (Fig. 3.8) that result in blocky disconnected contours in the direction of the passageway, (III) segmentation of the apical and basal slices becomes a more difficult task without adequate contextual details. Work has focused on various approaches as a solution to these problems: (I) motion correction on stacks of 2D SAX images prior to segmentation, (II) subpixel segmentation using only the LR image data, and (III) super-resolution cardiac image.

FIG. 3.8

Cine CMR stacks are often acquired with relatively thick slices (8–10mm). As slices are acquired over multiple breath-holds, there could be respiratory motion artefacts *(right)*, which can hamper quantitative assessment when it is combined with large slice thickness.

3.2.2 Imaging artifacts in cardiac 3D-US images

Due to its large availability and cost-effectiveness, ultrasound (US) imaging was chosen to be the primary imaging modality for initial evaluation of cardiac function [20]. However, the quality of the acquired images and the accuracy of quantitative assessments are always operator-dependent; as such, the quality of the US images can differ considerably depending on the location and angle of the transducer. Typical imaging artifacts [20] (Fig. 3.9) that could be observed in clinical cardiac US data are (I) narrow field of view of cardiac chambers (US beam profile); (II) signal drop-out caused by highly reflective anatomical structures (ribs) that can prevent the imaging of the entire endocardium; (III) stationary reverberations due to high reflective anatomic structures (ribs), which can prevent imaging of the entire endocardium; (III) stationary reverberations due to multiple reflections of the ultrasound beams, which often occlude the apical part of the myocardium.

Such objects may introduce inaccuracies in the segmentation of cardiac ventricles, where image data cannot be self-sufficient for precise analysis. On top of that, as shown on the left in Fig. 3.9, the low-intensity contrast between myocardium and endocardium may make the segmentation problem even more difficult. Frameworks for image processing have attempted to overcome these problems by using templates of anatomical form [24, 25] and techniques such as multiacquisition stitching or compounding [26].

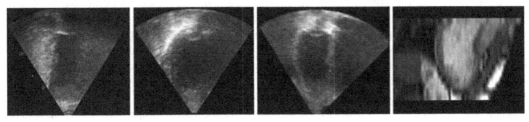

FIG. 3.9

From left to right: (I) Stationary reverberations covering the anterior wall (AW) in the 2-CH image, (II) signal drop-out of the AW in the 2-CH view due to a lung shadow distant from the probe. (III–IV) 3D-US and MR scans acquired from the same subject. Some of the structures are difficult to identify and locate in the apical ultrasound view such as the apex and right ventricle. This situation introduces a challenge in multimodal image alignment.

3.2.3 Identification of correspondences in multi-modal imaging data

Multimodal imagery may provide additional information that cannot be collected through a single mode alone. For example, 3D-US data provide valuable guidance in surgical procedures by visualizing the papillary muscles and providing high-resolution temporal information [20] that is not usually captured by CMR images. Most specifically, CMR is not compatible with other surgical instruments and is thus difficult to use during surgery. Nonetheless, the fusion of multimodal data also involves spatial synchronization of multimodal images, so it is important to recognize at least on a sparse level correspondences between US and MR images. This is a daunting task, as certain anatomical structures are not simultaneously visualized in both modalities and their manifestations can be substantially different as seen in Fig. 3.9 on the right. In addition, manual delineations of the endocardial boundary in both modalities frequently display no agreement with each other as has been shown in clinical studies [27, 28]. The volumetric measurements obtained from 3D-US and CMR frequently show a systematic discrepancy, for this reason. In conclusion, the registration of multimodal ultrasound images is a complex topic and the focus of ongoing research.

3.2.4 User interaction requirement in semi-automatic segmentation methods

In addition to the problems the imaging systems face, the accessibility of image processing techniques is another thing that needs to be addressed. Specifically semiautomatic segmentation tools (multiatlas, deformable models) also require an operator's guidance to perform the delineation function. Operator input is often needed to initialize these algorithms by defining a particular set of landmarks in the images. This can, however, be a constraint on the implementation of these algorithms in the processing of large imaging cohorts such as UK Biobank [29], where thousands of images are needed for population studies to be analyzed. To overcome this limitation, several research efforts have concentrated on developing a technique for automated landmark localization, which must ensure consistent and precise segmentation accuracy while automating the frameworks of study.

3.2.5 Edge-maps for multi-modal image analysis

We propose a novel technique of representing images, which we call probabilistic edge-maps (PEMs). PEM is an intermediate function space where before study, multimodal image data is first projected into. Subsequent image analysis benefits from this function space because it is unique to the organ and only shows the anatomy's structural detail, which is especially useful in the analysis of images in the US. We show its applicability for multimodal cardiac image processing, multiatlas US image segmentation, and MR respiratory motion correction problems with cardiac cine. The proposed approach differs from existing types of representation of image features by using a trained decision forest (DF) to carry out the feature mapping, which provides supervision and robustness against image objects.

3.2.6 Automatic anatomical landmark localization in CMR images

We show that a hierarchical DF-based regression model can solve the anatomical landmark localization problem in cardiac imaging in a very robust and accurate way. The suggested methodology is used as a preprocessing technique for achieving a fully automatic segmentation pipeline in a multiatlas segmentation system. A new decision tree model is viewed from a more technological point of view, which can leverage local and global image annotations such as subject-specific metainformation-like target anatomy size and scale.

3.2.7 Cardiac MR Image super-resolution with convolutional neural networks

In cardiac imaging, image super-resolution (SR) can be used to reduce the quantitative measurement errors that arise due to thick slice acquisitions. In that regard, we propose one of the first approaches that employ a convolutional neural network (CNN) model for the cardiac image SR problem and demonstrate the performance improvement in terms of accuracy and inference time by comparing it to state-of-the-art SR approaches. The presented SR framework fuses the information from multiple input images that are acquired from different imaging planes (e.g., SAX, LAX). More importantly, we show that the accuracy of subsequent image analysis (e.g., segmentation, myocardium tracking) can be improved when the input images are preprocessed with the proposed SR technique.

3.2.8 Learning anatomical shape priors with convolutional neural networks

The latest state-of-the-art segmentation of medical images and SR structures are based on CNN models; however, widely used training objectives do not specifically oversee these models to learn the global structure of the target space, such as label form and topology. This may pose a potential issue where the image data is not self-sufficient for analysis due to image objects, where the analysis involves anatomical priors. In that regard, we are exploring new model training objectives which could allow more efficient use of manual annotations and thus provide better model supervision. A novel training technique for integrating anatomical priors into a typical CNN model is being suggested. With this approach the trained models are guided in their predictions by respecting the underlying anatomical constraints. For example, SR is an ill-posed problem and a given LR image may have several valid inverse HR solutions. The proposed SR model would pick the most anatomically correct solution of all possible options in our approach. In addition, we show the benefit of end-to-end network training in circumventing conventional pre and postprocessing imaging strategies such as motion correction, super-resolution, and conditional random fields. We further show that application-driven model learning in widely used frameworks can remove the need for intermediate steps in image analysis. In other words, to know the direct relationship between the image data and the target goal, the models may be supervised. For example, high-resolution 3D segmentations are obtained directly from the 2D-SAX stack data without the need for respiratory motion correction or super-resolution.

3.3 Conclusions

Convolutionary neural networks and features derived from them seem to function surprisingly well for medical images. As large data sets for the training of complex models are often not available, fine-tuning the domain of a previously trained model can help. This speeds up the learning process and makes better predictions. Even models trained for general object recognition could be a great baseline. In our case, network surgery by removing the final layer and fine-tuning the pretrained model allowed us to make significant progress in the identification of the cardiac view from the image contents without drafting features or training with additional annotations. This also made it possible for us to gain improvement over models learned from scratch. However, even the performance of models learned from scratch is very encouraging for further exploration. More recent and much deeper network architectures have achieved significant improvements in the performance of image recognition over AlexNet and are likely to help further improve the performance of view recognition. Features extracted from our network should be useful as descriptors for new views (e.g., pathology specific views such as those used in congenital heart disease) and acquisition sequences other than SSFP, but also for the recognition of the acquisition sequences themselves. Several recommendations have recently been proposed to simplify and remove vendor-specific naming of acquisition sequences. Such efforts are crucial to improving communication in cardiology. The methods presented in this chapter could help us to learn how to map the image content to these standardized nomenclatures and to further clean up inconsistent and missing metadata for better organization and organization. As we can see later in this article, the features of our fine-tuned network can also be used to predict the locations of cardiac landmarks. These are valuable additions to the arsenal of resources for managing noisy metadata in our data sets and are already helping us to organize cardiac image collections. In the future, our method can be used for the semantic image retrieval and analysis of a medical liter. Image recognition can also be incredibly useful for the expensive question of quality assurance to check enhanced contrast images.

References

[1] S. Standring, Gray's Anatomy E-Book: The Anatomical Basis of Clinical Practice, Elsevier Health Sciences, 2015.

[2] L.H. Opie, Heart Physiology: From Cell to Circulation, Lippincott Williams & Wilkins, 2004.

[3] W.F. Boron, E.L. Boulpaep, Medical Physiology, third ed., Elsevier Health Sciences, 2016.

[4] E. Chou, J. Carrino, Magnetic Resonance Imaging, vol. 1, Elsevier Inc, 2006, pp. 106–117.

[5] R.W. Brown, Y.-C.N. Cheng, E.M. Haacke, M.R. Thompson, R. Venkatesan, Magnetic Resonance Imaging: Physical Principles and Sequence Design, John Wiley & Sons, 2014.

[6] M. Sutton, N. Sharpe, Left ventricular remodeling after myocardial infarction, Circulation 101 (25) (2000) 2981–2988.

[7] E. Castillo, D.A. Bluemke, Cardiac MR imaging, Radiol. Clin. 41 (1) (2003) 17–28.

[8] M. Lustig, D. Donoho, J.M. Pauly, Sparse MRI: the application of compressed sensing for rapid MR imaging, Magn. Reson. Med. 58 (6) (2007) 1182–1195.

[9] J.P. Ridgway, Cardiovascular magnetic resonance physics for clinicians: part I, J. Cardiovasc. Magn. Reson. 12 (1) (2010) 71.

[10] J.P. Finn, K. Nael, V. Deshpande, O. Ratib, G. Laub, Cardiac MR imaging: state of the technology, Radiology 241 (2) (2006) 338–354.

[11] A. Oppelt, R. Graumann, H. Barfuss, H. Fischer, W. Hartl, W. Schajor, et al., FISPa new fast MRI sequence, Electromedica 54 (1) (1986) 15–18.

[12] J.C. Carr, O. Simonetti, J. Bundy, D. Li, S. Pereles, J.P. Finn, Cine MR angiography of the heart with segmented true fast imaging with steady-state precession, Radiology 219 (3) (2001) 828–834.

[13] C.B. Higgins, A. de Roos, MRI and CT of the Cardiovascular System, Lippincott Williams & Wilkins, 2006.

[14] C. Rickers, N.M. Wilke, M. Jerosch-Herold, S.A. Casey, P. Panse, N. Panse, J. Weil, A.G. Zenovich, B.J. Maron, Utility of cardiac magnetic resonance imaging in the diagnosis of hypertrophic cardiomyopathy, Circulation 112 (6) (2005) 855–861.

[15] M. Foppa, B.B. Duncan, L.E. Rohde, Echocardiography-based left ventricular mass estimation. How should we define hypertrophy? Cardiovasc. Ultrasound 3 (1) (2005) 17.

[16] A.F. Frangi, W.J. Niessen, M.A. Viergever, Three-dimensional modeling for functional analysis of cardiac images, a review, IEEE Trans. Med. Imaging 20 (1) (2001) 2–5.

[17] J.-Y. Lu, H. Zou, J.F. Greenleaf, Biomedical ultrasound beam forming, Ultrasound Med. Biol. 20 (5) (1994) 403–428.

[18] P.R. Hoskins, K. Martin, A. Thrush, Diagnostic Ultrasound: Physics and Equipment, Cambridge University Press, 2010.

[19] I.S. Salgo, Three-dimensional echocardiographic technology, Cardiol. Clin. 25 (2) (2007) 231–239.

[20] J.A. Noble, N. Navab, H. Becher, Ultrasonic image analysis and image-guided interventions, Interface Focus 1 (4) (2011) 673–685.

[21] J.A. Noble, D. Boukerroui, Ultrasound image segmentation: a survey, IEEE Trans. Med. Imaging 25 (8) (2006) 987–1010.

[22] P. Lancellotti, C. Tribouilloy, A. Hagendorff, B.A. Popescu, T. Edvardsen, L.A. Pierard, L. Badano, J.L. Zamorano, Recommendations for the echocardiographic assessment of native valvular regurgitation: an executive summary from the European association of cardiovascular imaging, Eur. Heart J. Cardiovasc. Imag. 14 (7) (2013) 611–644.

[23] F. Sardanelli, M. Quarenghi, G. Di Leo, L. Boccaccini, A. Schiavi, Segmentation of cardiac cine MR images of left and right ventricles: interactive semi-automated methods and manual contouring by two readers with different education and experience, J. Magn. Reson. Imaging 27 (4) (2008) 785–792.

[24] N. Paragios, M.-P. Jolly, M. Taron, R. Ramaraj, Active shape models and segmentation of the left ventricle in echocardiography, in: Scale-Space, Springer, 2005, pp. 131–142.

[25] M.V. Stralen, A. Haak, K. Leung, G.V. Burken, J. Bosch, Segmentation of multicenter 3D left ventricular echocardiograms by active appearance models, in: Proceedings of MICCAI CETUS Challenge, 2014, pp. 73–80.

[26] C. Yao, 3D Echocardiography Image Compounding, PhD Thesis, King's College London, University of London, 2012.

[27] S. Shernand, Evaluation of the left ventricular size and function, in: Comprehensive Atlas of 3D Echocardiography, Lippincott Williams and Wilkins, 2012.

[28] S. Malm, S. Frigstad, E. Sagberg, H. Larsson, T. Skjaerpe, Accurate and reproducible measurement of left ventricular volume and ejection fraction by contrast echocardiography, J. Am. Coll. Cardiol. 44 (5) (2004) 1030–1035.

[29] S.E. Petersen, P.M. Matthews, J.M. Francis, M.D. Robson, F. Zemrak, R. Boubertakh, A.A. Young, S. Hudson, P. Weale, S. Garratt, R. Collins, S. Piechnik, S. Neubauer, UK biobanks cardiovascular magnetic resonance protocol, J. Cardiovasc. Magn. Reson. 18 (1) (2015) 8, https://doi.org/10.1186/s12968-016-0227-4.

Cardiac function review by machine learning approaches

4

I. Lakshmi

Department of Computer Science, Stella Maris College, Chennai, India

Chapter outline

Image Processing for Automated Diagnosis of Cardiac Diseases. https://doi.org/10.1016/B978-0-323-85064-3.00012-1

4.1 Cardiac MR and ultrasound image segmentation

Due to its nonionizing and high-contrast tissue visualization of heart chambers and arteries, cardiac MR (CMR) imaging is vitally important in clinical cardiology. More specifically, clinical indices derived from CMR images assist in assessing heart function and anatomy, from which clinicians can diagnose cardiovascular diseases (CVDs). Stroke volume (SV), ejection fraction (EF), and wall thickness measurements are collected for the functional evaluation of the left ventricle in normal practice [1] and are useful markers of nonischemic cardiomyopathies such as dilated LV and hypertrophy [2]. In clinical practice, the estimation of these measurements or biomarkers involves manual or automated ventricle-bound delineation. Manual contouring is a repetitive, operator-dependent, and time-consuming task; as shown in Fig. 4.1, researchers have examined semiautomated and automated ventricle segmentation approaches to obtain coherent and precise delineations from SAX and LAX images for these reasons. As reported in the recent survey [3], CMR approaches to segmentation can be classified as image driven and model-d into two classes. In the latter group, the approaches make use of the size, meaning, and anatomical information gained from expert annotations to identify pixels of photographs. The segmentation thus is less sensitive to low contrast, noise strength, and artifacts of acquisition. On the other hand, image-based methods are based on minimizing a predefined energy function consisting of the image strength, contour interaction, and label smoothness energy terms.

4.1.1 Energy minimization methods

The early work [4] on cardiac image segmentation used thresholding to define boundaries of objects by clustering each individual pixel based on a defined intensity threshold, which is also prone to variations in intensity and results may be spatially inconsistent. Region-growing techniques [5] operate on the basis of preselected seed points, and anatomical structures are segmented by propagating the seed labels to neighboring pixels based on their intensity values. Oversegmentation and ventricle boundary leakage were reported [3] as the principal limitation of these approaches. On the other hand, the active-contour and level-set segmentation techniques [6] do not resolve the problem by pixel classification but through contour fitting by iterative energy minimization. The topology and smoothness of the curve are

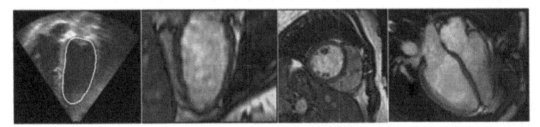

FIG. 4.1

Examples of automatic cardiac MR and US image segmentation results obtained with a convolutional neural network. Cardiac short-axis (second from left) and long-axis (rightmost) MR images are partitioned into semantic parts: LV myocardium, LV blood pool, and background. The number of pixels labeled into blood pool and myocardium classes is calculated to obtain clinical measurements such as ejection fraction and ventricular mass.

regularized during optimization of the objective function, while the gradients in the image intensities direct the fitting process. In some cases [7], type priors are also used in the operation of the energy. However, these techniques rely more on precise initialization of the contour. For example, mathematical models (e.g., shape PCA [8]) were used to model the shape of the ventricles and are used to implement anatomically realistic delineations in image segmentation algorithms. In such methods, optimization is achieved over a collection of learned modes of variation characterizing the distribution of surface points representing the shapes of the organ. Particular examples are active type models (ASM) [9] and appearance models (AAM) [10] that involve the identification of landmark correspondences between target and training images. As pointed out by Peng et al. [3], during the surface fitting process, these models can be computationally very challenging and may not always generalize well to previously unseen forms. Graph-cutting techniques [11] were also commonly used in cardiac MR [12] and segmentation problems in the US [13]. It uses the maximum flow algorithm [14] to find the minimum cut on a graph, which in polynomial time gives optimal solutions. It has the advantage of being fast in that regard and providing optimum results globally. It is also not sensitive to initialization, whereas model-based deformable approaches are sensitive to initialization. In later years, extensions to the original algorithm have been suggested, including computationally efficient 3D+T CMR segmentation [15] and forming prior energy-dependent formulations [16].

4.1.2 Gaussian mixture models

Gaussian mixture modeling (GMM) of image intensities was suggested as another way to segment cardiac LV [17]. This method, in its simplest form, classifies pixels based on a fitting intensity distribution, modeled as normal weighted sum distributions as shown in Fig. 4.2. The optimization of probability is carried out using the maximization of expectations (EM) algorithm [18]. A spatially coherent GMM is suggested in follow-up work [19] to ensure accuracy of the output mark, which is accomplished with a Markov random field (MRF). In addition, spatially distorted 3D+T probabilistic cardiac atlases are used in the same algorithm to direct the optimization of the EM, where prior knowledge from the atlas

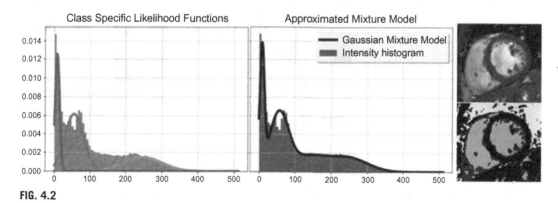

FIG. 4.2

Cardiac MR image segmentation with a Gaussian mixture model using expectation maximization algorithm. The intensity histogram is modeled with weighted normal distributions shown in the middle and the class-likelihood distributions shown on the left.

is used to estimate the initial GMM parameters. Similarly, a probabilistic atlas is used to initialize the GMM-EM framework [20]; however, the authors suggested a multivariate mixture model to perform joint multisequence segmentation of multisequence CMR images. Shi et al. [21] incorporated the techniques of EM and graph-cut optimization into the myocardium segment infarct regions within the same system. Recent work [22] has suggested a collaborative approach to CMR image restoration and segmentation of GMM-EM. In this process, the optimization of compressed sensing energy is driven by a mixture model so that for the segmentation function the reconstructed intensity values can be more accurately modeled.

4.1.3 Multiatlas segmentation methods

Multiatlas mark fusion (MALF) technique is another segmentation method that was used in cardiac MR [23, 24] and 3D-US [25] images to delineate ventricles. As shown in Fig. 4.3, using affine and deformable transformation models, manually annotated atlases are warped to target image. The computed spatial transformations are added to manual segmentations and fused together to form the final segmentation of the LV. MALF requires several atlases to target image registrations, and the algorithm's efficiency depends mainly on the accuracy and robustness of the atlas to target

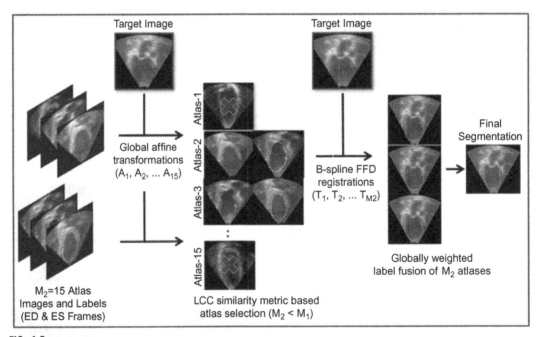

FIG. 4.3

Diagram of a standard multiatlas label fusion segmentation method. The atlases shown on the left are spatially warped to the target image (in red) using affine (A) and deformable (T) transformation models. The computed spatial mappings are later applied to atlas LV segmentation maps and fused together to obtain the LV delineation of the target image.

image registration. MALF approaches have two key features that make them accurate segmentation tools: (1) segmentation label accuracy and object shape are ensured in label predictions because the atlas system operates directly on manual annotations and (2) a large number of training data are effectively fused through the label fusion algorithm so that the ensemble of all deformed annotations leads to further deformities. However, it can be computationally costly to perform several registrations, and in some cases, anatomical landmarks can be needed to obtain an initial alignment between aim and atlas images. Multiatlas segmentation methods have consistently performed well compared with other approaches and obtained state-of-the-art performance in benchmarks for RV segmentation [26]. It is also important to notice that more accurate and computationally faster methods have been proposed and benchmarked in cardiac LV segmentation challenges over the past 2 years (e.g., convolutionary neural networks) [27]. In addition, clinical index estimation cannot always require an algorithm for image segmentation. Zhen et al. [28] proposed a method focused on machine learning to estimate the EF and LVM values directly. Since there have been various methods of measuring LV volume, such as Simpson's rule [29], a machine learning model can theoretically leverage an efficient way of learning the relationship between image data and volumetric measurements in an end-to-end manner without requiring precise ventricle delineations. Image segmentation approaches that involve more advanced machine learning models are discussed in Section 4.5.2 and a short comparison to traditional methods is provided.

4.1.4 **Anatomical priors in cardiac segmentation**

In segmentation of cardiac MR, ventricle boundaries do not generally align with edges of the pressure. For example, trabeculae in the LV blood pool are usually found in LV endocardial segmentations [30], though the contrast between the blood pool and trabeculae is strong in strength. That is why contrasting images alone cannot always be a valid source of information for automatic delineation tools. Similar conditions may be found in echocardiographic images; the myocardial contour may be incomplete simply because it is out of the transducer coverage area. In addition, noise in ultrasound images combined with signal drop-out artifacts can lead to higher prediction errors in the methods of segmentation and recording. Section 4.1.2 allows for a more detailed explanation of these weaknesses (e.g., motion artifacts). For these reasons, anatomical details need to be taken into account in the design of the energy role in image-driven segmentation approaches. This can be accomplished by adding additional energy function constraints which are related to the heart's cardiac structure, form statistics, or physical properties. Tavakoli et al. [31] supported a survey study on the use of anatomical priors in cardiac image analysis methods to resolve the problems of segmentation and registration. In this section, we focus briefly on the prior-based methods applicable to the scope of this thesis. We are especially interested in priors based on a statistical model, and also the deterministic ones used in optimization as a regularization concept, such as adjacency and edge polarity. For example, PCA-based statistical shape models [32] (ASM, AAM) were widely used to refine the results of level sets [33] and active contour segmentation algorithms [34]. Similarly, Pszczolkowski et al. [35] used these models to parameterize fields of deformation in nonrigid image recordings. The trained generative models are used in both cases to calculate shape distances which direct algorithms to generate more plausible anatomical results. Anatomical priors have been encoded as a regularization concept in other segmentation systems, without needing a computational model or training dataset. Some specific examples used in cardiac imaging can be summarized as follows: (1) Thickness prior—the radial distance between endocardium and epicardium labels was used as a restriction in a level-set US segmentation framework [36]. (2) Topological prior—many anatomical objects in medical pictures have a particular topology form. For example, surface segmentation of the LV endocardium is supposed to be a connected object without any holes. By imposing this constraint (Fig. 4.4) [37], the topology of segmentation maps can be conserved. (3) Prior motion—segmentation and monitoring have different applications in both cardiac MR and US imaging. This group of techniques relies on the mechanical, optical, or physiological properties of the heart, such as models of finite elements [38], myocardial incompressibility [39], and optical or elasticity laws as constraints for cardiac image segmentation and motion estimation. Multiatlas techniques [11, 19] that implicitly use similar anatomical constraints (e.g., adjacency and shape) by propagating the manually annotated labels to the target image space are shown in Fig. 4.3. Similarly, image registration and segmentation approaches based on machine learning will implicitly incorporate prior information into its system by learning from external annotated datasets.

4.2 Super-resolution in magnetic resonance images

The sensor resolution of a medical imaging system is determined according to the physical constraints which limit the data sampling frequency and signal-to-noise ratio of the acquired data. In MR imaging, the problem arises from the need for long signal recovery between excitations to enable the operation of the spin-echo mechanism that provides tissue contrast. In addition to these limitations, acquisition time is another factor determining the resolution of acquired images as in the case of cardiac MR imaging, where repeated breath-holds and temporal data acquisition are required. For these reasons, the acquisition of high-resolution 3D+T cardiac images is very difficult to perform within clinically acceptable time frames. On the other hand, high-resolution (HR) 3D imaging is the key to more accurate understanding of the anatomy and function of the human body. Therefore, in clinical practice [17], multiple low-resolution (LR) cardiac MR images are acquired from different imaging planes (e.g., SAX and LAX stacks) and clinical assessment is performed through analyzing the anatomy from these LR images as shown in Fig. 4.5. In the context of MR imaging, a common approach [40] assumes that LR images (x) can be modeled as a weighted average of the corresponding HR image (y) plus a noise signal (η). In cardiac imaging, due to respiratory and heart motion, a spatial transformation operator (M) is included in this forward model which can be formulated as $x = DBSMy + \eta$. Here, S and B

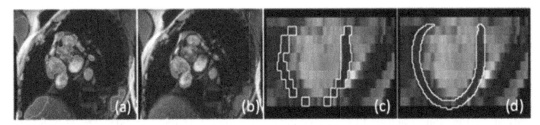

FIG. 4.4

Use of anatomical priors in cardiac image left ventricle segmentation. Topological prior is used in [37] to obtain a connected single segmentation object (A, B). Similarly, statistical shape model is used to regularize the CMR SAX image segmentation output (C, D) [86].

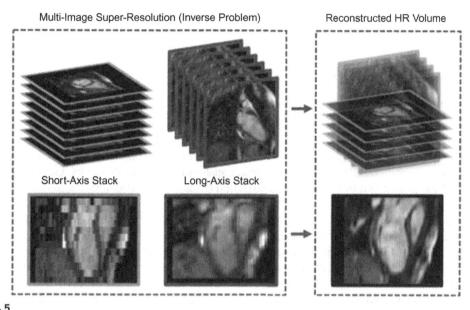

Multi-Image Super-Resolution (Inverse Problem)   Reconstructed HR Volume

Short-Axis Stack   Long-Axis Stack

FIG. 4.5

Stack of 2D cardiac MR slices acquired along the short- (SAX) and long-axis (LAX) planes. Information from multiple stacks can be merged into a single high-resolution volume (shown on the right) through an image super-resolution algorithm [40].

correspond to slice selection and blurring operators, respectively. The blurring kernel is associated with the slice profile of the scanner and usually approximated by a Gaussian function [17]. The last operator D corresponds to image decimation. In the interest of providing more detailed visualizations, some studies [23, 41] have proposed to tackle these hardware limitations through inverse solution techniques such as image super-resolution (SR). In standard SR approaches, a single image with a high pixel resolution is synthesized by combining independent LR acquisitions of the same organ. In other words, combination of several sources provides more information than each of the individual sources. Besides the improved image quality and resolution, SR can provide better guidance for subsequent computer-aided image analysis techniques such as image segmentation. Zhen et al. [28] demonstrated that precision of brain tissue segmentation can be improved by preprocessing the input low-resolution MR image data with a SR algorithm. Similarly, other studies have shown that SR can be a useful image preprocessing technique in fetal MR [42] and PET imaging [43] for better visualization of the brain tissues.

Image SR is usually an ill-posed inverse problem that requires the approximation of the HR image data from the given LR image(s) [44]. SR approaches can be characterized in terms of two main properties: (1) whether they operate on multiple LR image data acquired from different directions or require only single LR image data and (2) whether they operate based on a learned inverse model or relies solely on the given image data. Traditional variational approaches (e.g., total variation [45]) solve the inverse problem iteratively through energy minimization. On the other hand, model-driven approaches [46, 47], in particular single-image SR, require a generative or regression model to approximate the inverse function and are learnt from an external dataset containing LR–HR image pairs. In exceptional cases, single-image SR techniques may not require external training data as in the case of nonlocal means based image upsampling methods proposed previously [48, 49].

4.2.1 Variational inverse methods

The iterative back-projection algorithm (IBP) [49] is a traditional multiimage SR approach that attempts to solve the inverse problem by making an initial guess on the high-resolution image, which is later iteratively updated by back projecting the error signal originating from the synthetically generated LR images and original input data. To obtain anatomically plausible results, the standard IBP energy function is modified by including regularization terms such as cross-image self-similarity [50] or total variation terms. Similarly, Odille et al. [51] proposed an energy minimization based SR approach that performs joint reconstruction and motion compensation for cardiac 2D image stacks, which includes denoising with Beltrami regularization.

Energy minimization based SR reconstruction techniques require a good initial approximation of the solution for both the HR volume and also for the motion model [51]; otherwise, optimization techniques such as Gauss–Newton [25] are not guaranteed to converge to reliable SR results. More importantly, multiple stack input data might not always be available and are not acquired in standard imaging protocols. As discussed in Section 4.1.3, cardiac images acquired along the LAX plane do not necessarily always cover the whole heart.

4.2.2 Regression models for image super-resolution

In general, single-image super-resolution techniques are more flexible and have more application areas as they do not require multiple data acquisitions from different views. However, external training data are often required to learn a generative SR model. Bhatia et al. [41] proposed a coupled dictionary learning approach to model the relationship between low- and high-resolution image patches collected from cardiac MR data. Similarly, O'Regan and Rueckert [41] used a multiatlas technique to transfer high-resolution information from atlases to a low-resolution target image grid. Although multiatlas techniques do not have an explicit parametric model, as they make use of an external dataset, they are included in this review. As shown in Fig. 4.6, a regression model can be learnt to perform the mapping from LR to HR patches. Rickers et al. [2] proposed a regression forest-based approach to upsample diffusion tensor images. In general, these approaches differ from each other in terms of the way they model the inverse mapping between low- and high-resolution image patches. In the recent years, machine learning approaches in particular CNNs have been shown to be capable of learning inverse functions very effectively, and Tanno et al. [53] have shown their applicability in diffusion MR image SR problem. However, the presented experiments do not show whether subsequent image analysis (e.g., pathology classification) does actually benefit from SR preprocessing or not. Since HR pixel values are generated as a result of an optimization process, resultant intensity values may not be considered as reliable as the ones in the original images which are directly generated by the reconstruction methods. In contrast, by showing the benefits of SR for subsequent analysis, one can provide a scientific evidence for its use as a preprocessing technique in analysis frameworks.

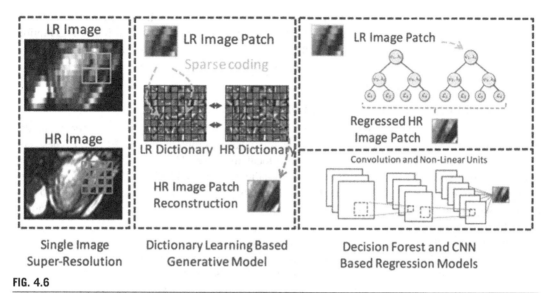

FIG. 4.6

Model-based single-image super-resolution approaches: coupled low- (LR) and high-resolution (HR) dictionaries are used to synthesize HR image patches [23], similarly regression models can be trained to solve this inverse mapping problem [2, 52].

4.3 Multimodal cardiac image registration

Imaging techniques play an essential role in the evaluation of cardiac-related pathologies, interventional treatment guidance, and prognosis throughout the patient's follow-up. Integration of several imaging techniques provides multimodal data that contain both functional and anatomical information [54]. For instance, in image-guided cardiac surgery, overlaying 3D MR/CT images on real-time fluoroscopic or ultrasound data enables tissue characterization and precise localization of instruments and catheters with respect to the underlying anatomy [55]. Similarly, image fusion of CT angiography with cardiac perfusion MRI has facilitated detailed assessment of coronary artery disease [56]. Image fusion, which is also referred as image registration, is the task of spatially aligning and visualizing different aspects of human anatomy simultaneously. This can be performed by means of a dedicated combined imaging system (e.g., PET/MRI, PET/CT) or through image registration techniques. Despite extensive research, these image registration algorithms have not been widely adopted in clinical practice due to two main reasons: (1) most registration algorithms still require manual interaction for initialization and (2) anatomical knowledge is needed to be integrated into algorithms to understand and match correspondences between different imaging modalities. The latter can be considered as the main challenge in multimodal image registration. In general, image registration can be performed between two or more images. In the current context, we only consider methods that involve two images. A registration algorithm typically minimizes an energy function that is composed of dissimilarity (S) and regularization (R) terms:

$$\arg_a \min S\,(I, J \circ T) + R(T) \tag{4.1}$$

Optimization techniques allow us to minimize the energy function and find an optimal spatial transformation (T) that maps a source image (J) to a target image (I). In summary, an image registration algorithm mainly consists of three main building blocks: a transformation model, an optimization strategy, and an objective function measuring the image similarity.

4.3.1 Transformation models and optimization techniques

Optimization techniques can be roughly grouped into two categories: continuous and discrete methods. In the latter case, registration is expressed as a discrete labeling problem over a MRF [57]. These approaches have been shown to be more robust against local minima problem due to nonconvex nature of the optimization task [58] and they are inherently gradient free. In addition to that, major speed improvements can be achieved as parallel architectures can be used in several discrete algorithms to perform nonsequential tasks. A more detailed comparison on registration optimization techniques can be found in Sotiras et al. [59].

Transformation models, which define the warping function between source and target images, can be categorized into two subgroups as linear (rigid/affine) and deformable. The latter can be further divided into two subcategories as physical model and interpolation based deformation models. Common examples for the former are elastic body [60], fluid flow [61], and flow of diffeomorphism models [62], which regulate displacement fields based on some underlying physical phenomena such as bending energy. The interpolation based deformation models use smooth basis functions with local or global spatial support such as free-form deformations (FFD) [63], radial basis functions [64], and locally affine models [65]. Further details about deformable models can be found in the recent survey paper [64].

4.3.2 Image similarity criteria in multimodal image registration

In multimodal image registration, the formulation of similarity metric has more importance and is more challenging compared to monomodal registration due to a few reasons: (1) Some anatomical structures may not always be visible in both modalities (e.g., US and MRI) due to physical properties of the imaging systems. (2) Anatomical tissues might be visualized with different intensity statistics and the relationship between the two image signals might vary depending on the spatial location and scanner configuration (e.g., US probe location). These factors are more pronounced particularly in the cardiac US multimodal image registration problem. The focus of this review and thesis will be on the development of reliable image similarity metrics to identify correspondences between multimodal images (Fig. 4.7).

The diagram shown in Fig. 4.8 visualizes the standard categorization of the existing similarity criteria used in multimodal registration methods. Information theoretic measures such as mutual information (MI) [64] and correlation ratio [65] have been common choices in alignment of multimodal MR image data. Nevertheless, in US image analysis, global similarity metrics do not always capture the true tissue correspondences since image intensity statistics can vary spatially. For this reason, the focus has shifted to development of local intensity similarity metrics such as local MI [66] and conditional MI [52]. King et al. [68] proposed a physical model-based US dense similarity metric and used to align CT and US cardiac images. Other methods, on the other hand, have approached the multimodal registration problem by converting it to a monomodal registration problem. This goal can be achieved either by simulating one modality from another or by mapping both modalities into a

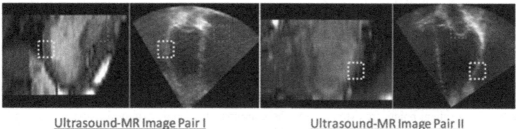

Ultrasound-MR Image Pair I   Ultrasound-MR Image Pair II

FIG. 4.7

Two pairs of cardiac 3D-US and MR images, acquired from same subject, are shown. Identifying the anatomical correspondences between the two modalities is not an easy task due to spatially varying intensity statistics. Additionally, some anatomical structures might not be visible in ultrasound due to limited field of view and signal drop-out (shown in red). For instance, papillary muscles (#2) and right ventricle (#1) are not visible in the shown US images, which needs to be taken into account in design of similarity metrics or optimization.

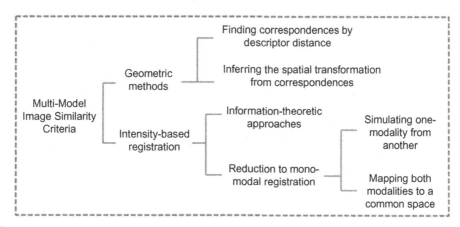

FIG. 4.8

Categorization of image similarity metrics that are used in multimodal medical image registration problem.

common space. Simulation methods have been used to align abdominal CT/US [68], fetal MR/US [69], and cardiac US/CT/MR data [70]. The main drawback of the methods in this category is that they require tissue segmentation prior to registration. Furthermore, the intensity models used in modality simulations may not reflect the true intensity characteristics of the scanner. For this reason, research has focused on techniques that map the images into a common feature space. Multichannel feature-based alignment techniques were the early examples, such as wavelets coefficients [71] and Gabor features [1]. A particular feature type, namely local phase representation, was used as a similarity metric in the cardiac MR/US registration problem [2]. The proposed approach extracts ventricle boundaries from both US and MR images by analyzing the phase signal in a multiscale fashion. Recent work [10] has shown improved performance over these approaches by proposing the use of local self-similarity measures. It has achieved state-of-the-art performance in CT lung and US/MR brain image registration [9].

Although these methods have achieved good performance in benchmarks, their translation to clinical use is still limited due to the low US imaging quality. In particular, the generated representations may not always be robust toward noise and the registration accuracy strongly depends on the image quality. To overcome this problem, research needs to focus on development of machine learning based image similarity techniques. A trained model can be utilized to map intermodality data into a common feature space to highlight the tissue correspondences. In addition to intensity-based metrics, sparse geometric descriptors have been used in multimodal image alignment as a similarity metric. Typically two sets of landmarks or salient points are extracted and these are matched via descriptor distance or geometric constraints such as graph matching algorithms [42]. For instance, SIFT feature-based 3D MR/CT image alignment [26] is one particular example. Similarly, surface-based cardiac US/MR image alignment techniques [13, 69] have been proposed. Procrustes analysis [10] has been commonly used to align surface point sets, which require prior surface segmentation for image alignment.

4.3.3 Evaluation of image registration algorithms

The evaluation of registration algorithms is another important subject of study. Since the underlying ground truth spatial transformation information is not always available, except for phantom data, several techniques have been developed to quantify the accuracy of registration algorithms. Surrogate measures (e.g., SSD or MI) may not always be a good indicator of spatially meaningful registration results. For this reason, quantification based on spatial distance of physically attached markers is a more reliable way to evaluate registration algorithms [67], which is referred as fiducial localization error. Similarly, it can also be achieved through sparsely located landmark correspondences or through comparison of object surface segmentations performed on both target and source images [24]. However, manual identification of landmarks or fiducial points is a tedious and error-prone task even for clinical experts. Therefore, interobserver variability in landmark localization accuracy often has to be taken into account in registration algorithm evaluation.

4.4 Machine learning models in image analysis

An overview of two machine learning models commonly used in image analysis is given in this section. In particular, we discuss machine learning approaches based on decision forests and convolutional neural networks. Our analysis focuses on model parameterization, design rules in image analysis frameworks, and practical requirements in terms of training data size and computation power. Moreover, we compare the two models in terms of how they make use of training data to learn decision rules and reason about it. Finally, we summarize their applications in cardiac image analysis and discuss about the ongoing practical challenges: model interpretability and computation resource management.

4.4.1 Ensemble of decision trees (decision forests)

The decision tree model [30] is a nonparametric model commonly used for classification and regression tasks. The model predicts the value of a target variable by using simple decision rules based on comparing the input data features to a fixed threshold value. As shown in Fig. 4.9, the tree model is composed of split and leaf nodes, which define the tree model parameters. Split

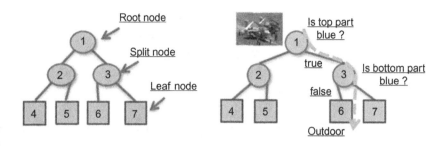

FIG. 4.9

The definition of nodes in a decision tree structure. Image class label prediction is decided by routing the samples through the split nodes based on sequential decision rules.

nodes characterize the decision rules applied on input data, branches represent the outcome of each decision, and leaf nodes contain target posterior information for given input. As explained in the recent survey by Criminisi [46], decision tree training algorithms allow us to come up with an optimal set of sequential decision rules, used in split nodes, to minimize tree transversal and maximize information about output label for given input data, which is also known as minimization of output space uncertainty or entropy. The learned decision rules are stored in split nodes (weak classifiers), and in the standard tree model they are based on a decision stump. In a simple classification task, shown in Fig. 4.10, the tree decision boundaries are composition of horizontal and vertical lines defined along a single dimension in feature space due to decision stumps in each split node. However, in canonical correlation based splits [21] and oblique splits [17], split node decision rules can be based on multidimensional information obtained from training samples, which can reduce model bias (under fitting) in training. At testing time, each sample is routed to its corresponding leaf node through learned decision rules as shown in Fig. 4.9. Decision stump threshold values are determined by considering the information gain after each binary split of training data. The formulation of different information gain objectives are discussed in Glatz et al. [55]. Decision trees offer design flexibility as such different kind of labels (e.g., numerical, categorical) can be utilized simultaneously within the same model as long as training data can be clustered in a meaningful way. Some examples include structured learning [64] and multitask Hough forest models [52]. Similarly, the local leaf node models can store different sorts of information (regression, classification, image metadata) at the same time. In several studies [25, 56], the Bayesian uncertainty of a tree model is stored in leaf nodes to understand model prediction confidence. Another useful feature is tree pruning, through which model overfitting can be avoided by simply reducing the depth of trained decision trees. For these given reasons, decision trees and ensemble models have been widely studied in image analysis in the last decade as it provides design flexibility. Ensemble of decision trees [11], also known as decision forests, combine several uncorrelated decision trees into a single model through bootstrap aggregating (bagging) [29], where different subsets of training data and features are used to train each tree. In this way, the model variance is reduced and better data generalization is achieved. In ensemble models, the final outcome is usually obtained by aggregating individual tree predictions, and weighted averaging is one way to merge multiple predictions as in the case of regression forest [56]. Another advantage of decision forests is that they are simple to understand and interpret. By analyzing the information gain obtained at each split node for the selected image feature, we can categorize input features in terms of their importance for the

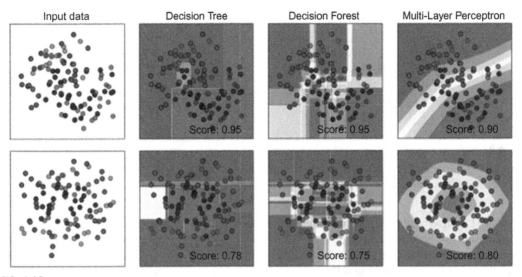

| Input data | Decision Tree | Decision Forest | Multi-Layer Perceptron |

Score: 0.95 — Score: 0.95 — Score: 0.90

Score: 0.78 — Score: 0.75 — Score: 0.80

FIG. 4.10

Visual comparison of different classification models and their decision boundaries. In this toy classification example, we observe that decision forests and MLP models generalize to the underlying data distribution in different ways.

given task. Additionally, by analyzing the leaf nodes and adjacency of each sample stored in the leaf nodes, one could get insights into the local leaf models and visualize how samples are clustered within the tree model.

For example, a proximity analysis [31] is used by Lorenzo-Vald´es et al. [19] to visualize how the cardiac images are clustered. Finally, decision tree models do not require significant computation power and large amounts of data unlike convolutional neural networks which will be discussed next.

4.4.2 Convolutional neural networks

A convolutional neural network (CNN) [39] is a feed-forward artificial neural network model that has been successfully applied in image classification benchmarks such as ImageNet [32].

The neural connectivity pattern of a CNN model was inspired by the biological processes in the human visual system [17]. From a technical perspective, CNN models are parameterized by convolutional filters (learnt weights) that are shared across each neuron within the same layer, which reduces model complexity and exploits the statistical correlation between neighboring pixels in an effective way. Therefore, the number of model parameters can be reduced significantly and the training of deep models become practically easier [10]. The connectivity pattern of CNNs is shown in Fig. 4.11.

A cascade of convolutional layers build a CNN model, as shown in Fig. 4.12, which was initially used for digit recognition in the MNIST dataset [39]. The back-propagation algorithm [29] is used to learn the optimal set of image filters for the given task and training objective such as classification or regression. The updates on each layer parameters are computed by back propagating the error signal originating from the loss function. The error signal is differentiated with respect to the weight and bias

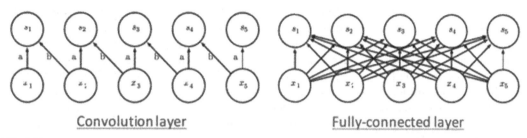

Convolution layer   **Fully-connected layer**

FIG. 4.11

Neural connectivity comparison between convolutional and dense layers. In the former case, the connections are sparser and they are shared across the neurons, which reduces the number of parameters used in the model and partially avoids the overfitting problem.

The figure is adapted from [10].

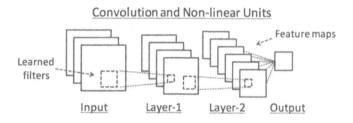

Convolution and Non-linear Units

Learned filters | Feature maps

Input   Layer-1   Layer-2   Output

FIG. 4.12

Structure of a standard convolutional neural network model that is composed of series of convolution layers and nonlinear units. Each layer is characterized by a set of image filters that are trained to map the input data to the desired output space.

terms using the chain rule [10]. As long as the loss function can be differentiated with respect to model parameters, the error originating from the loss function can be back propagated to the input layer to optimize the model parameters. Due to nonconvex nature of commonly used objective functions, CNNs are trained iteratively with stochastic optimization methods. At each iteration, gradient updates are computed using a small subset of training data also known as mini-batch, which provides tolerance to noisy data and reduces the chance of the network getting stuck in local minima [67]. Additionally, iterative mini-batch update scheme enables the use of large-scale datasets for model training.

End-to-end learning and back propagation also reduce the dependency of CNN models on hand-engineered image features and ad hoc preprocessing techniques. This could be seen as the main advantage of CNN models over its counterparts as the generated intermediate representations are customized for the given training objective as shown in Fig. 4.15. Indeed, this is the main reason why some studies [8, 28] proposed the use of autoencoder models to extract domain-specific image features from unlabeled image datasets. The learnt features are later used in an ensemble model (e.g., decision forest) for classification and regression tasks. Similar to DFs, in neural network models, ensemble learning can be achieved using the drop-out technique [46] that is commonly used in densely connected layers to avoid model overfitting. Due to its sparse connectivity structure, drop-out technique has not provided a substantial performance improvement when it is used in the CNN models. Recent research has focused on development of CNN-based image analysis frameworks, and these approaches have consistently outperformed other ML models (e.g., decision forests) in common benchmarks in both computer vision [32] and cardiac imaging [37]. Also, it is shown [43] that deeper network architectures are better at capturing nonlinear mappings between input and output spaces for fixed amount of model capacity (number of trainable parameters). From these perspectives, one can argue that CNN models can potentially outperform tree models in image analysis tasks since CNNs can learn more complex mapping functions through a large number of hidden layers and nonlinear operations. In the next section, we demonstrate how these models have been applied in medical image analysis tasks.

4.5 Applications of ML models in medical imaging

Traditional image analysis techniques such as graph-cut and level-set segmentation methods operate according to a handcrafted optimization objective that drive segmentation algorithm. Ventricle boundaries are delineated along high image contrast based on intensity data and some regularization term that ensures smoothness and connectivity of predicted labels. However, these methods have underachieved in segmentation benchmarks (e.g., PASCAL VOC'12 [71]) in comparison to recent submissions done with neural network frameworks since no external learning and algorithm supervision is involved. In the medical imaging domain, one can observe a similar performance difference in the recent cardiac segmentation challenge [37]. With the advent of increased medical imaging data and annotations, the focus has shifted toward development of learning and pattern recognition based image analysis approaches that map input data into abstract representations to better exploit the connection between input and output spaces. As it can be seen in Fig. 4.13, the interest in development and application of machine learning (ML) techniques has exponentially increased over the last decade. Although most of the ML models, such as CNNs [39] and decision forests [13], were initially proposed long time ago, their widespread use in image-processing frameworks has been delayed due to unavailability of large training data and computation power. Indeed, neural networks have seen a significant progress in the last few years and been commonly used in image-processing pipelines since the availability of large computation power. The recent survey [14] presents a historical perspective on neural networks and their widespread use in medical image analysis. In the context of cardiac imaging, researchers have trained various types of discriminative and generative models using imaging data: boosting trees, support vector machines, sparse coding, and dictionary learning. The applications include semantic segmentation [68], landmark localization [58], pathology classification [18], image reconstruction [34], and super-resolution [23]. The main factors that determine the performance of these ML approaches have been (1) the availability of training data, (2) the representation power of the model, and (3) the ability for generalization of the trained model to different input data distributions such as images obtained from different scanners. The requirement of training data has been the main limitation of learning based approaches; however, in the last years more and more cardiac image datasets have become available such as UK Biobank [26] and Second Annual Data Science Bowl [27]. On such large-scale datasets, the main performance difference between ML-based image analysis algorithms arises from how they make use of the annotations to generalize and learn a discriminative or generative model. Additionally, smart preprocessing and augmentation techniques play an important role as well,

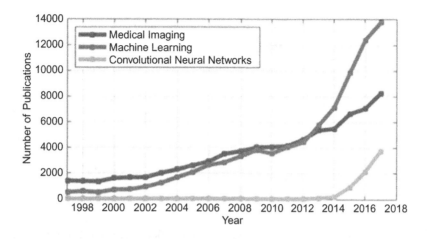

FIG. 4.13

Number of scientific publications according to topic search on https://www.webofknowledge.com/. The figures show that attention to machine learning research has increased exponentially in the recent years. More importantly, convolutional neural network studies constitute substantial part of the machine learning research lately.

which are discussed in detail in Lombaert et al. [15]. In that regard, convolutional neural network (CNN) models have dominated the medical image analysis field in the last years since they can learn complex and task-specific abstract representations to model the relationship between input and output. Moreover, they can scale to large training images well and do not require large number of model parameters in comparison to multilayer densely connected neural networks. Therefore, the differentiating point between ML models arises from compact parameterization of training data while having a strong representation power. Ensemble models have also shown good generalization power on different medical imaging data; as such, decision forest (DF)-based frameworks were proposed by Criminisi et al. [46] to analyze cardiac CT and MR data in various problems. In the next section, we discuss about the existing work on DF- and CNN-based cardiac imaging.

4.5.1 Decision forests in medical imaging

In Table 4.1, we have a short list of cardiac image analysis research that used decision forests in its pipeline. It is important to note that the current work applied by DF in medical imaging is not limited only to those listed in the table. What we find is that researchers used the DF model initially in default applications such as object localization and the functions of classification marking. The emphasis has moved in the following years to applications in other fields, such as super-resolution or evaluating quality control. In addition, we also note that DF model design versatility has allowed researchers to make adjustments to the DF model structure to improve performance. Some examples are organized learning [19], specific goals for classification and regression training [7], and hashing forest [47]. The same pattern of study can also be found in studies of natural image processing as shown in Table 4.2. In addition to the properties of DF models discussed, there are a few limiting factors for their widespread use in medical imaging: (1) DF models do not always well scale up to a large

Table 4.1 Applications of decision forest in medical image analysis.

Reference	Model	Application; remarks
Alexander et al. [46] [MICCAI'14]	Regression forest	Single-image super- resolution method: applied to diffusion MR images.
Lombaert et al. [15] [MICCAI'14]	Laplacian forest	Decision trees are used to select neighboring atlases in multilabel propagation. It is an efficient way of clustering and selecting images for analysis.
Odille et al. [51] [MICCAI'15]	Hough forest	Cardiac ultrasound LV segmentation. Regression votes are used to identify relative location of each patch, which are later utilized to propagate and merge labels from multiatlas dataset.

Table 4.2 Variants of decision forest model have been developed to solve different natural image analysis tasks. This includes joint classification and regression training, and structured learning of the output space.

Reference	Model	Application; remarks
Roche et al. [52] [TPAMI'11]	Hough forest	Pedestrian detection and localization in natural images. Joint training of classification and regression objectives.
Stolzmann et al. [56] [CVPR'11]	Regression forest	Human body joint localization in kinect depth images for pose estimation.
Shi et al. [41] [ICCV'13]	Structured forest	Object boundary map extraction in natural images. Structured forest stores segmentation patches in its leaf nodes instead of storing label posterior distributions.

number of training data because batches of samples must be processed simultaneously during the training of each split node; while CNN models can solve this problem by stochastic learning with small subsets of training data using mini-batches. This could, for example, be a limiting factor in training a DF model with thousands of annotations from the UK Biobank dataset [26]. (2) DF models are typically expected to be retrained from scratch upon the acquisition of new training data. (3) The flow of information from input to output space is built to be deterministic and each sample typically ends in a single leaf node; however, in CNN models this flow can be linked by interleafed parallel neural connections through several directions. The power of representation for the DF model is constrained in that regard. In addition to these aforementioned factors, we include a more comprehensive comparison of CNN and DF models in the next section. The following chapters provide technical information about the organized and regression trees.

4.5.2 Convolutional neural networks in medical imaging

Research on convolutionary neural networks [10] has shown that CNN models can use cascaded convolution and nonlinear operations to learn complex decision boundaries. We can also expect CNN models to be more appropriate for medical image analysis, including cardiac MR images, as long as adequate training data are given, as mentioned in the previous parts. Fig. 4.14 demonstrates the

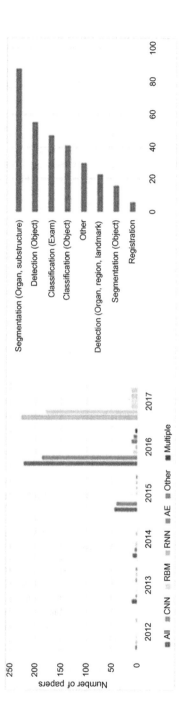

FIG. 4.14

The bar plot shows the number of medical image analysis publications over the recent years which are related to neural networks. On the right, the distribution of these publications with respect to the application type is shown. Segmentation and CNNs have been the most commonly studied research areas in the recent years.

Image courtesy Litjens [47].

number of medical imaging publications using a CNN model within the proposed system of analyzes, which has expanded exponentially. More specifically, most studies focused on applying the CNN models for the task of image segmentation, particularly the U-Net architecture [25] was widely used in this issue. As with decision forest, the focus of the recent CNN-based medical imaging work has changed to other applications such as cardiac image quality assessment [28], MR image super-resolution [11], and image reconstruction [34]. In addition to these areas of research, recurrent models and adversarial learning techniques [11] attracted interest in medical imaging and were applied to the issue of CMR segmentation [10, 71]. In comparison, adversarial learning [11] enables the formulation of custom training targets, which may not be easily formulated in a closed form. The last two chapters in this study are devoted to cardiac image analysis based on CNN, and the target applications are super-resolution image and segmentation. The related CNN research on these subjects is discussed further next.

4.5.3 Medical image segmentation

Table 4.3 offers a representative list of current segmentation research, which uses a neural network model in its processing pipeline. In early work [12], deep belief network models (cascaded Boltzmann machines) were integrated into feature extraction and nearest neighbor patch search problems. Follow-up studies [42, 61] conducted end-to-end learning between input and label spaces using a completely convolutionary model (FCN) [51], which outperformed previous handcrafted segmentation MIC-CAI'12 RV segmentation demanding data pipelines like multiatlas and graph-cut techniques [27]. The medical imaging group has also discussed the disparity in output between the 2D and 3D image kernels used in cardiac segmentation frameworks based on CNN [15]. Since specific benchmarks (e.g., ACDC'171) were evaluated according to manual annotations performed on each slice independently, 3D CNN models showed no substantial change in efficiency.

Table 4.3 A list of cardiac MR and ultrasound image segmentation frameworks that utilize deep neural network architectures.

Reference	Model and modality	Application; remarks
Tanno et al. [53] [Arxiv'16]	Active contour and CNN, MRI	CNN model is used to predict dense flow fields which guide active contour fitting. The framework is used to segment LV in CMR images.
Paragios et al. [6] [MEDIA'16]	Stacked AE, MRI	Autoencoder is used to perform coarse LV segmentation which is later fine-tuned using a deformable model and level-set optimization.
	RNN model, MRI	Recurrent model is utilized across through-plane direction and combined with in-plan CNN model, which is used for CMR LV segmentation.
Tanno et al. [53] [Arxiv'16]	CNN model, MRI	Fully convolutional network is trained in an end-to-end manner for CMR LV segmentation.

Table 4.4 Single-image super-resolution frameworks that make use of a trained CNN model. The application areas range from natural images to medical images including cardiac MRI [191] and brain diffusion imaging.

Reference	Model and modality	Application; remarks
Shi et al. [21] [CVPR'16]	CNN model, natural images	Single-image SR on natural 2D images. Subpixel convolution technique is proposed to reduce model runtime by an order of magnitude.
Ledig et al. [41] [CVPR'17]	CNN model, natural images	Single-image SR on natural 2D images. Adversarial learning is used in SR training to synthesize realistic looking high-resolution images at test time.
Tanno et al. [53] [MICCAI'17]	CNN model, diffusion MRI	Single-image super-resolution for brain DT images. Empirical Bayesian SR uncertainty is estimated using the drop-out technique.

4.5.4 Image super-resolution and other applications

Single-image super-resolution (SR) is another application area of CNN models, which is discussed extensively throughout this chapter. Table 4.4 gives a short summary of the CNN-based SR studies in natural and medical image analysis. The approach was evaluated on natural images, and it has outperformed previous state-of-the-art SR techniques by a significant margin in terms of both PSNR and SSIM [66] metrics. Later, Shi et al. [21] has proposed a subpixel convolution method as an improvement to Dong's architecture. The new SR model performs all convolution and nonlinear operations on the low-resolution image grid to reduce the computational complexity of the network. As an application of similar models in medical imaging, a multiinput SR framework is proposed [11], which utilizes both LAX and SAX stack cardiac data to synthesize a high-resolution isotropic image volume. In follow-up work, Tanno et al. [53] have recently shown that with the same CNN model, SR regression uncertainty can be obtained empirically by sampling from the posterior distribution, which is often done with multiple forward passes and drop-out at each forward pass as suggested previously [9]. Finally, Ledig et al. [41] applied adversarial learning to SR CNN models to obtain qualitatively more appealing HR natural image synthesis. However, the experimental results show that the improved image quality may degrade the performance. CNN models have found other uses in cardiac imaging, in addition to the segmentation and super-resolution methods. One of them is deformable image registration using ML techniques, and it is still a specific field of research that has not been explored in detail. Recent research [23, 55], as shown in Table 4.5, used the U-Net model to approximate FFD and SVF deformable parameters. These techniques will implicitly know the underlying similarities of the pairwise image and classify the tissue correspondences. In Chapter 2, we demonstrate that the proposed probabilistic representation of the surface is one way of exploring multimodal image correspondence through qualified decision forests. Another interesting area of application is automated image quality control for MR image stacks in the cardiac cine. However, CNN-based methods could theoretically explore a more discriminative intermediate space where similarities can be better established between multimodal results. Similarly, decision-making forest-based cardiac landmark localization techniques [10] against a novel CNN architecture and efficiency improvements have been

Table 4.5 A list of other application areas of CNN models in cardiac imaging, which includes quality control, landmark localization, and deformable registration.

Reference	Model and modality	Application; remarks
Tanno et al. [53] [DLMI'17]	CNN model, cardiac MRI	Automatic anatomical landmark localization for cardiac long-axis view generation.
Alexander et al. [46] [SASHIMI'16]	CNN model, cardiac MRI	Automatic image quality assessment. The trained model identifies whether the apical or basal slice is missing in the acquired stack data.
Alexander et al. [46] [MICCAI'17]	CNN model, ultrasound	FFD-based myocardial tracking method is regularized with a spatiotemporal CNN model.
Mahapatra and Sun [12] [MICCAI'16]	Reinforcement learning, cardiac MRI	Artificial agent-based automatic anatomical landmark localization, which is trained using Q-learning.

recorded [38]. Alexander et al. [46] addressed this issue with a CNN model and with the qualified models automatically checked slice coverage of the acquired cardiac MR stacks.

4.5.5 Incorporating anatomical priors in neural networks

As mentioned in Section 4.1.4, anatomical priors were integrated into conventional cardiac segmentation algorithms to provide useful guidance in optimizations. For medical imaging, however, the incorporation of shape and mark prior knowledge into CNN models was not studied for detail except for a few studies: boundary-aware segmentation [19] and topology-aware segmentation of CNN [72]. In recent research, the key component analysis model [18] for regularization has been integrated into CNN models to provide prior shape information in the question of cardiac ultrasound segmentation. In the last chapter, this subject is explored with a more detailed survey about the relevant research published in the field of computer vision.

4.5.6 Current limitations

Although CNN models can learn complex nonlinear mappings and perform well in the tasks of image analysis, they are often represented as black boxes. Accountability is critical particularly in medical image analysis and it is often not enough to have precise predictions. It have shown that we may have a better understanding of what each layer in the network is specialized in by examining the intermediate feature maps. Similarly, directed gradient back-propagation technique [45] was proposed as another way of visualizing the salient image features that contribute to the prediction of the model. Future research is therefore necessary to explore the question of interpretability more thoroughly to understand what these models are actually learning. In addition to the interpretability of the model, hardware limitations (e.g., GPU memory) are another limiting factor in the analysis of broad image contexts particularly in isotropic 3D images (e.g., abdominal CT data). Recent studies have attempted to resolve this problem by exploring large-scale background sparse convolution techniques that minimize computational demand and feature maps [18] (Fig. 4.15).

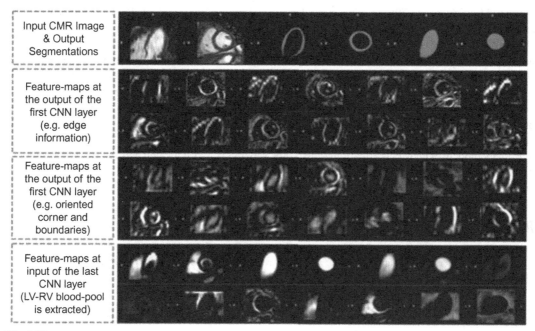

FIG. 4.15

Visualization of intermediate feature maps generated with a cardiac LV segmentation CNN model. The input image shown on the top figure is passed through a series of convolutional layers. In the early stages, the model extracts low-level features such as the ventricle boundaries. In the following layers, oriented boundary information is computed. Toward the end, the model extracts semantic labels by aggregating the inferred contextual information.

4.6 Conclusion

In this chapter, we have shown that segmentation can be learned directly from voxel-wise labels using forest classification. We have also shown how segmentation can be learned for spatial-temporal images. Although this method is only applied to MR and CT images in this work, it is quite straightforward to apply it to other modalities and other structures of interest. Very little prior information is included and the method can automatically select the relevant features from the given set and improve with more input data. However, when less examples are given, the use of extra (more handcrafted) feature channels helps to improve segmentation and allows you to learn how to segment fewer training pictures. However, a few improvements to the method are needed to allow us to reliably index and query cardiac images using volumetric measurements. More research on the segmentation of cardiac structures and other organs using semantic voxel-wise machine learning classification techniques have emerged after this study. These include various sets of features or image channels to define voxels that use more than two layers to more intelligently pick subsets, e.g., training images for each tree, or to use unmarked data as well. Many of the ideas in these approaches are orthogonal to ours and could further help to improve the quality of our segmentations. By itself, the dice coefficient increased from 66.6% to 79% by a smarter selection of training image subsets for each tree. The use of classification forests for segmentation greatly simplifies the problem of learning how to segment directly from voxel-wise ground truth without hardcoding the rules for segmentation. However, the algorithm still requires the definition of feature families and the design of image channels that enhance relevant regions, and the improvement of smoothness and contour matching. In addition, the structure of the tree is optimized and fixed during training. For growing databases, when new training examples are continually added to the training set, the forest can be retrained from scratch. More recent CNN-based segmentation approaches automatically learn optimal image channels to solve segmentation, and can update network parameters with SGD when new data becomes usable. Finally, there was a hybrid method in which classification forests are separated and educated within CNN using back propagation.

References

[1] N.G. Bellenger, J.M. Francis, C.L. Davies, A.J. Coats, D.J. Pennell, Establishment and performance of a magnetic resonance cardiac function clinic, J. Cardiovasc. Magn. Reson. 2 (1) (2000) 15–22.

[2] C. Rickers, N.M. Wilke, M. Jerosch-Herold, S.A. Casey, P. Panse, N. Panse, J. Weil, A.G. Zenovich, B.J. Maron, Utility of cardiac magnetic resonance imaging in the diagnosis of hypertrophic cardiomyopathy, Circulation 112 (6) (2005) 855–861.

[3] P. Peng, K. Lekadir, A. Gooya, L. Shao, S.E. Petersen, A.F. Frangi, A review of heart chamber segmentation for structural and functional analysis using cardiac magnetic resonance imaging, MAGMA 29 (2) (2016) 155–195.

[4] Y.-L. Lu, K.A. Connelly, A.J. Dick, G.A. Wright, P.E. Radau, Automatic functional analysis of left ventricle in cardiac cine MRI, Quant. Imaging Med. Surg. 3 (4) (2013) 200.

[5] H.-Y. Lee, N.C. Codella, M.D. Cham, J.W. Weinsaft, Y. Wang, Automatic left ventricle segmentation using iterative thresholding and an active contour model with adaptation on short-axis cardiac MRI, I.E.E.E. Trans. Biomed. Eng. 57 (4) (2010) 905–913.

[6] N. Paragios, A variational approach for the segmentation of the left ventricle in cardiac image analysis, Int. J. Comput. Vis. 50 (3) (2002) 345–362.

[7] T. Chen, J. Babb, P. Kellman, L. Axel, D. Kim, Semiautomated segmentation of myocardial contours for fast strain analysis in cine displacement-encoded MRI, IEEE Trans. Med. Imaging 27 (8) (2008) 1084–1094.

[8] T.F. Cootes, C.J. Taylor, Combining point distribution models with shape models based on finite element analysis, Image Vis. Comput. 13 (5) (1995) 403–409, https://doi.org/10.1016/0262-8856(95)99727-I.

[9] K. Lekadir, R. Merrifield, G.-Z. Yang, Outlier detection and handling for robust 3-D active shape models search, IEEE Trans. Med. Imaging 26 (2) (2007) 212–222.

[10] S.C. Mitchell, J.G. Bosch, B.P. Lelieveldt, R.J. Van der Geest, J.H. Reiber, M. Sonka, 3-D active appearance models: Segmentation of cardiac MR and ultrasound images, IEEE Trans. Med. Imaging 21 (9) (2002) 1167–1178.

[11] Y.Y. Boykov, M.-P. Jolly, Interactive graph cuts for optimal boundary & region segmentation of objects in nd images, in: Computer Vision, 2001. ICCV 2001. Proceedings. Eighth IEEE International Conference on, IEEE, vol. 1, 2001, pp. 105–112.

[12] D. Mahapatra, Y. Sun, Orientation histograms as shape priors for left ventricle segmentation using graph cuts, in: Medical Image Computing and Computer-Assisted Intervention–MICCAI 2011, Springer, 2011, pp. 420–427.

[13] M. Rajchl, J. Yuan, T.M. Peters, Real-time segmentation in 4D ultrasound with continuous max-flow, in: Medical Imaging: Image Processing, International Society for Optics and Photonics, 2012, p. 83141F.

[14] C.H. Papadimitriou, K. Steiglitz, The max-flow, min-cut theorem, in: Combinatorial Optimization: Algorithms and Complexity, Courier Corporation, 1998, pp. 120–128. ch. 6.

[15] H. Lombaert, Y. Sun, F. Cheriet, Fast 4D segmentation of large datasets using graph cuts, in: Medical Imaging: Image Processing, Vol. 7962, International Society for Optics and Photonics, 2011, p. 79622H.

[16] D. Mahapatra, Cardiac image segmentation from cine cardiac MRI using graph cuts and shape priors, J. Digit. Imaging 26 (4) (2013) 721–730.

[17] M.-P. Jolly, Automatic segmentation of the left ventricle in cardiac MR and CT images, Int. J. Comput. Vis. 70 (2) (2006) 151–163.

[18] A.P. Dempster, N.M. Laird, D.B. Rubin, Maximum likelihood from incomplete data via the EM algorithm, J. R. Stat. Soc. Ser. B Methodol. (1977) 1–38.

[19] M. Lorenzo-Valdés, G.I. Sanchez-Ortiz, A.G. Elkington, R.H. Mohiaddin, D. Rueckert, Segmentation of 4D cardiac MR images using a probabilistic atlas and the EM algorithm, Med. Image Anal. 8 (3) (2004) 255–265.

[20] X. Zhuang, Multivariate mixture model for cardiac segmentation from multi-sequence MRI, in: International Conference on Medical Image Computing and Computer-Assisted Intervention, Springer, 2016, pp. 581–588.

[21] W. Shi, X. Zhuang, H. Wang, S. Duckett, D. Oregan, P. Edwards, S. Ourselin, D. Rueckert, Automatic segmentation of different pathologies from cardiac cine MRI using registration and multiple component EM estimation, in: International Conference on Functional Imaging and Modeling of the Heart, Springer, 2011, pp. 163–170.

[22] J. Caballero, W. Bai, A.N. Price, D. Rueckert, J.V. Hajnal, Application-driven MRI: Joint reconstruction and segmentation from undersampled MRI data, in: International Conference on Medical Image Computing and Computer-Assisted Intervention, Springer, 2014, pp. 106–113.

[23] W. Bai, W. Shi, D.P. O'Regan, T. Tong, H. Wang, S. Jamil-Copley, N.S. Peters, D. Rueckert, A probabilistic patch-based label fusion model for multi-atlas segmentation with registration refinement: application to cardiac MR images, IEEE Trans. Med. Imaging 32 (7) (2013) 1302–1315, https://doi.org/10.1109/TMI.2013.2256922.

[24] M.A. Zuluaga, M.J. Cardoso, M. Modat, S. Ourselin, Multi-atlas propagation whole heart segmentation from MRI and CTA using a local normalised correlation coefficient criterion, in: International Conference on Functional Imaging and Modeling of the Heart, Springer, 2013, pp. 174–181.

[25] O. Oktay, A. Gomez, K. Keraudren, A. Schuh, W. Bai, W. Shi, G. Penney, D. Rueckert, Probabilistic edge map (PEM) for 3D ultrasound image registration and multiatlas left ventricle segmentation, in: International Conference on Functional Imaging and Modeling of the Heart, Springer, 2015, pp. 223–230.

[26] C. Petitjean, M.A. Zuluaga, W. Bai, J.-N. Dacher, D. Grosgeorge, J. Caudron, S. Ruan, I.B. Ayed, M.J. Cardoso, H.-C. Chen, et al., Right ventricle segmentation from cardiac MRI: A collation study, Med. Image Anal. 19 (1) (2015) 187–202.

[27] Second Annual Data Science Bowl, 2017. https://www.kaggle.com/c/second-annualdata-science-bowl, Accessed: 2017-09-12.

[28] X. Zhen, Z. Wang, A. Islam, M. Bhaduri, I. Chan, S. Li, Multi-scale deep networks and regression forests for direct bi-ventricular volume estimation, Med. Image Anal. 30 (2016) 120–129.

[29] K. Hergan, A. Schuster, J. Frühwald, M. Mair, R. Burger, M. Töpker, Comparison of left and right ventricular volume measurement using the Simpson's method and the area length method, Eur. J. Radiol. 65 (2) (2008) 270–278.

[30] T. Papavassiliu, H.P. Kuhl, M. Schroder, T. Suselbeck, O. Bondarenko, C.K. Bohm, A. Beek, M.M. Hofman, A.C. van Rossum, Effect of endocardial trabeculae on left ventricular measurements and measurement reproducibility at cardiovascular MR imaging, Radiology 236 (1) (2005) 57–64.

[31] V. Tavakoli, A.A. Amini, A survey of shaped-based registration and segmentation techniques for cardiac images, Comput. Vis. Image Underst. 117 (9) (2013) 966–989.

[32] T.F. Cootes, C.J. Taylor, Combining point distribution models with shape models based on finite element analysis, Image Vis. Comput. 13 (5) (1995) 403–409, https://doi.org/10.1016/0262-8856(95)99727-I.

[33] A. Tsai, A. Yezzi, W. Wells, C. Tempany, D. Tucker, A. Fan, W.E. Grimson, A. Willsky, A shape-based approach to the segmentation of medical imagery using level sets, IEEE Trans. Med. Imaging 22 (2) (2003) 137–154.

[34] J. Folkesson, E. Samset, R.Y. Kwong, C.-F. Westin, Unifying statistical classification and geodesic active regions for segmentation of cardiac MRI, IEEE Trans. Inf. Technol. Biomed. 12 (3) (2008) 328–334.

[35] S. Pszczolkowski, L. Pizarro, R. Guerrero, D. Rueckert, Nonrigid free-form registration using landmark-based statistical deformation models, in: Medical Imaging 2012: Image Processing, Vol. 8314, International Society for Optics and Photonics, 2012, pp. 8314–8319.

[36] T. Dietenbeck, M. Alessandrini, D. Barbosa, J. Dhooge, D. Friboulet, O. Bernard, Detection of the whole myocardium in 2d-echocardiography for multiple orientations using a geometrically constrained level-set, Med. Image Anal. 16 (2) (2012) 386–401.

[37] Y. Zeng, D. Samaras, W. Chen, Q. Peng, Topology cuts: A novel min-cut/maxflow algorithm for topology preserving segmentation in N–D images, Comput. Vis. Image Underst. 112 (1) (2008) 81–90.

[38] D. Rueckert, L.I. Sonoda, C. Hayes, D.L.G. Hill, M.O. Leach, D.J. Hawkes, Nonrigid registration using free-form deformations: Application to breast MR images, IEEE Trans. Med. Imaging 18 (8) (1999) 712–721.

[39] A. Bistoquet, J. Oshinski, O. Skrinjar, Left ventricular deformation recovery from cine MRI using an incompressible model, IEEE Trans. Med. Imaging 26 (9) (2007) 1136–1153.

[40] H. Greenspan, Super-resolution in medical imaging, Comput. J. 52 (1) (2008) 43–63, https://doi.org/10.1093/comjnl/bxm075.

[41] W. Shi, J. Caballero, C. Ledig, X. Zhuang, W. Bai, K. Bhatia, A. de Marvao, T. Dawes, D. O'Regan, D. Rueckert, Cardiac image super-resolution with global correspondence using multi-atlas patchmatch, in: MICCAI, 2013, pp. 9–16.

[42] M. Kuklisova-Murgasova, G. Quaghebeur, M.A. Rutherford, J.V. Hajnal, J.A. Schnabel, Reconstruction of fetal brain MRI with intensity matching and complete outlier removal, Med. Image Anal. 16 (8) (2012) 1550–1564.

[43] J.A. Kennedy, O. Israel, A. Frenkel, R. Bar-Shalom, H. Azhari, Super-resolution in PET imaging, IEEE Trans. Med. Imaging 25 (2) (2006) 137–147.

[44] S.C. Park, M.K. Park, M.G. Kang, Super-resolution image reconstruction: A technical overview, IEEE Signal Process. Mag. 20 (3) (2003) 21–36.

[45] S.D. Babacan, R. Molina, A.K. Katsaggelos, Total variation super resolution using a variational approach, in: Image Processing, 2008. ICIP 2008. 15th IEEE International Conference on, IEEE, 2008, pp. 641–644.

[46] D.C. Alexander, D. Zikic, J. Zhang, H. Zhang, A. Criminisi, Image quality transfer via random forest regression: Applications in diffusion MRI, in: MICCAI, Springer, 2014, pp. 225–232.

[47] K.K. Bhatia, A.N. Price, W. Shi, D. Rueckert, Super-resolution reconstruction of cardiac MRI using coupled dictionary learning, in: IEEE ISBI, 2014, pp. 947–950.

[48] F. Rousseau, A.D.N. Initiative, et al., A non-local approach for image super-resolution using intermodality priors, Med. Image Anal. 14 (4) (2010) 594–605.

[49] H. Greenspan, G. Oz, N. Kiryati, S. Peled, MRI inter-slice reconstruction using super-resolution, Magn. Reson. Imaging 20 (5) (2002) 437–446.

[50] E. Plenge, D. Poot, W. Niessen, E. Meijering, Super-resolution reconstruction using cross-scale self-similarity in multi-slice MRI, in: MICCAI, 2013, pp. 123–130.

[51] F. Odille, A. Bustin, B. Chen, P.-A. Vuissoz, J. Felblinger, Motion-corrected, super-resolution reconstruction for high-resolution 3D cardiac cine MRI, in: MICCAI, Springer, 2015, pp. 435–442.

[52] A. Roche, G. Malandain, X. Pennec, N. Ayache, The correlation ratio as a new similarity measure for multimodal image registration, in: Medical Image Computing and Computer-Assisted Intervention (MICCAI), Springer, 1998, pp. 1115–1124.

[53] R. Tanno, D.E. Worrall, A. Ghosh, E. Kaden, S.N. Sotiropoulos, A. Criminisi, D.C. Alexander, Bayesian image quality transfer with CNNs: exploring uncertainty in DMRI super-resolution, ArXiv preprint arXiv:1705.00664, 2017.

[54] J.F. Rodríguez-Palomares, M.A.G. Fernández, J.B. Cosials, Integrating multimodal imaging in clinical practice: The importance of a multidisciplinary approach, Rev. Esp. Cardiol. 69 (05) (2016) 477–479.

[55] A.C. Glatz, X. Zhu, M.J. Gillespie, B.D. Hanna, J.J. Rome, Use of angiographic CT imaging in the cardiac catheterization laboratory for congenital heart disease, JACC Cardiovasc. Imaging 3 (11) (2010) 1149–1157.

[56] P. Stolzmann, H. Alkadhi, H. Scheffel, A. Hennemuth, C. Kuehnel, S. Baumueller, S. Kozerke, V. Falk, B. Marincek, O.F. Donati, Image fusion of coronary ct angiography and cardiac perfusion MRI: A pilot study, Eur. Radiol. 20 (5) (2010) 1174–1179.

[57] S.Z. Li, Markov random field models in computer vision, in: European Conference on Computer Vision, Springer, 1994, pp. 361–370.

[58] E. Ferrante, N. Paragios, Slice-to-volume medical image registration: a survey, Med. Image Anal. 39 (2017) 101–123.

[59] A. Sotiras, C. Davatzikos, N. Paragios, Deformable medical image registration: a survey, IEEE Trans. Med. Imaging 32 (7) (2013) 1153–1190.

[60] R. Bajcsy, S. Kovačič, Multiresolution elastic matching, Comput. Vision Graph. Image Proc. 46 (1) (1989) 1–21.

[61] G.E. Christensen, R.D. Rabbitt, M.I. Miller, Deformable templates using large deformation kinematics, IEEE Trans. Image Process. 5 (10) (1996) 1435–1447.

[62] M.F. Beg, M.I. Miller, A. Trouvé, L. Younes, Computing large deformation metric mappings via geodesic flows of diffeomorphisms, Int. J. Comput. Vis. 61 (2) (2005) 139–157.

[63] D. Rueckert, L.I. Sonoda, C. Hayes, D.L.G. Hill, M.O. Leach, D.J. Hawkes, Nonrigid registration using free-form deformations: Application to breast MR images, IEEE Trans. Med. Imaging 8 (1999) 18.

[64] F.L. Bookstein, Principal warps: thin-plate splines and the decomposition of deformations, IEEE Trans. Pattern Anal. Mach. Intell. 11 (6) (1989) 567–585.

[65] P. Hellier, C. Barillot, E. Mémin, P. Pérez, Hierarchical estimation of a dense deformation field for 3-D robust registration, IEEE Trans. Med. Imaging 20 (5) (2001) 388–402.

[66] F. Maes, A. Collignon, D. Vandermeulen, G. Marchal, P. Suetens, Multimodality image registration by maximization of mutual information, IEEE Trans. Med. Imaging 16 (2) (1997) 187–198.

[67] C. Studholme, C. Drapaca, B. Iordanova, V. Cardenas, Deformation-based mapping of volume change from serial brain MRI in the presence of local tissue contrast change, IEEE Trans. Med. Imaging 25 (5) (2006) 626–639.

[68] A.P. King, K.S. Rhode, Y. Ma, C. Yao, C. Jansen, R. Razavi, G.P. Penney, Registering preprocedure volumetric images with intraprocedure 3-D ultrasound using an ultrasound imaging model, IEEE Trans. Med. Imaging 29 (3) (2010) 924–937.

[69] D. Loeckx, P. Slagmolen, F. Maes, D. Vandermeulen, P. Suetens, Nonrigid image registration using conditional mutual information, IEEE Trans. Med. Imaging 29 (1) (2010) 19–29.

[70] M. Kuklisova-Murgasova, A. Cifor, R. Napolitano, A. Papageorghiou, G. Quaghebeur, M.A. Rutherford, J.V. Hajnal, J.A. Noble, J.A. Schnabel, Registration of 3D fetal neurosonography and MRI, Med. Image Anal. 17 (8) (2013) 1137–1150.

[71] V. Potesil, T. Kadir, G. Platsch, M. Brady, Personalized graphical models for anatomical landmark localization in whole-body medical images, Int. J. Comput. Vis. 111 (1) (2014) 29–49, https://doi.org/10.1007/s11263-014-0731-7.

[72] A. Rueda, N. Malpica, E. Romero, Single-image super-resolution of brain MR images using overcomplete dictionaries, Media 17 (1) (2013) 113–132.

Despeckling in echocardiographic images using a hybrid fuzzy filter

Arun Balodi

Department of Electronics and Communication Engineering, Atria Institute of Technology, Bangalore, India

Chapter outline

5.1 Introduction

An ultrasound-based imaging modality popularly known as echocardiography is the first choice for diagnosis and analysis of heart abnormalities. The main advantages of this technique are that it is non-invasive, low cost, and portable. A transthoracic echocardiogram (TTE) is mostly used to analyze valvular abnormalities such as stenosis and regurgitation. Mitral regurgitation (MR) is a state in which the mitral valve doesn't close properly, and because of this blood flows backwards from the left ventricle (LV) to the left atrium (LA) in the heart [1, 2]. Accurate identification of MR is essential for medical treatment and determining whether surgical intervention is needed (depending on the severity of the MR stage). Accurate image analysis is very important for pre- and postmitral valve replacement. In general, the nature of speckle noise is granular, like salt and pepper, which degrades the visual information of ultrasound, synthetic aperture radar (SAR), and optical coherence tomography images. The speckle noise reduces the contrast resolution and masks the texture details, which often makes quantitative measurements and automatic analysis difficult [3–5]. Speckle noise is considered multiplicative noise, which restricts edge preservation during despeckling [6]. Goodman et al. [7] presented an analysis of speckle properties based on the characterization of laser speckle, which was then further studied by several other authors [8, 9]. Speckle reduction is generally used before image segmentation and registration as a preprocessing step. Existing techniques of speckle reduction include averaging, resolution enhancement, and postprocessing approaches. The SAR community investigated adaptive despeckling filters based on local statistics that use a moving window, including Lee, Frost, and Kuan filters. The Lee filter estimates the intensity by local average intensity within the fixed window. The Frost filter convolves the pixel inside a fixed-size window with a flexible exponential impulse reaction. The Kuan resampling filter decides the dark level for each pixel by superseding the center pixel with a weighted normal of the focal pixel and the mean of the qualities in a square kernel incorporating the pixel [10–12]. The available despeckling filters based on anisotropic diffusions (AD) such as speckle reducing anisotropic diffusion (SRAD) [10] and detail preserving anisotropic diffusion (DPAD) [11] preserve the edges along with intraregion smoothing. The nonlocal means (NLM) approach, introduced in [12], became popular because of its edge preservation and speckle reduction capabilities. The concept of the NLM filter is to filter the image by taking an average of the intensity of similar pixels block-wise instead of geometrically. Coupe et al. [13] proposed an NLM filter using a Bayesian framework for despeckling in ultrasound images. This algorithm evaluates every pixel value as a weighted average of other comparative noisy pixels. Fuzzy filters are based on the concepts of moving average and median, and have been used effectively for additive noise but less analyzed for multiplicative noise [14, 15]. Several filtering techniques have been proposed to reduce speckle noise without flattening the image features [4, 16–19]. Each of these despeckling techniques has advantages and disadvantages. The performance of despeckling filters can be tuned by combining the present approaches [20]. In this chapter, we propose hybrid fuzzy filters (HFFs) that integrate homomorphic fuzzy (HF) filters (TMAV, TMED, and ATMED) and an NLM filter. The study shows that the proposed HFFs perform very well in terms of removing speckle noise as well as preserving edges compared to several existing methods.

The rest of the chapter is arranged as follows. Section 5.2 discusses the hypothetical foundation of despeckling filtering. Section 5.3 introduces the proposed approach of the hybrid filters. Section 5.4 presents the experimental results of the proposed techniques and Section 5.5 presents concluding remarks.

5.2 Background of despeckle filtering

5.2.1 Mathematical model of speckle noise for ultrasound images

The nature of speckle noise is multiplicative and mathematically represented as:

$$y(i,j) = x(i,j)\, n(i,j) \tag{5.1}$$

where $y(i,j)$ is the noisy image, which is the product of the noise-free image $x(i,j)$, $n(i,j)$ is the multiplicative noise, and i and j are spatial coordinates [18, 20, 21]. The logarithm operation converts the multiplicative noise into additive noise [20]:

$$\log[y(i,j)] = \log[x(i,j) \cdot n(i,j)] = \log[x(i,j)] + \log[n(i,j)] \tag{5.2}$$

$$y_{ij} = x_{iyj} + n_{ij} \tag{5.3}$$

where $y_{ij} = log\,[y(i,j)]$, $x_{ij} = log[x(i,j)]$, and $n_{ij} = log[n(i,j)]$. The denoising filters proposed for additive noise can be utilized for despeckling in the logarithmic domain, and the output is acquired by converting the filtered image in the exponential domain by:

$$\hat{x}(i,j) = \exp\left(Filter\left(\log\left(y(i,j)\right)\right)\right) \tag{5.4}$$

in the above expression, "Filter" represents the technique in the denoising process.

5.2.2 Despeckling filters

5.2.2.1 Local adaptive filters

In a Lee [22] filter the speckle noise is approximated by a linear model and then the minimum mean square error (MMSE) is applied. This filter enhances the image details, but it induces a blocky effect and removes sharp features. Since it does not require any transformation, it has very high efficiency. The Frost filter [23] uses adaptive least-squares estimation criterion. The center pixel value is replaced by a weighted sum of the intensity values in the $n \times n$ moving kernel. As the variance of the kernel increases, the weighting factors also increase for the central pixels. The drawback of this filter is the significant loss in image details and blurred boundaries. The Kuan filter [24] is based on a different weighting function. The advantage of this filter is that it preserves the image structure. The drawbacks of this filter are over-smoothing and blurring of edges.

5.2.2.2 Local statistics filtering

In these types of filters, a fixed-size kernel window is moved and the estimation of the pixel of interest is supplanted by the neighborhood statistics, for example, mean, variance, skewness, and kurtosis. The local window size may vary from 3×3 to 15×15. The Wiener filter is a pixel-wise adaptive filter that expands the optical recognition of the ultrasound image. It is otherwise called the least mean squares (LMS) filter. It preserves edges and high-recurrence data of the image [18, 21]. In the median filter, the center pixel in the window is supplanted with the median value of its neighbors. This filter is satisfactorily appropriate for upgrading the optical perception, however, much of the time it is used to annihilate the image boundaries. The Kuwahara filter is a nonlinear noise-reduction filter that preserves edges [17]. It uses a sliding window approach to access every pixel in the image. The center pixel of the 1×5 neighborhood is supplanted by the median gray estimation of the 1×5 masks. A geometric filter is also a nonlinear approach that analyzes the intensity of the central pixel of 3×3 window and the value of the center pixel depend on the values of its neighborhood pixels.

5.2.2.3 Anisotropic diffusion filter

Perona and Malik [25] introduced the anisotropic diffusion (AD) filter to remove high-frequency additive noise while preserving edges of existing images. This filter diminished the constraints of spatial filtering by altogether decreasing the speckle noise and improving the image quality. The upside of this technique is intra-region smoothing and edge protection. However, it corrupts image contrast and obscures edges. It utilizes the idea of heat diffusion, and the numerical model that simulates the diffusion process is:

$$\frac{\partial s(x,y;t)}{\partial t} = \text{div}\left(g\|\nabla s(x,y;t)\| \cdot \nabla s(x,y;t)\right) \tag{5.5}$$

where div, $g(.)$ is divergence operator and diffusion parameter, respectively. The coefficient $g\|\nabla s(x,y;t)\|$ allows the controlling of the diffusion regularization process more accurately in the range $[0,1]$.

Keeping g independent concerning image position (x, y) or time t, then the above equation can be written for linear diffusion as:

$$\frac{\partial s}{\partial t} = \text{div}\left(g \cdot \nabla s(x, y; t)\right) = g \nabla^2 s(x, y; t)) \tag{5.6}$$

To preserve image edges, Perona and Malik also suggested the following two diffusion parameters that can be explicit:

$$g\|\nabla s(x, y; t)\| = \frac{1}{1 + \left(\frac{\|\nabla s(x, y; t)\|}{K}\right)^2} \tag{5.7}$$

$$g\|\nabla s(x, y; t)\| = \exp\left(-\left[\frac{\|\nabla s(x, y; t)\|}{K}\right]\right)^2 \tag{5.8}$$

where K is the edge magnitude parameter, which is responsible for the response of the AD filter. If $I\nabla s(x, y; t)I \gg K$, then the diffusion coefficient becomes zero $(g(I\nabla s(x, y; t)I) \rightarrow 0)$ and we achieve an all-pass filter. However, if $I\nabla s(x, y; t)I \ll K$, then the diffusion coefficient becomes one $(g(I\nabla s(x, y; t)I) \rightarrow 1)$ and becomes isotropic diffusion. Yu and Acton [10] proposed an extension of this approach that is considered more sensitive for the edges in the processed image.

5.2.2.4 Fuzzy filter (TMED, TMAV, ATMED)

Kwan et al. [14, 15] defined fuzzy filters from which they have derived various types of other fuzzy filters based on various membership function. The output of fuzzy filters for the input $f(i, j)$ is defined as:

$$y(i, j) = \frac{\sum_{(r, s) \in A} F[f(i+r, j+s)] \cdot f(i+r, j+s)}{\sum_{(r, s) \in A} F[f(i+r, j+s)]} \tag{5.9}$$

where $F[f(i, j)]$ is the window function defined in terms of fuzzy membership functions and "A" is the area. The various types of fuzzy filters can be derived by different window functions such as a fuzzy filter with symmetrical triangular with median center (TMED), fuzzy filter with asymmetrical triangular function with median center (ATMED), and fuzzy filter with moving average (TMAV). The center value of a fuzzy filter with a triangular function and the median value is defined as:

$$F[f(i+r, j+s)] = \begin{cases} 1 - \frac{|f(i+r, j+s) - f_{med}(i, j)|}{f_{mm}(i, j)} \\ \text{for } |f(i+r, j+s) - f_{med}(i, j)| \leq f_{mm}(i, j) \\ 1 \text{ for } f_{mm} = 0 \end{cases} \tag{5.10}$$

$$f_{mm}(i, j) = \max\left[f_{max}(i, j) - f_{med}(i, j), f_{med}(i, j) - f_{min}(i, j)\right] \tag{5.11}$$

where $f_{max}(i,j), f_{min}(i,j)$, and $f_{med}(i,j)$ represent the maximum, minimum, and median values, respectively, with $s, r \in A$ the window at indices (i, j). The fuzzy filter with a triangular function and moving average value within a window is defined as:

$$[f(i+r,j+s)] = \begin{cases} 1 - \dfrac{|f(i+r,j+s) - f_{mav}(i,j)|}{f_{mm}(i,j)} \\ \text{for } |f(i+r,j+s) - f_{mav}(i,j)| \leq f_{mm}(i,j) \\ 1 \text{ for } f_{mv} = 0 \end{cases} \qquad (5.12)$$

$$f_{mv}(i, j) = \max[f_{max}(i,j) - f_{mav}(i,j) f_{mav}(i,j) - f_{min}(i,j)] \qquad (5.13)$$

where $f_{max}(i,j), f_{min}(i,j)$, and $f_{mav}(i,j)$ represent the maximum, minimum, and moving average values, respectively, with $s, r \in A$ the window at indices (i, j).

Median filtering using fuzzy ATMED is defined as follows:

$$F[f(i+r,j+s)] = \begin{cases} 1 - [f_{med}(i,j) - f(i+r,j+s)]/f_{mm}(i,j) - f_{min}(i,j) \\ \text{if } f_{min}(i,j) \leq f(i+r,j+s) \leq f_{med}(i,j) \\ 1 - \dfrac{[f(i+r,j+s) - f_{med}(i,j)]}{[f_{max}(i,j) - f_{med}(i,j)]} - f_{min}(i,j) \\ \text{if } f_{med}(i,j) \leq f(i+r,j+s) \leq f_{max}(i,j) \\ 1, \text{if } f_{med}(i,j) - f_{min}(i,j) = 0 \text{ or } f_{max}(i,j) - f_{med}(i,j) = 0 \end{cases} \qquad (5.14)$$

5.2.2.5 Nonlocal means filter

Buades et al. [12] introduced the NLM filter, which is highly capable of removing additive white Gaussian noise (AWGN) and preserving edges. Unlike other despeckling filters, the NLM filter compares the gray level in the geometrical configuration in a whole neighborhood. Various modified versions of the NLM filter have been allied to remove signal-dependent multiplicative speckle noise. The restored intensity of a pixel $NL(u)(i)$ for a pixel i can be estimated as a weighted average of all the pixels in the neighborhood where the discrete noisy image is $u(i) | i \in I$.

$$NL(u)(i) = \sum_{j \in I} w(i,j).u(j) \qquad (5.15)$$

where $\{w(i,j)\}_j$ estimates the affinity between i and j with a restriction such as $\{w(i,j)\} \in [0,1]$ and $\sum_j w(i,j) = 1$. The gray intensity vectors $u(N_i)$ and $u(N_j)$ define the kinship between two pixels i and j, where N_k is the square neighborhood of fixed size and k is the center pixel. The pixels with a similar gray level neighborhood to $u(N_i)$ have larger weights in the average. These weights are calculated as:

$$w(i,j) = \frac{1}{Z_i} e^{-\frac{\|u(Ni)-u(Nj)\|_{2,a}^2}{h^2}} \qquad (5.16)$$

$$Z_i = e^{-\frac{\|u(Ni)-u(Nj)\|_{2,a}^2}{h^2}} \qquad (5.17)$$

where N_i and N_j are intensities of local neighborhood centers on pixels i and j, Z_i represents the normalization constant, and h is the degree of filtering that controls the decay of the exponential function. To reduce the computational complexity of the NLM filter, a probabilistic early termination (PET)-based fast NLM [26] was introduced.

5.3 Proposed hybrid fuzzy filters (HFFs)

Here, we propose a new despeckling approach by embedding the NLM filter with an HF filter and test it on ultrasound images of MR. The fuzzy filters are used in the logarithmic domain. The NLM filters are very good in terms of edge preservation when used for speckle noise reduction. Therefore, the edge preservation capability of NLM is integrated with the fuzzy filters. The proposed technique is termed a hybrid fuzzy filter (HFF) and illustrated in Fig. 5.1.

The procedural steps of the proposed approach are step-wise as follows:

Step 1: In the first step, all images are resized to 512×512, and converted to grayscale image and then speckle noise is added.

Step 2: The noisy image is given as an input to the logarithmic space. The output image is of form $f = log\ (double\ (f) + 1)$, where f is the noisy image.

Step 3: Fuzzy filters (TMED, TMAV, and ATMED) are applied to the noisy image in the logarithmic space.

Step 4: The output of the fuzzy filter in the nonlogarithmic domain. It is represented by $g = \exp(y) - 1$, where y is the output of the fuzzy filter.

Step 5: The output image at step 4 is given as an input to the NLM filter.

Step 6: The output of the last step is the denoised image, on which we perform a performance parameter and visual quality assessment.

5.3.1 Ultrasound image database

We used the echocardiographic images of MR in this study to check the performance of the despeckling filters (Fig. 5.2). We used an image dataset from Swami Rama Himalayan University, Dehradun, India [27, 28].

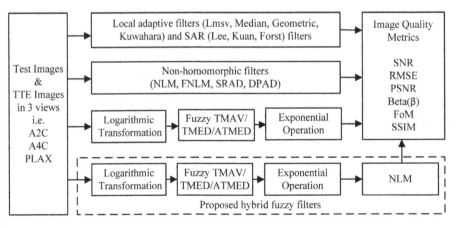

FIG. 5.1

Flowchart of the proposed methodology.

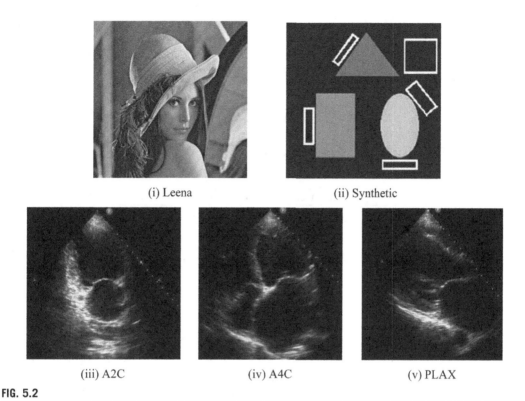

(i) Leena   (ii) Synthetic

(iii) A2C   (iv) A4C   (v) PLAX

FIG. 5.2

Image dataset used in the study.

5.3.2 Image quality metrics (IQM) for performance evaluation

Countless researchers have used standard full reference-based estimations for surveying the performance of despeckling channels. These parameters require the reference image and include signal-
to-noise ratio (SNR) [8], peak signal-to-noise ratio (PSNR) [20], mean square error (MSE) [4, 20],
and structural similarity index measure (SSIM) [4, 18, 29, 30]. Ultrasound images inevitably have
speckle noise, so noise-free reference images are not available. In this case, we have to use blind
image-quality parameters such as speckle suppression index (SSI) [31, 32], speckle suppression
and mean preservation index (SMPI), normalized correlation coefficient (NCC), Laplacian mean
square error (LMSE), and normalized error summation (Err3, Err4) [4, 18]. The edge preservation
is estimated by calculating Pratt's figure of merit (FoM) [4] and the beta (β) metric [33].

$$\text{PSNR}\left(f_{den}, f_{org}\right) = 20\text{x}\log_{10}\left(\frac{255}{\sqrt{\text{MSE}\left(f_{den}, f_{org}\right)}}\right) \tag{5.18}$$

$$\text{SSIM}(f_{org}, f_{den}) = \frac{1}{M} \sum \frac{\left(2\mu_{f_{org}}\mu_{f_{den}} + c_1\right)\left(2\sigma_{f_{org}f_{den}} + c_2\right)}{\left(\mu_{f_{org}}^2 + \mu_{f_{den}}^2 + c_1\right)\left(\sigma_{f_{org}}^2 + \sigma_{f_{den}}^2 + c_2\right)} \tag{5.19}$$

$$\text{FoM}(f_{den}, f_{ref}) = \frac{1}{\max(N_{den}, N_{ref})} \sum_{j=1}^{N_{den}} \frac{1}{1 + \gamma d_j^2} \tag{5.20}$$

$$SSI = \frac{\sqrt{VAR(f_{den})}}{Mean(f_{den})} \frac{Mean(f_{org})}{\sqrt{VAR(f_{org})}} \tag{5.21}$$

$$\beta = \frac{D\left(\Delta f_{den} - \overline{\Delta} f_{org}, \Delta f_{org} - \overline{\Delta} f_{org}\right)}{\sqrt{D\left(\Delta f_{den} - \overline{\Delta} f_{den}, \Delta f_{den} - \overline{\Delta} f_{den}\right) D\left(\Delta f_{org} - \overline{\Delta} f_{org}, \Delta f_{org} - \overline{\Delta} f_{org}\right)}} \tag{5.22}$$

$$MSE(f_{den}, f_{org}) = \frac{1}{MN} \sum_{i=1}^{M} \sum_{j=1}^{N} \left(f_{den} - f_{org}\right)^2 \tag{5.23}$$

$$SMPI = Q \frac{\sqrt{VAR(f_{den})}}{\sqrt{VAR(f_{org})}} \tag{5.24}$$

with $Q = K + |\text{Mean}(f_{den}) - \text{Mean}(f_{org})|$, $K = \dfrac{\max(\text{Mean}(f_{den})) - \min(\text{Mean}(f_{den}))}{\text{Mean}(f_{org})}$

$$SNR = 10 \log_{10} \left(\frac{var(f_{org})}{MSE(f_{den}, f_{org})} \right) \tag{5.25}$$

where γ is the penalization factor with a fixed value of 1/9, and and n_r are the number of pixels in the original and processed images, respectively, d_j is the Euclidean distance, Δf_{den} and Δf_{org} represent the filtered versions of the original and processed images, pixel mean intensities in the region Δf_{den}, Δf_{org} is represented by Δf_{den} and Δf_{org}, respectively, c_1 and c_2 are constants, σf_{org}, σf_{den}, and $2\mu f_{org}$, μf_{den} are the standard deviations and mean of image compared, $\sigma f_{org} f_{den}$ represents the covariance, $c_1, c_2 \leq 1$ are the constants, $C_1 = (K_1 L)^2$, $C_2 = (K_2 L)^2$, where L is the dynamic range of pixel intensities (255, for 8-bit grayscale images), $K_1, K_2 \ll 1$.

5.4 Experimental results and discussion

We assessed the despeckling filters using standard test images and clinical echocardiographic images. We further examined these filters by using image quality estimations and observations of specialists. We used the MATLAB in-assembled function "imnoise" to add speckle noise with variance 0.01–0.1 to the test images, although echocardiographic images are naturally noisy. Table 5.1 lists the parameters of the filters.

Table 5.1 Parameters used in the implementation of despeckling filters.

Category	Filter name	Abbreviation	Parameters
Local adaptive	Local statistics mean-variance	LSMV	Window size $= 5 \times 5$ Iterations $= 2$
	Wiener	Wiener	Window size $= 5 \times 5$ Iterations $= 1$
	Median	Median	Window size $= 5 \times 5$ Iterations $= 2$
	Kuwahara	Kuwahara	Window size $= 5 \times 5$
	Geometric	Geometric	Window size $= 5 \times 5$
Synthetic aperture radar (SAR)	Lee		Window size $= 5 \times 5$
	Frost		Window size $= 5 \times 5$
	Kuan		Window size $= 5 \times 5$
Anisotropic diffusion	Perona-Malik's anisotropic diffusion	PMAD	Diffusion constant $= 30$ Rate of diffusion $= 0.25$ Iteration $= 20$
	Speckle reducing anisotropic diffusion filter	SRAD	Diffusion constant $= 30$ Time step $= 0.02$, $\rho = 1$
Nonlocal means	Nonlocal means	NLM	
	Fast nonlocal means	FNLM	
Fuzzy	Triangular function with median center	TMED	Window size $= 3 \times 3$
	Triangular moving average center filter	TMAV	Window size $= 3 \times 3$
	Asymmetrical triangular function with a median filter	ATMED	Window size $= 3 \times 3$
Proposed	Hybrid fuzzy filter (TMAV+NLM)	HFF1	
	Hybrid fuzzy filter (TMED+NLM)	HFF2	
	Hybrid fuzzy filter (ATMED+NLM)	HFF3	

Table 5.2 presents the performance of the speckle filters for two test images based on IQM such as PSNR, SSIM, FoM, SSI, beta, NCC, MSE, IQI, and SNR. The first image is a standard test image and the second is a synthetic image using HF filters (TMED, TMAV, and ATMED) along with an NLM filter. As shown in Table 5.2, the performance of the fuzzy filters integrated with an NLM filter degraded with an increase in noise variance for the two test images. The outcomes demonstrate that the NLM filter is better than the other three filters followed by the HF filter based on ATMED regarding traditional performance parameters such as PSNR, MSE, and SNR. Results also show that the value of

Table 5.2 Performance comparison of IQM for test images using TMED, TMAV, ATMED, and NLM filters.

Image	Noise	PSNR				SSIM				FoM			
		TMED	TMAV	ATMED	NLM	TMED	TMAV	ATMED	NLM	TMED	TMAV	ATMED	NLM
Lena	0.01	32.25	35.36	35.80	36.63	0.7620	0.8828	0.8050	0.8908	0.8492	0.8797	0.7487	0.7944
	0.03	29.10	32.35	30.70	32.97	0.6070	0.7767	0.6444	0.7100	0.5095	0.7157	0.4638	0.7794
	0.05	26.68	29.96	28.60	29.02	0.5212	0.7033	0.5574	0.5522	0.4434	0.5636	0.4283	0.5961
	0.10	22.44	25.55	26.57	22.87	0.3935	0.5705	0.4392	0.3676	0.3749	0.4319	0.3807	0.4243
Synthetic	0.01	30.95	34.22	36.78	40.83	0.8829	0.9430	0.9038	0.9606	0.4339	0.4781	0.4356	0.6063
	0.03	28.86	32.02	32.82	34.31	0.8101	0.8917	0.8333	0.8596	0.4082	0.4368	0.4036	0.4409
	0.05	26.95	30.17	30.70	30.39	0.7705	0.8588	0.7945	0.8003	0.3771	0.4226	0.3630	0.3591
	0.10	23.51	26.55	27.61	25.56	0.6999	0.7960	0.7340	0.7504	0.3487	0.3887	0.3516	0.3325

Image	Noise	SSI				Beta				NCC			
		TMED	TMAV	ATMED	NLM	TMED	TMAV	ATMED	NLM	TMED	TMAV	ATMED	NLM
Lena	0.01	0.9623	0.9576	0.9627	0.9523	0.1173	0.3326	0.3796	0.5356	0.9822	0.9859	0.9936	0.9958
	0.03	0.9058	0.8975	0.9124	0.9071	0.1089	0.2577	0.2293	0.1817	0.9566	0.9681	0.9865	0.9922
	0.05	0.8600	0.8496	0.8714	0.8832	0.0935	0.2178	0.1758	0.1073	0.9275	0.9475	0.9775	0.9894
	0.10	0.7869	0.7638	0.7980	0.8666	0.0719	0.1562	0.1226	0.0600	0.8516	0.8927	0.9552	0.9820
Synthetic	0.01	0.9860	0.9869	0.9878	0.9900	0.2103	0.4846	0.5280	0.7039	0.9492	0.9631	0.9825	0.9934
	0.03	0.9703	0.9716	0.9742	0.9783	0.1678	0.3729	0.3618	0.2871	0.9206	0.9422	0.9683	0.9869
	0.05	0.9539	0.9571	0.9624	0.9717	0.1471	0.3187	0.2863	0.1759	0.8845	0.9178	0.9533	0.9813
	0.10	0.9234	0.9271	0.9369	0.9634	0.1082	0.2358	0.2079	0.0938	0.8027	0.8582	0.9188	0.9640

Image	Noise	MSE				IQI				SNR			
		TMED	TMAV	ATMED	NLM	TMED	TMAV	ATMED	NLM	TMED	TMAV	ATMED	NLM
Lena	0.01	75.61	37.00	42.06	27.60	0.5703	0.6937	0.6078	0.6264	26.62	29.74	29.21	31.05
	0.03	156.20	74.01	108.11	80.66	0.4590	0.5778	0.4851	0.4842	23.37	26.65	25.09	26.39
	0.05	273.05	128.30	175.51	200.26	0.3997	0.5162	0.4268	0.4001	20.82	24.18	22.96	22.44
	0.10	723.65	353.79	352.29	656.51	0.3087	0.4197	0.3481	0.2973	16.29	19.54	19.85	17.31
Synthetic	0.01	104.42	49.22	27.28	10.75	0.3808	0.4884	0.4219	0.3371	22.40	25.72	28.36	32.45
	0.03	168.98	81.70	67.88	48.22	0.3016	0.3972	0.3316	0.3166	20.19	23.43	24.35	25.91
	0.05	262.26	125.20	110.62	118.91	0.2671	0.3523	0.2932	0.3041	18.14	21.47	22.17	21.98
	0.10	579.14	287.56	225.40	361.11	0.2162	0.2859	0.2500	0.2731	14.37	17.61	18.95	17.14

SSIM and FoM for the TMAV filter was better compared to the other three filters. In terms of beta and NCC, the NLM filter responded the best out of all the filters. The higher values of the SSIM and FoM show lesser distortion and greater edge protection in the denoised image. Relative assessments have been carried out on TTE images without including speckle noise and those results resemble those for standard test images.

In the local statistics-based filters (LSMV, Wiener, median, Kuwahara, and geometric), the denoised image gets blurry as the window size increases, which causes the loss of image texture. Fig. 5.4C–G shows that there is smoothing at the output of the LSMV filter. The geometric filter preserves edges in despeckling, but the edge noise remains the same. The Wiener filter removes speckle noise and preserves edges efficiently. The geometric filter preserves the texture as it has a good edge-preservation index beta, but the image contains small speckle noise.

The outcome of Lee and Kuan filters incites visual artifacts as observed in Fig. 5.4H–J, whereas the Frost filter brings about a loss of texture. The Lee and Frost filters have similar values for the SSIM metric. The Frost and Kuan filters likewise protect the edge information. Average edge pixel distortion because of filtering is minimal in SAR filters as observed by the high FoM. Generally, SAR filters are easy to implement and reduce speckle noise as well. NLM and FNLM have strong speckle reduction while having high computational complexity, as shown in Fig. 5.4K and L. As per IQM, it is observed that the value of FoM and SSIM are high for NLM filters, demonstrating the filters' effectiveness for preserving edges. Fig. 5.4M and N show the output of PMAD and SRAD filters. These filters remove speckle noise, but have smoothing at edges. Furthermore, fuzzy filters such as TMED, TMAV, and ATMED performed well, with the ATMED filter partially preserving texture.

Tables 6.3 and 6.4 compare the performance of the proposed HFFs in terms of edge-preserving parameters and traditional parameters, respectively. The performance of each filter is tabulated and compared. Strong speckle suppression is observed in the proposed hybrid filter HFF3, followed by FNLM in terms of PSNR. The PSNR of the HFF3 filter (42.65 dB) is improved compared to HF (42.62 dB) and NLM filters (39.68 dB). MSE is lesser for the HFF when compared to many of the filters.

The performance for the proposed hybrid filter HFF3 was found to be superior in comparison to HF, AD, and NLM filters in terms of the traditional parameters such as PSNR, MSE, SNR, and NCC. Fig. 5.3 shows the despeckling performance of the proposed HFFs compared to the other filters in terms of IQM. Results show that HFF3 responded very well in terms of SSI. The values of SMPI and FoM are also superior in HFF3 compared to the SAR filters. Overall, the fuzzy filters responded very well in terms of all quality metrics except for beta. The performances of the Wiener, Frost, FNLM, and ATMED filters are similar in terms of PSNR. The beta value of the proposed filters increased when compared to hybrid and NLM filters. The correlation coefficient value was also improved in the HFFs. All the edge-preserving parameters (PSNR, SSIM, FoM, SSI, beta, and NCC) exhibited improved values compared with those of the fuzzy and NLM filters.

Further, we compared the performance of the proposed approach with fifteen despeckling filters. Figs. 5.4–6.8 depict this visual performance. As per visual quality, HFF3 outperformed all other filters.

Table 5.3 Comparison of edge-preserving parameters for ultrasound images in three views.

Methods	A2C	A4C	PLAX	A2C	A4C	PLAX	A2C	A4C	PLAX
	PSNR (dB)			SSIM			FoM		
LSMV	37.50	38.77	37.44	0.9342	0.9472	0.9475	0.8683	0.8729	0.8880
Wiener	41.17	41.72	41.98	0.9263	0.9399	0.9393	0.8323	0.8542	0.8880
Median	38.74	40.23	38.29	0.9416	0.9528	0.9554	0.8804	0.8981	0.9029
Kuwahara	36.43	37.59	37.53	0.9510	0.9586	0.9531	0.9488	0.9362	0.9332
Geometric	40.17	40.98	40.25	0.9729	0.9772	0.9796	0.9119	0.8663	0.9162
Lee	40.08	41.29	39.42	0.9619	0.9689	0.9633	0.9537	0.9606	0.9601
Frost	41.86	43.10	42.13	0.9543	0.9609	0.9638	0.9661	0.9709	0.9712
Kuan	37.78	39.08	37.84	0.9583	0.9648	0.9609	0.8748	0.8406	0.8618
PMAD	37.35	38.67	38.13	0.9288	0.9389	0.9382	0.7798	0.7152	0.7607
SRAD	36.47	39.36	39.41	0.9491	0.9608	0.9673	0.7711	0.9064	0.9148
NLM	39.68	40.76	40.58	0.9353	0.9430	0.9488	0.7035	0.7279	0.7081
FNLM	42.12	43.09	42.93	0.9637	0.9674	0.9709	0.8472	0.7922	0.8398
TMED	37.91	38.78	37.40	0.9666	0.9658	0.9724	0.9107	0.9136	0.9123
TMAV	40.81	41.77	40.05	0.9882	0.9898	0.9878	0.9363	0.9396	0.9388
ATMED	42.62	42.96	41.80	0.9913	0.9925	0.9911	0.9529	0.9639	0.9599
HFF1	39.49	40.62	39.68	0.9583	0.9626	0.9583	0.9674	0.9259	0.9595
HFF2	40.54	41.61	40.71	0.9786	0.9812	0.9776	0.9599	0.9217	0.9461
HFF3	42.65	43.88	43.11	0.9899	0.9916	0.9896	0.9720	0.9978	0.9813
	SSI			Beta			NCC		
LSMV	0.9510	0.9586	0.9531	0.5107	0.4886	0.3565	0.9841	0.9730	0.9704
Wiener	0.9729	0.9772	0.9796	0.8686	0.9134	0.9134	0.9951	0.9934	0.9937
Median	0.9619	0.9689	0.9633	0.4398	0.4791	0.3858	0.9866	0.9752	0.9716
Kuwahara	0.9543	0.9609	0.9638	0.3214	0.3408	0.3408	0.9955	0.9874	0.9861
Geometric	0.9666	0.9658	0.9724	0.8280	0.8071	0.8551	0.9975	0.9970	0.9971
Lee	0.9882	0.9898	0.9878	0.7854	0.7829	0.7475	0.9938	0.9896	0.9879
Frost	0.9913	0.9925	0.9911	0.7869	0.7839	0.7560	0.9962	0.9933	0.9917
Kuan	0.9583	0.9648	0.9609	0.6081	0.5931	0.5496	0.9843	0.9734	0.9711
PMAD	0.9288	0.9389	0.9382	0.5011	0.4773	0.5043	0.9828	0.9704	0.9714
SRAD	0.9874	0.9948	0.9939	0.3292	0.3334	0.4792	0.9962	0.9990	0.9962
NLM	0.9353	0.9430	0.9488	0.7532	0.7394	0.7611	0.9891	0.9782	0.9798
FNLM	0.9637	0.9674	0.9709	0.7637	0.7448	0.7786	0.9837	0.9882	0.9889
TMED	0.9442	0.9572	0.9575	0.1781	0.1299	0.1225	0.9613	0.9502	0.9478
TMAV	0.9363	0.9499	0.9393	0.5457	0.5110	0.4602	0.9645	0.9536	0.9487
ATMED	0.9516	0.9628	0.9654	0.7422	0.7557	0.6959	0.9812	0.9650	0.9643
HFF1	0.9583	0.9626	0.9583	0.7231	0.7094	0.7407	0.9750	0.9596	0.9545
HFF2	0.9786	0.9812	0.9776	0.7276	0.7818	0.7592	0.9818	0.9704	0.9660
HFF3	0.9899	0.9916	0.9896	0.7696	0.7668	0.7602	0.9916	0.9854	0.9831

Table 5.4 Comparison of traditional parameters for ultrasound images in three views.

Methods	A2C	A4C	PLAX	A2C	A4C	PLAX	A2C	A4C	PLAX
	MSE			SMPI			SNR (dB)		
LSMV	22.07	16.35	22.38	3.0956	2.7293	3.6485	24.75	22.50	21.14
Wiener	4.74	3.30	3.13	3.1486	2.8358	3.7839	31.46	29.53	29.75
Median	16.56	11.67	18.40	3.3318	2.9591	3.8902	26.00	23.97	21.99
Kuwahara	28.23	21.41	21.89	3.5294	3.1612	4.0536	23.73	21.40	21.30
Geometric	4.75	3.91	3.70	3.5344	3.1532	4.0357	31.47	28.80	29.04
Lee	4.85	3.64	5.65	3.1074	2.7690	3.7129	31.36	29.08	27.17
Frost	3.22	2.40	3.80	3.1836	2.8425	3.7757	33.15	30.91	28.90
Kuan	20.70	15.20	20.41	3.1522	2.7605	3.6741	25.03	22.82	21.54
PMAD	22.81	16.72	19.07	3.0859	2.6992	3.6386	24.60	22.39	21.83
SRAD	27.92	14.24	14.19	3.2912	2.8592	3.8334	23.78	23.21	23.22
NLM	13.36	10.31	10.85	3.2407	2.8686	3.8082	26.94	24.52	24.30
FNLM	7.61	6.03	6.31	3.1923	2.8383	3.7795	29.40	26.88	26.69
TMED	27.85	21.29	26.61	3.6631	3.2226	4.1339	23.68	21.26	20.29
TMAV	34.61	26.88	33.33	3.5416	3.1331	4.0628	22.71	20.21	19.27
ATMED	21.32	15.93	19.15	3.2849	2.9191	3.8682	24.88	22.58	21.78
HFF1	20.08	16.28	22.57	3.6406	3.1823	4.0808	25.12	22.46	21.03
HFF2	10.30	8.18	12.26	3.7660	3.2685	4.1456	28.04	25.49	23.71
HFF3	4.28	3.12	5.17	3.3842	2.9752	3.9002	31.89	29.73	27.53
	Err3			Err4			LMSE		
LSMV	7.68	6.87	8.55	11.31	10.34	13.41	0.7700	0.7890	0.8811
Wiener	3.06	2.60	2.63	3.84	3.30	3.39	0.2517	0.2497	0.1709
Median	7.47	6.60	8.84	11.95	10.82	14.78	0.8931	0.8416	0.9176
Kuwahara	8.63	7.75	8.27	12.08	10.99	12.24	6.1957	6.1100	3.9853
Geometric	3.07	2.84	2.88	3.80	3.56	3.67	0.3205	0.3536	0.2687
Lee	3.78	3.26	4.33	6.03	4.97	6.72	0.4275	0.4332	0.4981
Frost	3.08	2.63	3.54	4.94	4.02	5.48	0.3990	0.4030	0.4544
Kuan	7.87	7.67	9.16	12.18	13.97	16.55	0.6679	0.6797	0.7456
PMAD	6.96	6.16	6.74	9.00	8.16	8.93	0.7629	0.7924	0.7553
SRAD	7.70	6.18	6.37	9.89	8.45	8.82	5.1155	6.4074	2.9236
NLM	5.03	4.56	4.91	6.27	5.79	6.39	0.4538	0.4775	0.4483
FNLM	3.97	3.64	3.94	5.31	4.99	5.57	0.4187	0.4476	0.3949
TMED	8.11	7.36	8.89	11.49	10.58	13.43	1.7854	1.9269	1.8130
TMAV	9.18	8.44	10.10	12.98	12.24	15.33	0.7183	0.7664	0.8174
ATMED	7.00	6.21	7.32	10.02	8.88	10.90	0.4496	0.4301	0.5139
HFF1	7.47	6.92	8.66	10.96	10.17	13.29	0.6647	0.6768	0.7418
HFF2	5.49	4.98	6.60	8.42	7.54	10.50	0.7442	0.7788	0.8713
HFF3	4.02	3.41	4.70	7.05	5.73	7.93	0.5952	0.5979	0.6253

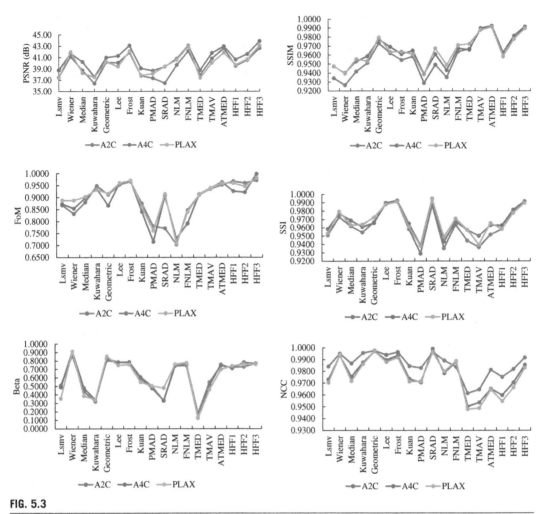

FIG. 5.3

Comparison of TTE images in three views (A) PSNR, (B) SSIM, (C) FoM, (D) SSI, (E) beta, (F) NCC.

5.5 **Conclusion**

In this chapter, we tested a proposed HFF on test images and ultrasound images based on blind and full-reference image parameters. We compared three HFFs with fifteen existing types of despeckling filters. Conventional parameters are not sufficient to check the performance of despeckling filters without a noise-free reference image. As such, we investigated conventional parameters including SMPI, FoM, IQI, and SSI along with blind-quality metrics such as SSI and beta. Because different kinds of benchmark filters are accessible, it is extremely hard to pick the best clinically adequate filter. It is likewise important to expel speckle noise while protecting the edges.

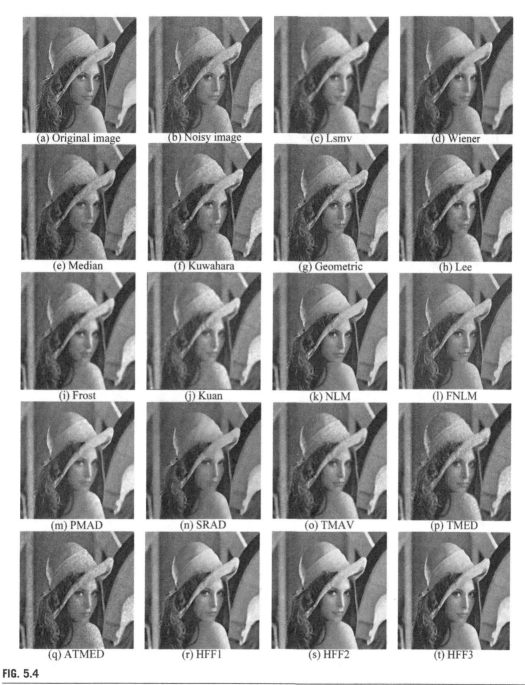

FIG. 5.4

Perceptual quality comparisons for noise variance 0.01 using different filters for Lena image.

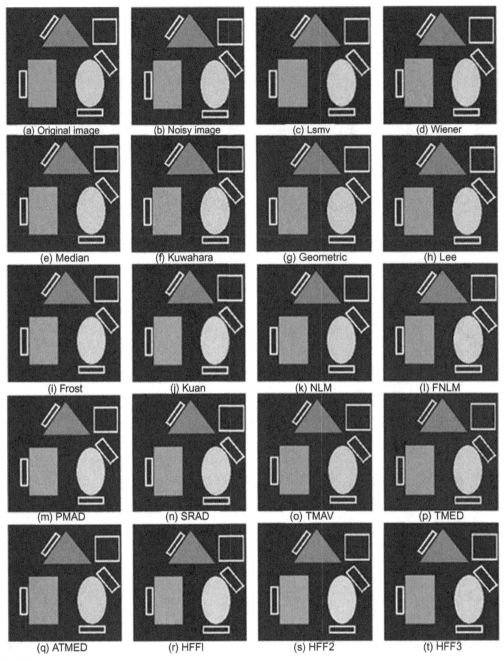

(a) Original image   (b) Noisy image   (c) Lsmv   (d) Wiener

(e) Median   (f) Kuwahara   (g) Geometric   (h) Lee

(i) Frost   (j) Kuan   (k) NLM   (l) FNLM

(m) PMAD   (n) SRAD   (o) TMAV   (p) TMED

(q) ATMED   (r) HFFI   (s) HFF2   (t) HFF3

FIG. 5.5

Perceptual quality comparisons for noise variance 0.01 using different filters for artificial image.

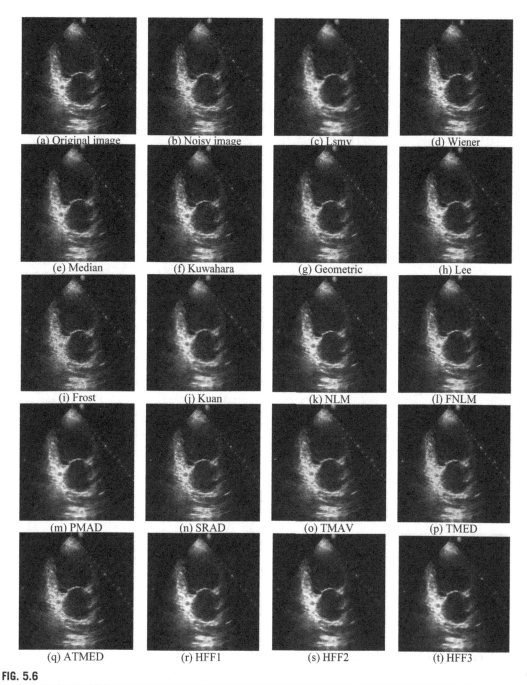

FIG. 5.6

Perceptual quality comparisons using different filters in A2C view.

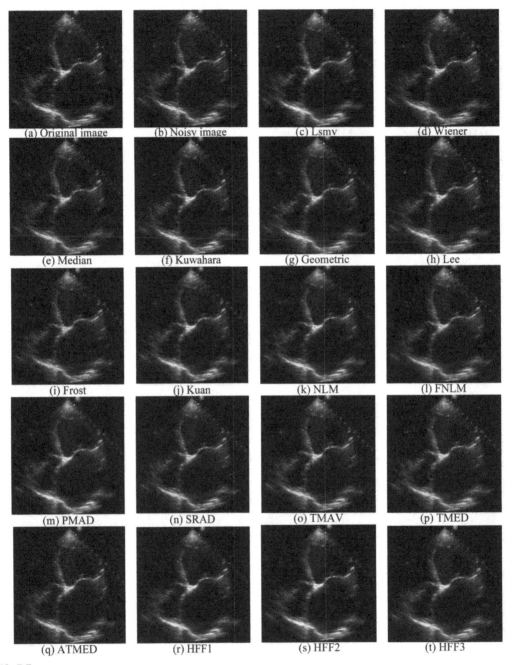

FIG. 5.7

Perceptual quality comparisons using different filters in A4C view.

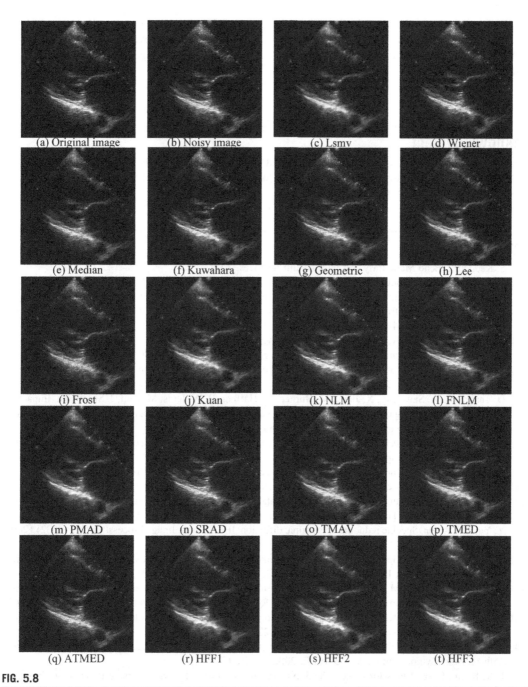

FIG. 5.8

Perceptual quality comparisons using different filters in PLAX view.

This study helps in choosing the best filters for clinical TTE images among a wide range of filters and their constituents. Results of quantitative assessment and clinical approval show that the proposed HFF3 performed the best compared to other filters in terms of edge safeguarding and denoising of speckle noise.

Acknowledgment

The author, Arun Balodi, would like to extend deep and sincere appreciation to the Department of Cardiology, Swami Rama Himalayan University, Dehradun, India, for providing the dataset of ultrasound images and their constant support for carrying out this research.

References

[1] S. Kaddoura, Echo Made Easy, Elsevier Health Sciences, 2012.
[2] P. Lancellotti, C. Tribouilloy, A. Hagendorff, B.A. Popescu, T. Edvardsen, L.A. Pierard, L. Badano, J.L. Zamorano, et al., Recommendations for the echocardiographic assessment of native valvular regurgitation: an executive summary from the european association of cardiovascular imaging, Eur. Heart J. Cardiovasc. Imaging 14 (2013) 1–34.
[3] X. Zong, A.F. Laine, E.A. Geiser, Speckle reduction and contrast enhancement of echocardiograms via multiscale nonlinear processing, IEEE Trans. Med. Imaging 17 (4) (1998) 532–540.
[4] S. Finn, M. Glavin, E. Jones, Echocardiographic speckle reduction comparison, IEEE Trans. Ultrason. Ferroelectr. Freq. Control 58 (1) (2011) 82–101.
[5] D. Tenbrinck, A. Sawatzky, X. Jiang, M. Burger, W. Haffner, P. Willems, M. Paul, J. Stypmann, Impact of physical noise modeling on image segmentation in echocardiography, in: Eurographics Workshop on Visual Computing for Biology and Medicine, 2012, pp. 33–40.
[6] A. Ozcan, A. Bilenca, A.E. Desjardins, B.E. Bouma, G.J. Tearney, Speckle reduction in optical coherence tomography images using digital filtering, JOSA A 24 (7) (2007) 1901–1910.
[7] J.W. Goodman, Some fundamental properties of speckle, JOSA 66 (11) (1976) 1145–1150.
[8] C.B. Burckhardt, Speckle in ultrasound b-mode scans, IEEE Trans. Son. Ultrason. 25 (1) (1978) 1–6.
[9] R.F. Wagner, M.F. Insana, S.W. Smith, Fundamental correlation lengths of coherent speckle in medical ultrasonic images, IEEE Trans. Ultrason. Ferroelectr. Freq. Control 35 (1) (1988) 34–44.
[10] Y. Yu, S.T. Acton, Speckle reducing anisotropic diffusion, IEEE Trans. Image Process. 11 (11) (2002) 1260–1270.
[11] S. Aja-Fernández, C. Alberola-López, On the estimation of the coefficient of variation for anisotropic diffusion speckle filtering, IEEE Trans. Image Process. 15 (9) (2006) 2694–2701.
[12] A. Buades, B. Coll, J.-M. Morel, A non-local algorithm for image denoising, in: 2005 IEEE Computer Society Conference on Computer Vision and Pattern Recognition (CVPR'05), vol. 2, IEEE, 2005, pp. 60–65.
[13] P. Coupé, P. Hellier, C. Kervrann, C. Barillot, Nonlocal means-based speckle filtering for ultrasound images, IEEE Trans. Image Process. 18 (10) (2009) 2221–2229.
[14] H. Kwan, Y. Cai, Fuzzy filters for image filtering, in: Circuits and Systems, 2002. MWSCAS-2002. The 2002 45th Midwest Symposium on, vol. 3, IEEE, 2002. pp. III–672.
[15] H.K. Kwan, Fuzzy filters for noise reduction in images, in: Fuzzy Filters for Image Processing, Springer, 2003, pp. 25–53.

[16] Y. Sheng, Z.-G. Xia, A comprehensive evaluation of filters for radar speckle suppression, in: Geo- Science and Remote Sensing Symposium, 1996. IGARSS'96.'Remote Sensing for a Sustainable Future, International, vol. 3, IEEE, 1996, pp. 1559–1561.

[17] C.P. Loizou, C.S. Pattichis, C.I. Christodoulou, R.S. Istepanian, M. Pantziaris, A. Nicolaides, Comparative evaluation of despeckle filtering in ultrasound imaging of the carotid artery, IEEE Trans. Ultrason. Ferroelectr. Freq. Control 52 (10) (2005) 1653–1669.

[18] C.P. Loizou, C. Theofanous, M. Pantziaris, T. Kasparis, Despeckle filtering software toolbox for ultrasound imaging of the common carotid artery, Comput. Methods Programs Biomed. 114 (1) (2014) 109–124.

[19] A. Balodi, M. Dewal, A. Rawat, Comparison of despeckle filters for ultrasound images, in: Computing for Sustainable Global Development (INDIACom), 2015 2nd International Conference on, IEEE, 2015, pp. 1919–1924.

[20] J.L. Mateo, A. Fernández-Caballero, Finding out general tendencies in speckle noise reduction in ultrasound images, Expert Syst. Appl. 36 (4) (2009) 7786–7797.

[21] N. Biradar, M.L. Dewal, M.K. Rohit, Speckle noise reduction in b-mode echocardiographic images: a comparison, IETE Tech. Rev. 32 (6) (2015) 435–453.

[22] J.-S. Lee, Digital image enhancement and noise filtering by use of local statistics, IEEE Trans. Pattern Anal. Mach. Intell. 2 (1980) 165–168.

[23] V.S. Frost, J.A. Stiles, K.S. Shanmugan, J.C. Holtzman, A model for radar images and its application to adaptive digital filtering of multiplicative noise, IEEE Trans. Pattern Anal. Mach. Intell. 2 (1982) 157–166.

[24] D. Kuan, A. Sawchuk, T. Strand, P. Chavel, Adaptive restoration of images with speckle, IEEE Trans. Acoust. Speech Signal Process. 35 (3) (1987) 373–383.

[25] P. Perona, J. Malik, Scale-space and edge detection using anisotropic diffusion, IEEE Trans. Pattern Anal. Mach. Intell. 12 (7) (1990) 629–639.

[26] R. Vignesh, B.T. Oh, C.-C.J. Kuo, Fast non-local means (nlm) computation with probabilistic early termination, IEEE Signal Process. Lett. 17 (3) (2010) 277–280.

[27] A. Balodi, M. Dewal, R. Anand, A. Rawat, Texture based classification of the severity of mitral regurgitation, Comput. Biol. Med. 73 (2016) 157–164.

[28] A. Balodi, R. Anand, M. Dewal, A. Rawat, Computer-aided classification of the mitral regurgitation using multiresolution local binary pattern, Neural Comput. Applic. 32 (2019) 1–11.

[29] Z. Wang, A.C. Bovik, H.R. Sheikh, E.P. Simoncelli, Image quality assessment: from error visibility to structural similarity, IEEE Trans. Image Process. 13 (4) (2004) 600–612.

[30] J. Zhang, C. Wang, Y. Cheng, Comparison of despeckle filters for breast ultrasound images, Circuits Syst. Signal Process. 34 (1) (2015) 185–208.

[31] Y. Guo, Y. Wang, T. Hou, Speckle filtering of ultrasonic images using a modified non-local-based algorithm, Biomed. Signal Process. Control 6 (2) (2011) 129–138.

[32] M. Iqbal, J. Chen, W. Yang, P. Wang, B. Sun, Sar image despeckling by selective 3d filtering of multiple compressive reconstructed images, Prog. Electromagn. Res. 134 (2013) 209–226.

[33] N. Biradar, M. Dewal, M.K. Rohit, Speckle noise reduction in echocardiographic images of aortic valve and cardiac chambers, Optik 126 (2) (2015) 153–163.

Impetus to machine learning in cardiac disease diagnosis

T. Vani

Department of Computer Science, Rajeswari Vedachalam Government Arts College [Affiliated to University of Madras], Chengalpattu, Tamil Nadu, India

Chapter outline

Image Processing for Automated Diagnosis of Cardiac Diseases. https://doi.org/10.1016/B978-0-323-85064-3.00009-1

6.1 Impetus to machine learning in cardiac disease diagnosis

The most common dreadful disease in the world is coronary artery disease (CAD), a cardiovascular disease. This disease always leads to cardiac attacks and claims abundant human lives in the world. The early diagnosis may help to reduce the fatal rate. The conventional medical diagnosis available for CAD is angiography, which involves high-risk factors. The procedure for angiography is invasive, and it has many risks and limitations. Hence, there is a need for a noninvasive, fast, and accurate procedure for the diagnosis of CAD. The machine-learning-based medical diagnosis is a fast, noninvasive, time-saving, and more accurate method. As this method is noninvasive, this is preferred over the existing methods. In this chapter, the machine learning and its significance in the medical diagnosis of cardiac diseases are explained.

6.2 Introduction to medical imaging

Medical imaging has advanced along with the development of radiological imaging equipment such as computed tomography and magnetic resonance imaging. The process of medical imaging is very much complex and a challenging task for medical professionals. Earlier the medical image analysis was only qualitative. It needs a quantitative diagnosis about the severity and stage of the illness, the chance of treatment response, risk of recurrence, and expected survival in many diseases, such as oncology. The computer-aided diagnosis (CAD) is an emerging field to fulfill the above needs. The CAD facilitates accuracy, precision, consistency in the interpretation of diseases by evaluating the medical images. Eventually, this process generates large volumes of data, which leads to a more time-consuming diagnosis and a delay in decision-making. This delay will affect the patients' timely treatment pattern and end up in hazardous results, sometimes fatal. Hence, computer-based medical imaging techniques have to be refined systematically to cope with the above alarming threats and challenges.

6.3 Role of computers in medical imaging

In computer science, the digital image is a two-dimensional function $f(x,y)$ represented by a matrix of spatial coordinates x and y. The image is treated as a two-dimensional arrangement of pixels, and each pixel represents the gray or color value of one cell in the image. The cell values of the matrix indicate the pixel values. The range of the pixel values lies between (0,1), where 0 indicates pure black, and 1 represents pure white. The values between 0 and 1 represent the different shades of gray color. In the three-dimensional system, the pixels are termed as voxels as it considers volume. The variation in these values is analyzed in medical images for the diagnosis of a particular disease.

6.3.1 Computer-based medical image analysis

In early 2000, there is a revolution PACS (Picture Archiving and Communication System) in the medical image motivated by technological advancements [1]. Using PACS, the medical images are captured without using films (filmless radiology) from the acquisition devices such as CT, MRI, and ultrasound. They are archived and communicated to the respective medical practitioners. These images are stored in DICOM (Digital Imaging and Communication) format in an organized way in an extensive medical database, available to the medical professionals any time. This concept is the basis for developing many CAD models.

6.3.2 Computer-aided detection

In 1980, the first computer-aided detection (CAD) system came into existence, and it was mainly used for additional confirmation or the second opinion using radiological imaging [1]. The earlier CAD systems were designed by image processing techniques and computer vision methods. Then the purpose of the application of CAD shifted toward accuracy and precision. In medical image analysis, precision, accuracy, and consistency are the significant parameters to measure the characteristics of the outcome. Even a smaller degree of deviation in the outcome of these parameters will significantly result in a hazardous effect in treatment patterns.

Moreover, the medical image analysis is done in almost life-threatening diseases like cancers, cardiac failure, neurological disorders, and so on. In such cases, the analysis of radiological images must maintain a high accuracy to support the treatment plans. Another vital aspect of computer-based medical image analysis is that it is noninvasive. The other medical diagnosis techniques are all invasive, which is very harmful to the patients, sometimes lethal.

6.3.3 Computer-based image retrieval (CBIR)

Computer-based image retrieval is an efficient tool to search a set of similar images that are similar to the given image, irrespective of their external description associated with it. In this tool, there will be a database used to store several images in an organized manner. If one image is given to the search engine associated with the database, it will retrieve all the images similar to the given image. This tool will be handy for the medical professional if the database of the radiological image is well maintained. They can easily track similar care history and conclude in no time. This tool can also be used for training in medical fields.

6.3.4 Radiomics and radio genomics

This level is the advanced level of CAD, where quantitative characteristics of radiological images are derived for the prognosis of the disease and the treatment plan for the patients. Due to the technological evolution and computational advancement in algorithms, the radiologists' diagnosis will change drastically. The newly evolved computer science fields such as artificial intelligence, computer vision, and machine learning help the medical imaging and diagnosis prosper and overcome the setbacks in conventional radiological systems. The significant benefits realized due to these fields are precision, accuracy, timely, and automated diagnosis of diseases from the radiological images. It facilitates determining the appropriate planning of treatments and analysis of the outcome; besides, it faces the legal and ethical issues in some medical exams. The use of machine learning algorithms also incredibly supports multidisciplinary patient assessment.

6.4 Introduction to machine learning

Artificial intelligence (AI) is growing as a powerful and most promising technology due to the exponential growth of high computing devices. AI is applied almost in all fields wherever human intelligence can be replaceable. The field which is emerging from AI is machine learning. It consists of a set of efficient algorithms based on statistical methods such as regression and correlation. The supremacy of these machine learning algorithms is that they facilitate the power of autonomous working to any system by learning from past experiences without any human intervention. Machine learning algorithms are designed from combinations of computational, mathematical, and statistical methodologies. The principal objective of machine learning is to develop computer programs that can learn themselves from past experiences and making efficient decisions for necessitating further action in any domain. The machine learning comprises of a number of algorithms based on statistical techniques such as regression, classification, and correlation. The commonly used machine learning are support vector machines, decision trees, naïve Bayes, artificial neural networks, K-nearest neighbor. Machine learning is a subfield of computer science derived from the field of artificial intelligence (AI). There are four categories of machine learning methods based on the learning strategy, such as supervised learning algorithms, unsupervised learning algorithms, semisupervised algorithms, and reinforcement learning algorithms, which are explained below.

6.4.1 Categories of machine learning

Machine learning algorithms are divided into four categories, as supervised learning, unsupervised learning, semisupervised learning, and reinforcement learning based on their learning pattern. Each category has its unique functionality and limitations, and they are described below.

6.4.1.1 Supervised learning

Many of the machine learning algorithms are based on supervised learning strategy. In the supervised learning category, the set of input variables (X) and a set of output variables (Y) will be provided. The algorithm will learn the mapping function $Y = f(X)$ from the input to the output. The mapping function is designed such that for a new value of X, the output value Y can be predicted. This data is called as training data set as it acts as a supervisor for the learning process. The algorithm makes a number of iterations for predicting the value until it obtains optimum value. The supervised learning method is applied in regression and classification problems. In the supervised machine learning, the set inputs or features are directly associated with a known outcome. This attribute is useful for representing the real-world scenario by appropriately associating the objects with their characteristics. For example, the weight and age of a person can be associated with the onset of diabetic disease in the near future.

The well-trained supervised models make accurate predictions when new input data is given to it. The outcome prediction of a supervised model can be produced in the form of discrete or continuous values. The model that produces a discrete outcome is applied in classification algorithms, and the one that produces continuous outcome is applied in regression algorithms. Examples of machine learning algorithms belonging to this category are linear regression (LR) for regression problems, random forest (RF) for classification and regression problems, and support vector machines (SVM) for classification problems.

6.4.1.2 Unsupervised learning

Unsupervised machine learning algorithms will only be a set of input values (X), and the output value will be unknown. The objective of unsupervised learning is to build the underlying model on its own to learn more about the data. Here, there is no training data set to supervise the outcomes. Hence this is called an unsupervised learning method. Unsupervised learning can be applied in clustering and association problems. In an unsupervised learning method, there is no predefined outcome associated with the input. In this method, the system has to explore the appropriate outcome for the given input. When the input size is enormous, some dimension reduction techniques are to be applied to reduce the size. Some examples of unsupervised learning algorithms are the k-means algorithm for clustering problems and the apriori algorithm for association rule learning problems.

6.4.1.3 Semisupervised learning

In the semisupervised machine learning method, there will be provided a large amount of input data (X) and a partial set of the output data (Y), and the system can learn for the given set of data (Y). For the other data, it has to follow unsupervised learning. Hence, it is called semisupervised learning. Many real-world machine learning problems belong to this category that needs access to domain experts. Semisupervised learning is partially supervised and partially unsupervised learning, and hence it lies in between supervised and unsupervised learning. This category is mainly used in genetic sequencing, classification, and speech recognition.

6.4.1.4 Reinforcement learning

In reinforcement learning, the model is trained to make a set of decisions in a row. In this way, the model is practiced to make decisions in an unknown, unpredictable, and complex scenario. The approach for making decisions is based on trial and error methods. If the outcome is the desired or expected one, then the system is encouraged with rewards. If the outcome is not desirable, then the system has to face the consequence in terms of penalties. Hence, the objective of this method is to increase the number of rewards or minimize the number of penalties. This method aids to increase the creativity of the system by encouraging it with some rewards. This method is applied in game designing, self-driving cars. Examples for this method are temporal difference, deep adversarial networks, and Q-learning.

6.4.2 Machine learning algorithms

There are many numbers of machine learning algorithms devised based on computational and statistical methodology. Among them, the most accurate algorithms are logistic regression, support vector machine, artificial neural networks, naïve Bayes, and random forest. These algorithms provide an almost 80% accuracy rate in results. They are explained below.

6.4.2.1 Artificial neural networks (ANN)

Artificial neural networks are based on the biological inspiration of the human brain, and this is an attempt to simulate it. This technique is also called multilayer perceptron as this model can efficiently represent an exceptionally complex nonlinear function. This system is implemented to learn from the data set just as a human brain does. Hence, the term "neural" is used in the context. There are three layers in the neural network, namely the input layer, an output layer, and the hidden layer. The input layer's data are transmitted to the output layer in different patterns through the hidden layer. If the result is not the desired one, then the hidden layer will send back the signals to the input layer to make necessary arrangements in the form of feedbacks. This technique is called back propagation. The model is efficient in complex pattern analysis and matching, and hence it is most commonly used in pattern extraction.

6.4.2.2 Logistic regression (LR)

The logistic regression method is applied to predict the probability of the desired outcome for the given set of input values based on some categories, incessantly. There are three types of logic regression, namely, binary logistic regression, multinomial logistic regression, ordinal logistic regression. In binary logistic regression, there are precisely two categorical responses obtained as an outcome for the given input values. In multinomial logistic regression, the number of categorical responses will be three or more, and they will not follow any order. An ordinal logistic regression, the categorical responses will be three or more, but they follow some sequence. When the number of input values is getting large, the complexity of prediction also increases. Hence, this value must be kept as a minimum to achieve accurate prediction in the diagnosis. In such cases, the reduction algorithms such as principal component analysis and linear discriminator analysis are applied to reduce the dimensions. The logistic regression method is easy to implement in medical diagnosis and hence applied in many research works. This method is also used to classify medical images such as MRI segments, SPECT images.

6.4.2.3 Support vector machine (SVM)

Support vector machines (SVMs) are supervised machine learning algorithms, and they are used for classification and regression analysis. The SVM performs both linear classification and nonlinear classification. The nonlinear classification is performed using the Kernel function. In nonlinear classification, the kernels are homogenous polynomial, complex polynomial, Gaussian radial basis function, and hyperbolic tangent function. The SVM is performed excellently by the proper selection of kernel, the parameters of the kernel, notably the Gaussian kernel is preferred as it has a single parameter. The SVM method outperforms the other methods, and hence it is the most commonly used machine learning technique, especially in industrial applications. The SVM method is considered the best method for diagnosing coronary diseases. The SVM method has also suffered from potential setbacks such as high memory consumption when it processes large volumes of data. It is not easy to interpret the parameters of the solved SVM method. The SVM method requires all the input data to be correctly labeled before the process. The advantages of the SVM method are the better accuracy in classification and the best performance in the analysis.

6.4.2.4 Naive Bayes

Naive Bayes is one of the best machine learning methods used for predictive modeling. It is based on a famous statistical theorem Bayesian theorem of conditional probability. It is mainly used for classification, as there is a minimum error rate. This method is easy to implement, and it can be applied even for extensive data sets. This method is famous for giving better performance in classifications. This method is defined in terms of a hypothesis (h) and data sets (d). Then the Bayes' theorem is stated as

$$P(h \mid d) = P(d \mid h) \times P(h)/P(d)$$

where $P(h|d)$ is the probability of hypothesis h given the data d. This value is called the posterior probability. $P(d|h)$ is the probability of data d given that the hypothesis h was true. $P(h)$ is the probability of hypothesis when h is true (regardless of the data). This probability is called the prior probability of h. $P(d)$ is the probability of the data (regardless of the hypothesis).

6.4.2.5 Random Forest (RF)

Random Forest is one of the popular machine learning technique that is based on nonlinear structures called as decision tree. The random forest is ensemble learning by the construction of multiple decision trees. This method is well trained using different random sample data. Occasionally this method suffers high variance, which is addressed by proper training with random samples. As it reduces the generalizations error, this method serves as a powerful technique. In this method, the prediction is based on the mode or mean of all the predictions. The model is used for classification problems, and the mean is used for regression problems. This method is also called as bagging or bootstrap aggregation. A bootstrap is an efficient approach for finding the mean from the given set of values. The decision tree methods are used to calculate the value. The decision tree represents the prediction of the particular set. After obtaining all the decision trees, the mean of all predictions is estimated to get the consolidated prediction.

6.5 Impact of machine learning in everyday life

Machine learning has a high impact on our daily lives as tremendous growth in the supporting fields such as IoT, artificial intelligence and big data, and device development with high computational power. Hence, the machine learning starts to play a vital role in almost all fields globally, including energy sectors, financial sectors, healthcare, education, creative arts, manufacturing, media, and retail sectors. The inevitability of machine learning in these areas is described below.

6.5.1 Energy

With the tremendous support of machine learning, big data, and the internet of things, the global energy leaders are trying to build digital power plant and the internet of energy. For example, the global energy sources BP and GE are leading in realizing their visions by the applications of machine learning and artificial intelligence. They try to reach new levels of performance with the help of these technologies by improving their resources. They deploy sensors to monitor and increase the operations using AI technology continuously. Their engineers, scientists, and decision-makers are working with the help of these technologies to drive high performance. Another power source giant GE power uses big data, machine learning, and the internet of things (IoT) technology to construct an "internet of energy." Advanced analytics and machine learning also helps in predictive maintenance and power, operations, and business optimization.

6.5.2 Arts and culture

IBM designed a tool Chef Watson based on AI and big data for the world of arts and design. Using the machine learning technique, the tool was given as input, a series of artworks of famous artist Gaudi along with other information related to culture, song lyrics, historical articles, and biographies. On successful training with these data, Watson delivers inspired ideas and suggestions to the human artists who try to create the style of Gaudi. IBM's Watson also has the capability to guide us in cooking as perfect as a Master Chef. It suggests different recipes to prepare foods in unique flavor each time, but with a little human touch, i.e., it works with humans in the kitchen rather than cooking alone. Machine learning algorithms are now used in the field of music in composing different kinds of theme music, which is a wonder for musicians all over the world. They can use artificial intelligence-based models to come up with great tunes to inspire the audiences. IBM Watson BEAT is one such tool that offers different musical elements for the composers to make their music ever time hit.

6.5.3 Financial services

Finance industry is the one which involves complex rules and voluminous data (almost in PB) in making effective financial decision making. The data is collected from transactional records, customer, or general public information databases. To make fast and efficient decision making from the data out of these databases is a challenging task for the finance officials. The machine learning algorithms used in such tedious decision making will be a wise choice. Many financial sectors around the world start to realize it and implement them in their functionalities. Many business giants use machine learning to make online trend analysis. Eventually, it helps in preventing the losses due to poor decision making and minimizing the delay in decision-making.

6.5.4 Healthcare

Many healthcare applications are based on artificial intelligence, deep learning, and machine learning algorithms. These applications' main objective is to provide additional support in the decision-making process regarding radiological image analysis and the past history of the diseases. Machine learning applications are essential in places where the data is too large to study and analyze. When the medical images are to be reviewed within a short period, errors may occur due to human fatigue. The computer-based diagnosis helps to reduce such errors and make the treatment plan effectively.

However, in all the above applications, the Machine Learning algorithms are supportive tools, not as a replacement for the medical professionals. **Infervision** and **Deepmind** are two such applications of machine learning. Infervision is developed by China to analyze and review the radiological images effectively. Deepmind is developed by Google to simulate the human brain. Other than the fields as mentioned earlier, the machine learning algorithm is also used in the manufacturing sector, retail services, governmental services, media, and social media.

6.5.5 Machine learning in medical imaging

Computer-based medical imaging's main objective is to identify the image and check whether it is a healthy or disease-infected one. This process is called the classification of images, and machine learning algorithms can perform it. The machine-learning-based models are learning from experience (training data set) to make decisions for the present scenario. In medical images classification, the machine learning algorithms can be applied to classify the images based on the predefined factors or patterns of a particular disease. Hence, to apply machine learning algorithms, in medical image classifications, there are two steps involved. As a first step, the model should be trained by constructing a training data set. Once the training is successfully performed, the model can be validated by giving test data to check whether the model correctly classifies the images. If the result is not desirable, the feedback is added with the training data set, and the process is repeated until the outcome has arrived as expected.

The most widely used machine learning algorithm is an artificial neural network (ANN) model. The ANN is constructed as a model based on a human central nervous system. The ANN model consists of three layers: the input layer, hidden layer, and output layer, in which each layer consists of several neurons. The neurons of the input layer represent the features of the images, and the output layer represents the outcomes. The hidden layer consists of an activation function to match these data. The ANN model is also constructed as multilayer perceptron (MLP).

6.6 Applications of machine learning in disease diagnosis

The primary medical application areas of machine learning for diagnosis are liver diseases, Parkinson's diseases, ECG of human hearts [2–6]. In these applications, machine learning techniques are used for screening classification, assertion, prediction, and decision-making processes. The applications of various Machine Learning techniques and the specific process for diagnosing various diseases are described in Table 6.1.

6.7 Machine learning in cardiac disease diagnosis

Machine learning algorithms are widely used to diagnose cardiac disease by applying on various medical images ECG (echocardiography), cardiac MRI (magnetic resonance images), cardiac CT (computed tomography), and SPECT (single photon emission computed tomography) [7]. In CAD models, essential medical image processing is segmentation. The region of interest (ROI) can be easily separated and highlighted using Segmentation. Using ROI, the abnormal pattern of images can be easily differentiated from the normal patterns. The ROI is obtained by two processes, namely segmentation and feature extraction. Feature extraction from a segment can be performed by many algorithms, including contour recognition, texture classification, histogram construction, shape recognition. There are three types of features, namely, texture, gray level, and shape.

The extraction of the gray level is done by histogram analysis, and it can be applied directly as the images. This feature is the commonly used feature extraction technique. In gray level feature extraction, the difference in the gray level of the pixels is considered. However, in some images, the set of pixels will have the same set of gray values, which can be used for extraction. In such cases, the textures are instrumental in radiological imaging as they can be used to identify lesions easily. Shape features are also useful for differentiating the contours, curves, and polygonal regions of an image. To be more successful in this study, the performance of the segmentation algorithms should be excellent. Otherwise, the clinical investigation will not be efficient and proper decisions may not be possible to arrive.

Table 6.1 Machine learning algorithms in disease diagnosis.

S. no.	ML technique	Process	Findings/diagnosis
1.	Logistic regression	Classification Feature extraction	Myocarditis Obstructive CAD using SPECT images
2.	SVM	Diagnosis Identification Prediction Discrimination	Myocardial infarction CAD identification Predicting ACS ASD
3.	RF	Fast prediction Texture analysis Intensity analysis and motion modeling Identify biomarker difference	Clinical practices Cardiac MRI Infarction detection Echo and clinical data
4.	Cluster Analysis	Classification/discovery Hierarchical clustering of MRI data Grouping of CT data	Cardio-phenol groups Congenital heart disease Bicuspid aortic valve patients
5.	ANN	Feature extraction from ECHO Feature extraction from SPECT images	HCM and DCM patients Diagnose CAD
6.	CNN	Image analysis CAC detection ECHO images	Cardiac images CTA images HCM diagnosis amyloidosis, Pulmonary artery hypertension

There are many efficient algorithms in machine learning such as ANN, random forests (RF), and decision trees (DT), which serve these purposes.

Hence in the healthcare domain, especially in cardiac disease diagnosis, the machine learning algorithms are mostly preferred for the following factors:

- To handle with voluminous medical image data effectively
- To make the treatment plan efficiently without any delay
- To diagnose the disease without any errors
- Timely detection of disease efficiently

6.8 Potential challenges of using machine learning in disease diagnosis

Applications of machine learning face many challenges [8] in medical image analysis, especially in building decision support systems for psychiatry and neurology. The key challenges include lack of diagnostic reliability, presence of clinical heterogeneity, and absence of biomarkers. Each disease has its own degree of diagnostic reliability. Due to the absence of biomarkers, clinical heterogeneity, and diagnosis's reliability is uncertain in psychiatric disorders. However, it is possible to assess the diagnosis of neurological disorder with reduced uncertainty due to the presence of validated biomarkers. Hence, to access the presence of psychiatric illness Diagnostic and Statistical Manual of Mental Disorders (DSM) and the International Classification of Disease (ICD) have suggested diagnostic criteria to help the clinicians in the assessment. Nevertheless, these suggestions are not comprehensive and do not help in eliminating uncertainty.

Due to the lack of diagnostic reliability, the training, and evaluations of machine learning algorithms face complications, which lead to a biased classification. The biased classification hazardously leads to the wrong treatment regimen. All the diseases are heterogeneous in many aspects, such as treatment response, clinical presentations, and periodical progression. It poses a big challenge for implementing machine learning algorithms to achieve accuracy and precision in diagnosis, as it is tough to learn from the sample data with a high level of heterogeneity.

A biomarker is a clinical indicator used to measure and evaluate the pathogenic processor pharmacological responses normal biological process in response to therapy. If a biomarker is reliable, accurate, reproducible, and plausible in a clinical environment, it is said to be validated. The robust biomarkers are good at providing objective evidence, and they can be used to facilitate the diagnostic evaluation of patients. For some diseases like psychiatric disorders, there are no reliable, robust biomarkers. The unavailability of reliable biomarkers is a significant threat for developing implementing machine learning algorithms for accurate assessment and diagnosis, and it suffers severe discrimination in the outcome.

Another major challenge in the perspective of machine learning implementation is based on the type of learning it follows. Many machine learning models implemented in radiological imaging are based on the supervised learning category. In the supervised learning category, the algorithm is trained with an adequate data set, which includes a set of decisions made by the radiologists in the past similar cases. This data set is used to train the model to achieve 100% accuracy in a similar problem given as input.

When machine learning is applied in the medical domain, there arises two expectations: accuracy and robustness. The robustness can only be achieved when the machine learning model is trained with all possible imaging data sets. This aspect is challenging as many medical applications are lack of stored data. The lack of a comprehensive data set may not guarantee the robustness, and sometimes it may lead to biased results. The biased results will create havoc in the treatment regimen, which is fatal at times.

Other factors that pose a challenge to the implementation of machine learning in medical domains other than the size of the data set are data quality, feature selection, and data imbalance. The quality of trained data is essential for obtaining accurate results. As the model relies on the quality of data set for training, the poor-quality data will degrade the machine learning model's performance. This aspect will be more harmful to medical/clinical diagnosis applications. Similarly, feature selection is highly essential for implementing machine learning effectively in the medical domain. The medical images are consisting of rich features that are clinically insignificant. Low-level image feature extraction is challenging to apply in medical imaging. The high dimensional image features will be surplus for image-based operations like classification and image retrieval. Imbalanced data refers to the set of data where the set contains almost normal data with very few abnormal data. This kind of data set will affect the accuracy of the model and will lead to biased decision making.

6.9 Constraints of using machine learning

Although machine learning techniques have been implemented successfully in many sectors, they face some struggles in some aspects. Machine learning algorithms' performance is affected by many factors such as massive data sets, biased or incomplete data sets, verification of results, improper interpretation of results, and error-prone prediction [8,9]. These factors turn out to be the limitations of the machine learning algorithms, and they are described below.

1. The machine learning algorithm has to be adequately trained with a comprehensive set of trained data to obtain highly accurate results.
2. The trained data must be acquired from a sound source, and the data must also be unbiased to get the authentic prediction.
3. The one-fits-all approach cannot be applied in the use of machine learning because each algorithm can only be applied to a specific problem. The algorithm that gives better results in solving one particular problem may not yield the same accuracy to other problems. Hence, the selection of an algorithm must be appropriate to the problem which is taken for consideration. The selection of such an algorithm is a big challenge, and it must be resolved to get better results.
4. As the data set is extensive, it consumes more time during acquisition.
5. Sometimes the chosen algorithm may yield excellent outcomes, but it may fail if it is not correctly interpreted.
6. The results of the machine learning algorithms need to be verified whether they yield the same level of accurate results in all cases. The accuracy check needs a standard means of verification, which is not available now.
6. When machine learning algorithms are applied in the medical field, the errors must be carefully avoided. If one error in the prediction is left unnoticed, it may have severe consequences as the treatment patterns are designed.
8. Sometimes the machine learning algorithms struck up with local minima problems, which will affect the accuracy of diagnosis. Evolutionary computation algorithms can be applied to avoid such conflicts.
9. In CAD, machine learning models have been developed specifically for a particular problem. It can be revised by ensemble-based learning methods for achieving better performance.

6.10 How to develop a machine learning model for the medical domain?

When a machine learning model is constructed for medical diagnosis, the model must be trained with a complete set of past data [10]. Once the model is trained with a data set, it has to go through a number of clinical trials until it achieves 100% accuracy in outcomes. If the result is not desirable, the training has to be repeated. Because in many cases, the well-trained model produces considerably lower performances while it is undergone external exam. To avoid such things, the prebuilt model must offer an added facility to update periodically. Whenever a new update is added, the model should undergo training and testing to increase the performance and avoid bias. It is a significant challenge when the machine learning algorithm is applied in medical domains which is depicted in Fig. 6.1.

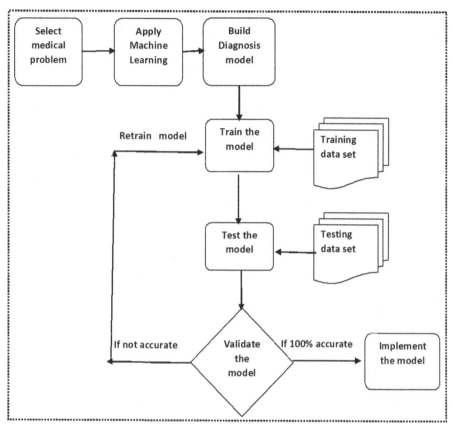

FIG. 6.1

Architecture of machine learning algorithms in disease diagnosis.

6.11 **Validation and performance assessment**

The major step in the implementation of the machine learning algorithm is to validate the model to measure its performance. For validation, there are many strategies available [1]. The most commonly used strategy is cross-validation. In cross-validation, a complete set of samples (N) is divided into two groups, in the ratio of (N-1,1) where the former group is used for training the model, and the latter group is used for testing the model. Another strategy is based on dividing the samples into three groups; one group is used for training the model, the second group is used for validation, and the third group is used for testing. Once the model is trained and appropriately tested using any one of the above strategies, the performance of the model has to be measured. The parameters used to measure the performance of the machine learning model are sensitivity (S_c), specificity (S_p), accuracy, and area under curve (AUC) for the receiver operating characteristic of the method. Sensitivity is defined as the ratio between the number of True Positive and the number of False Negative in a diagnosis. i.e., the number of positive cases of a disease currently identified by the model is called True Positive. The number of positive cases of a disease that are wrongly identified as negative is called False Negative. The ratio between the True Positive cases and the total number of cases of a disease is defined as Sensitivity, and it is measured as given below:

$$Sensitivity = \frac{True\ Positive}{True\ Positive + False\ Negative}$$

For a machine learning model, the high value of Sensitivity indicates that the True Positive value is high, and False Negative value is low. This result is the desired result for the ML algorithm when implemented in healthcare and financial domains.

The meter specificity is defined as the ratio between the number of True Negative cases and the total number of trials. Here, the True Negative indicates the total number of patients' negative results when they are actually healthy. In some cases, the result will be marked as positive for a healthy person by this machine learning model. This kind of result is called False Positive. The specificity of a machine learning model is measured using the parameters mentioned above as follows:

$$Specificity = \frac{True\ Negative}{True\ Negative + False\ Positive}$$

If the specificity is high for a model, then it indicates that True Negative values are high, and False Positive values are low for the diagnosis undertaken.

The difference between sensitivity and specificity is that the former indicates the number of positive results, and the latter indicates the number of negative results. The receiver operating characteristic (ROC) is plotted as a curve using the sensitivity and specificity values. The area under the ROC curve is defined as the AUC, and it is beneficial for measuring the performance of the underlying model.

The AUC is described as the probability that the implemented machine learning model predicts a positive value than the negative value. The value of AUC always lies in the range (0,1). If the prediction of the model is 100% accurate, then its AUC value is 1. For an unsuccessful machine learning model, the AUC value is 0. The analysis results of these ML techniques help diagnose the diseases summarized in Table 6.2. In this table, some major machine learning methods such as ANN, SVM, CNN, DT, and LR are described with their accuracy and AUC values when they are implemented for diagnosing the specific heart diseases.

6.12 Results and discussions

Since the last two decades, many successful pieces of research have been carried out to test the performance of machine learning algorithms in the process of cardiac disease diagnosis. The total number of research works that have been carried out around the world is 149 [9], and they include the implementations of various machine learning algorithms. Among them, artificial neural network, logistic regression, support vector machine, decision tree, naïve Bayes, convolutional neural networks, and random forest take the lead role in the diagnosis applications. The total number of research works of each algorithm out of these 149 is depicted in Fig. 6.2.

It is evident from the Fig. 6.2, that the most frequently applied algorithms are ANN, SVM, DT, and CNN. The performances of these algorithms are measured in terms of accuracy values, as described in Section 6.12. Among the validated algorithms, ANN and SVM algorithms achieved 100% accuracy

Table 6.2 Performance of machine learning algorithms.

S. no.	Cardiac disease name	Cohort size	Accuracy and AUC	Reference
1.	Myocardial infarctions	160	ANN – 0.94	[11]
		800	SVM – 0.99	[12]
		180	AUC LR – 0.92	[13]
2.	Cardio myopathies	83	DT – 0.79	[14]
			SVM – 0.92	[15]
			CNN – 0.78	[16]
			LR – 0.67	[17]
			SVM – 0.86	[17]
3.	Coronary artery disease	267	Pseudo-DT - 0.8	[18]
		115	Pseudo-DT – 0.77	[19]
		58	Pseudo-DT – 0.73	[20]
		308	ANN – 0.74	[20]
4.	Atherosclerosis		CNN – 0.77–0.8	[21]
5.	Valvular heart disease	102	SVM – 0.99	[22]
6.	Heart failure	397	SVM – 0.76	[23]
7.	Abnormal wall motion	20	SVM – 0.96	[24]
		58	SVM – 0.86	[25]

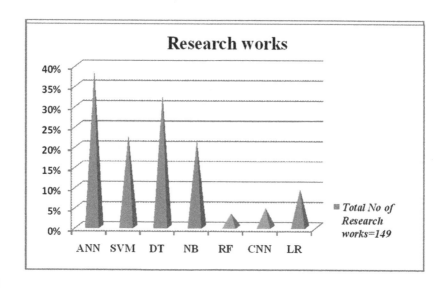

FIG. 6.2

Percentage of research works carried out for each algorithm.

[9], which is essential for disease diagnosis. The algorithms' results are categorized into three groups: a 100% accuracy level, above 90% accuracy level, and above 70% accuracy level. The results of these groups are described in Fig. 6.3.

It is evident from Fig. 6.3, the number of implementations with 100% accuracy is only 3 (ANN-1 and SVM-2) out of 149 research works. The algorithms with 90% accuracy are 15, which are obtained in ANN (3), SVM (4), DT (3), and CNN (5). The number of successful implementation is mentioned along with their names. The performance of DT and CNN algorithms are not obtained with 100% accuracy. To conduct the diagnosis effectively and efficiently, 100% accuracy is preferred as the treatment regimen highly depends on the diagnosis results' validity and robustness.

6.13 Conclusion

In this chapter, the impact of machine learning algorithms in the medical domain to serve as an efficient diagnostic tool is clearly explained. The field of radiological image analysis faces an uphill time as the data generated is growing exponentially. Due to this, the medical practitioners struggle to arrive at the right decision regarding the disease diagnosis and the appropriate treatment regimen. This threat is a significant one to the medical industry as the time delay in image analysis will lead to a haphazard effect in the treatment segments, sometimes fatal. Computer-based analysis and detection are applied in medical imaging with the help of machine learning algorithms to minimize such risks. Under machine learning, there are many kinds of algorithms, and each has its own set of benefits and limitations. If these setbacks are adequately addressed, the machine learning field will reap more benefits to the medical domain.

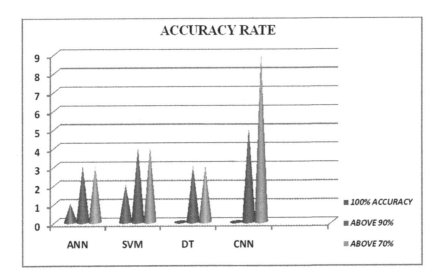

FIG. 6.3

Accuracy range of the algorithms [9].

References

[1] M. Koenigkam-Santos, et al., Artificial intelligence, machine learning, computer-aided diagnosis, and radiomics, Adv. Imag. Towards Precis. Med. 52 (6) (2019) 387–396.

[2] S. Razia, et al., Machine learning techniques for thyroid disease diagnosis: a systematic review, in: V.K. Gunjan, et al. (Eds.), Modern Approaches in Machine Learning and Cognitive Science: A Walkthrough Studies in Computational Intelligence, vol. 885, Springer, 2020.

[3] C. Scarpazza, et al., Applications of machine learning to brain disorders, Mach. Learn. (2020) 45–65, https://doi.org/10.1016/b978-0-12-815739-8.00003-1.

[4] M. Tanveer, et al., Machine learning techniques for the diagnosis of Alzheimer's disease: a review, ACM Trans. Multimedia Comput. Commun. Appl. (2020), https://doi.org/10.1145/3344998. 35 pp.

[5] R. Bernardes, et al., Machine learning approaches in OCT, in: A. Grzybowski, P. Barboni (Eds.), Application to Neurodegenerative Disorders, Springer, 2020.

[6] D. Raimondi, et al., An interpretable low-complexity machine learning framework for robust exome-based in-silico diagnosis of Crohn's disease patients, in: NAR Genomics and Bioinformatics, 2020, https://doi.org/10.1093/nargab/lqaa011.

[7] R. Alizadehsani, et al., Machine learning-based coronary artery disease diagnosis: a comprehensive review, Comput. Biol. Med. 111 (2019), https://doi.org/10.1016/j.compbiomed.2019.103346.

[8] J. Yanase, E. Triantaphyllou, The seven key challenges for the future of computer-aided diagnosis in medicine, Int. J. Med. Inform. 129 (2019) 413–422, https://doi.org/10.1016/j.ijmedinf.2019.06.017.

[9] R. Alizadehsani, et al., Machine learning-based coronary artery disease diagnosis: a comprehensive review, Comput. Biol. Med. (2019), https://doi.org/10.1016/j.compbiomed.2019.103346.

[10] J.A.M. Sidey-Gibbons, C.J. Sidey-Gibbons, Machine learning in medicine: a practical introduction, BMC Med. Res. Methodol. 64 (2019), https://doi.org/10.1186/s12874-019-0681-4.

[11] V.K. Sudarshan, et al., An integrated index for automated detection of infarcted myocardium from cross-sectional echocardiograms using texton-based features (Part 1), Comput. Biol. Med. 71 (2016) 231–240, https://doi.org/10.1016/j.compbiomed.2016.01.028.

[12] K.S. Vidya, et al., Computer-aided diagnosis of myocardial infarction using ultrasound images with DWT, GLCM, and HOS methods: a comparative study, Comput. Biol. Med. 62 (2015) 86–93, https://doi.org/10.1016/j.compbiomed.2015.03.033.

[13] B. Baeßler, et al., Texture analysis and machine learning of non-contrast T1-weighted MR images in patients with hypertrophic cardio myopathy–preliminaryresults, Eur. J. Radiol. 102 (2018) 61–67, https://doi.org/10.1016/j.ejrad.2018.03.013.

[14] V. Gopalakrishnan, et al., cMRI-BED: a novel informatics framework for cardiac MRI biomarker extraction and discovery applied to pediatric cardiomyopathy classification, Biomed Eng. Online (2015), https://doi.org/10.1186/1475-925X-14-S2-S7.

[15] I. Cetin, et al., A radiomics approach to analyze cardiac alterations in hypertension, in: IEEE 16th International Symposium on Biomedical Imaging, IEEE, Venice, 2019, pp. 640–643.

[16] G. Snaauw, et al., End-to-end diagnosis and segmentation learning from cardiac magnetic resonance imaging, in: 16th International Symposium on Biomedical Imaging, IEEE, Venice, 2019, pp. 802–805.

[17] U. Neisius, et al., Cardiovascular magnetic resonance feature tracking strain analysis for discrimination between hypertensive heart disease and hypertrophic cardiomyopathy, PLoS ONE 14 (2019) e0221061, https://doi.org/10.1371/journal.pone.0221061.

[18] L.A. Kurgan, et al., Knowledge discovery approach to automated cardiac SPECT diagnosis, Artif. Intell. Med. 23 (2001) 149–169, https://doi.org/10.1016/S0933-3657(01)00082-3.

[19] H. Bagher-Ebadian, et al., Neural network and fuzzy clustering approach for automatic diagnosis of coronary artery disease in nuclear medicine, IEEE Trans. Nucl. Sci. 51 (2004) 184–192, https://doi.org/10.1109/TNS.2003.823047.

[20] L.A. Guner, et al., An open-source framework of neural networks for diagnosis of coronary artery disease from myocardial perfusion, SPECT J. Nucl. Cardiol. 17 (2010) 405–413, https://doi.org/10.1007/s12350-010-9207-5.

[21] M. Zreik, et al., A recurrent CNN for automatic detection and classification of coronary artery plaque and stenosis in coronary CT angiography, IEEE Trans. Med. Imaging 38 (2018) 1588–1598, https://doi.org/10.1109/TMI.2018.2883807.

[22] H. Moghaddasi, S. Nourian, Automatic assessment of mitral regurgitation severity based on extensive textural features on 2D echocardiography videos, Comput. Biol. Med. 73 (2016) 47–55, https://doi.org/10.1016/j.compbiomed.2016.03.026.

[23] S.J. Shah, et al., Phenomapping for novel classification of heart failure with preserved ejection fraction, Circulation 131 (2015) 269–279, https://doi.org/10.1161/CIRCULATIONAHA.114.010637.

[24] J. Mantilla, et al., Machine learning techniques for LV wall motion classification based on spatio-temporal profiles from cardiac cine MRI, in: 12th International Conference on Machine Learning and Applications, vol. 1, IEEE, 2013, pp. 167–172.

[25] M. Afshin, et al., Regional assessment of cardiac left ventricular myocardial function via MRI statistical features, IEEE Trans. Med. Imag. 33 (2013) 481–494, https://doi.org/10.1109/TMI.2013.2287793.

Wavelet transform for cardiac image retrieval

7

Aswini K. Samantaray and Amol D. Rahulkar

Department of Electrical and Electronics Engineering, National Institute of Technology, Goa, India

Chapter outline

7.1 Introduction

With the innovation improvement in clinical field, there is a fast increment in clinical information of image data. Because of this, cardiac image retrieval turns out to be increasingly troublesome and tedious for diagnosis purpose [1]. Thus, there is a growing interest for developing proficient techniques for image retrieval from cardiac image databases. The image retrieval based on traditional techniques chiefly rely upon content depicting the scene. Hence, they are searching methods based on keywords. Nonetheless, it is troublesome and tedious to follow every cardiac image by its novel scene. So, cardiac images are listed by visual queries such as shape, texture, and color as opposed to content-based keywords [2]. Content-based image retrieval (CBIR) turned into a dynamic research area since last two decades. The advantage of CBIR system is its capacity to support the visual contents of an image. However, a few methods produce unsuitable results because of distinctive attributes of cardiac images. Therefore, it is necessary to develop efficient methods for CBIR systems with increased retrieval accuracy and reduced retrieval time.

The CBIR system performs the retrieval of a cardiac image from the database by comparing the query image to all the images present in the database and earmarking a similarity index to each pair. The automatic feature extraction from the cardiac images ensures the similarity between the images. The images are characterized by these features used for retrieval. Hence, the main aim in CBIR system is to devise the effective and efficient feature extraction techniques for the representation of cardiac images. In this context, there are four major classes of features considered, namely color [3], texture [4], edges [5, 6], and shapes [7]. There should be ideally the amalgamation of all these features for better discrimination in the measure of similarity. However, most of the CBIR systems perform with texture feature, as it gives better result as compared to other features.

The texture feature in cardiac images assume a significant role for acquiring data to diagnose the disease and data of different pathologies. The texture feature is considered the function of intensity variation with continual patterns and structures. Recently, wavelet transform with the mechanism of multichannel filtering concentrate on texture analysis of cardiac images. The outcome of the analysis of texture information mainly depends on the selection of basis function of the wavelet transform. The basis function selected for the transform should contain the desired properties of the wavelet such as symmetry, invariance in shifting, and support in both time domain and frequency domain. Due to this symmetric property, the dephasing can be avoided using the design of linear phase filters. The non-symmetric filters cause shift variance and this should be avoided in texture analysis for better result. It is found that Symlet which belongs to the orthogonal wavelet family is a compactly supported wavelet with least asymmetry. It also offers maximum number of vanishing moments for a given support length. Due to this property, the Symlet is a good choice for texture analysis.

For the last few years, the approaches based on wavelet transform gain popularity for cardiac image retrieval. A local feature descriptor based on Daubechies wavelet transform is used for the registration of cardiac images by Yelampalli et al. [8]. Another method based on binary feature descriptor is used by the same authors to distinguish the normal and abnormal chest computed tomography (CT) images [9]. Dubey et al. [10] used a local wavelet pattern for the cardiac image retrieval. To get better results, the level of decomposition in the wavelet transform is decided by the type of cardiac images in the database. Hence, these methods suffer from limited directionality.

One of the texture feature extraction techniques widely used is Gabor wavelet filter bank [11]. This filter bank uses a set of particular scales and orientations for the feature description. For each orientation and scale, the filter bank extracts the time frequency coefficients [12]. The database of cardiac images contains different modalities of images which differ in terms of different background pixels and rotation. With the fixed scales and orientations, the filter banks are unable to extract the textural content from the cardiac images [13]. Recently, a number of filters are derived from the original Gabor filter which are rotation invariant. These rotation-invariant filters can be used for the classification of texture feature [14, 15]. Manjunath and Ma [16] used circular Gabor to classify the texture which are rotation invariant and the texture segment. This technique shows better experimental results in feature extraction. However, high computational complexity is reported in extracting and analyzing the texture data [17]. Gao et al. [18] proposed Log-Gabor wavelet transform to solve this problem which has a low computational complexity. However, it is also designed with fixed directions which may not match with the texture directions of the cardiac images.

It is found from the literature survey that the Gabor wavelet filter bank along with its variants (Log-Gabor, Circular Gabor) are utilized for texture extraction and analysis purpose in large scale. However, the design of Gabor wavelet is difficult for different applications. This is because to design the Gabor wavelet, filter bank requires the major optimal parameters such as scale and orientation and other parameters such as phase offset, aspect ratio, and standard deviation along Gaussian major and minor axes. Ilonen et al. [19] explained the effect of these parameters in their research work for the retrieval of texture feature. However, the explanation is insufficient on the choice of the parameters. Particularly, the Gabor wavelet filter bank requires a particular set of orientations and scales for its design. Along with these major parameters, the smoothing parameters (standard deviation along Gaussian major and minor axes) which also play an important role are required for the design of the filter bank. It is difficult for the Gabor wavelet to extract the texture features with the fixed set of scales and orientations from the cardiac images. This is due the heterogeneous nature of the cardiac images which are different in size and modalities. It is found that the dominant features of the cardiac images do not match with the orientations used to design the Gabor wavelet filter bank. Due to this reason, the dominant features of the cardiac images cannot be extracted by the Gabor wavelet filter bank. This problem is solved by [20] where the Gabor filters are designed with the dominant texture directions present in the heterogeneous cardiac images.

In this chapter, the fundamentals of wavelets and their use in feature extraction from cardiac images are represented. The block diagram of a CBIR system is shown in Fig. 7.1. First, the fundamentals of orthogonal, biorthogonal, and Gabor wavelet is presented. All the cardiac images are preprocessed using some preprocessing techniques such as image enhancement and removal of noise to restore the minute details of the cardiac image. Next, the features from the cardiac images are extracted with the help of orthogonal, biorthogonal, and Gabor wavelets separately. A set of feature vectors are determined in terms of standard deviation and energy from the images filtered by all the wavelet. A match

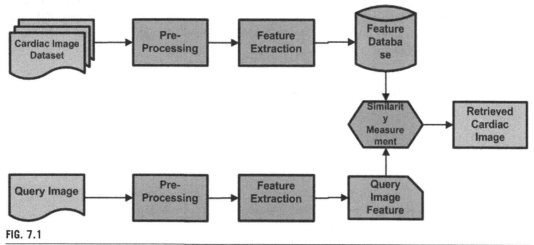

FIG. 7.1

General block diagram of image retrieval system.

between the query image and the images of the database is found using a similarity measurement technique to retrieve the image from the database. In this work, Manhattan distance is used as the similarity measurement technique due to its effectiveness over other similarity measurement techniques.

The rest of the chapter is organized as follows. The fundamentals of various orthogonal, biorthogonal, and Gabor wavelet transform is presented in Section 7.2. Section 7.3 presents the detailed discussion of databases, similarity measurement, and result analysis. The conclusion of the chapter is presented in Section 7.4.

7.2 Discrete wavelet transform

It is observed that the wavelet transform can be used in various applications such as image classification, analysis, enhancement, and compression [21]. The transform is used to represent the signals (in our case cardiac images) in various frequency bands. The frequency bands with a particular resolution matches with the scale of the transform [22]. Wavelet transform has an important characteristics of providing a compact representation of the images by removing the statistical redundancy among the pixels of the images. It is observed that the wavelet transform-based image indexing is more advantageous than the spatial domain-based image indexing design. This is because the wavelet transformed coefficient shows better distribution than the spatial domain image pixels [23]. The block diagram of two channel filter bank is shown in Fig. 7.2.

Wavelet transform decomposes the texture of low-frequency subband recursively. Fig. 7.3 shows the two-dimensional orthogonal wavelet transform decomposition structure and the coefficients of its corresponding wavelet. Wavelet transform goes through one-dimensional transform of the image signal twice (first transform along column and second transform along row) with help of a low-pass decomposition filter L and high-pass decomposition filter H. Hence, four subband of frequencies are obtained by different combinations of these low-pass and high-pass filters. These four subbands are as follows: (1) low-frequency approximation images LL, (2) horizontally high-frequency images HL, (3) vertically high-frequency images LH, and (4) diagonal high-frequency images HH. The low-frequency approximation images LL are decomposed recursively until the useful information and desired result are obtained.

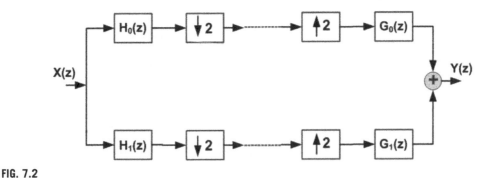

FIG. 7.2

Block diagram of 2 channel filter banks.

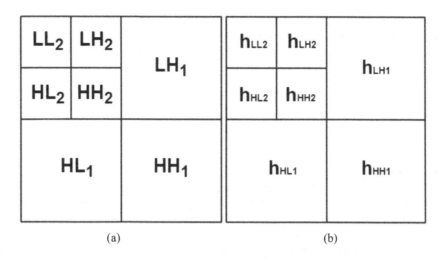

FIG. 7.3

(A) Wavelet transform decomposition structure. (B) The corresponding coefficient diagram.

7.3 Orthogonal wavelet transform

It is evident from the literature that the wavelet transform decomposes the image into different frequency subbands [24]. Each subband corresponds to a particular resolution matched to a particular scale of the transform. Wavelet transform is defined as a square integrable function of definite orthonormal series of wavelets where the series is either complex or real. Wavelet transform represents the signal in both time and frequency domain. The continuous wavelet transform (CWT) is defined as follows.

$$CWT_f^\psi(\tau, s) = \frac{1}{\sqrt{|s|}} \int f(t)\psi^*\left(\frac{t-\tau}{s}\right)dt \tag{7.1}$$

where s and τ are scaling and translation parameters, respectively. Similarly, the discrete wavelet transform (DWT) is defined by the following equation.

$$DWT_x^\psi[n, s] = \frac{1}{\sqrt{|s|}} \sum x[n]\psi_{n,s}^*[n] \tag{7.2}$$

where $\psi(t)$ in (7.1) and $\psi[n]$ in (7.2) represent the mother wavelet for CWT and DWT, respectively.

7.3.1 Haar wavelet transform

Haar wavelet transform is the simplest and oldest orthonormal wavelet transform which consumes less memory than other wavelets. This wavelet is also a recursive transform without having any influence on edges. Haar wavelet helps to change between the adjacent pixels of the image without any overlapping of the windows. This wavelet computes the average and difference between a pair of pixels using scale and wavelet as its two functions. The forward Haar wavelet computes a set of averages and wavelet coefficients in each step. With this computation, there are $n/2$ averages and $n/2$ coefficient values with n elements of a dataset. Scaling and Wavelet functions for Haar wavelet are given as follows.

$$a = \frac{(S_i + S_{i+1})}{2} \tag{7.3}$$

$$d = \frac{(S_i - S_{i+1})}{2} \tag{7.4}$$

where a is averaging, d is differencing with S_0 to S_{n-1} image data.

It is evident from the above equations that scaling function of Haar wavelet computes the average and wavelet function computes the coefficients. This wavelet works on horizontal adjacent pixels first and then on vertical adjacent pixels. The energy of the data is computed with each transform and is located at the top left corner. The resultant image is cut into two halves after each transformation. The two-dimensional transform of the image is obtained by two successive one-dimensional wavelet transform.

7.3.2 Daubechies wavelet transform

Ingrid Daubechies proposed the famous Daubechies wavelet transform [25]. This is an orthogonal wavelet transform consisting of scaling and wavelet function and defines the concept of number of vanishing moment. There are a number of Daubechies transforms such as Daub1, Daub2, Daub3, ..., Daub10. These wavelet transforms are defined based on the order of the filter coefficients. The popular wavelet among all is Daub2 which simple and effective for the texture retrieval. It has four scaling coefficients, namely $(\alpha_1, \alpha_2, \alpha_3, \alpha_4)$ and four wavelet coefficients, namely $(\beta_1, \beta_2, \beta_3, \beta_4)$. The coefficients, in each iteration, are shifted by a position of two. Hence, it causes outage of values in the last iteration. This is handled by either shifting the values or by computing the mirror image of the values [24]. Due to the smoother response, Daub2 is widely used with minimum (four) number of coefficients.

In the current chapter, the mother wavelet is one-dimensional Daub2 wavelet. This one-dimensional wavelet is applied recursively on cardiac images for local texture retrieval. The Daub4 scaling coefficients are given as follows.

$$\alpha_1 = \frac{1 + \sqrt{3}}{4\sqrt{2}}, \quad \alpha_2 = \frac{3 + \sqrt{3}}{4\sqrt{2}}, \quad \alpha_3 = \frac{3 - \sqrt{3}}{4\sqrt{2}}, \quad \alpha_4 = \frac{1 - \sqrt{3}}{4\sqrt{2}} \tag{7.5}$$

Similarly, the *Daub4* wavelet coefficients are defined as follows.

$$\beta_1 = \frac{1 - \sqrt{3}}{4\sqrt{2}}, \quad \beta_2 = \frac{-3 + \sqrt{3}}{4\sqrt{2}}, \quad \beta_3 = \frac{3 + \sqrt{3}}{4\sqrt{2}}, \quad \beta_4 = \frac{-1 - \sqrt{3}}{4\sqrt{2}} \tag{7.6}$$

Therefore, the forward transformation matrix of Daub2 with four element signal containing both scaling coefficient α and wavelet coefficient β is given as follows.

$$V_n = \frac{1}{4\sqrt{2}} \begin{pmatrix} 1+\sqrt{3} & 3+\sqrt{3} & 3-\sqrt{3} & 1-\sqrt{3} \\ 3-\sqrt{3} & 1-\sqrt{3} & 1-\sqrt{3} & -3+\sqrt{3} \\ 3-\sqrt{3} & 1-\sqrt{3} & 1+\sqrt{3} & 3+\sqrt{3} \\ 1-\sqrt{3} & -3+\sqrt{3} & 3-\sqrt{3} & 1-\sqrt{3} \end{pmatrix} \tag{7.7}$$

It is observed from the above matrix that α and β coefficient values in Daub2 are shifted around in the third and fourth rows to maintain the dimension balance of the matrix. Daubechies wavelet with six elements (Daub3) and higher order elements coefficient matrices can be defined in a similar manner. The dimension of the matrices depends on the decomposition performed at level one.

7.4 **Biorthogonal wavelet transform**

The system of wavelet transform should be orthogonal in both scaling and translations which provides a symmetric, robust, and clean formulation with Parseval's theorem. The system also puts some strong limitations on various possibilities. A number of degrees of freedom exist due to the orthogonality of the system. This results in preventing asymmetric analysis, preventing analysis of linear phase and synthesis of filter bank and complicated design. Hence, biorthogonal wavelets are developed with non-orthogonal and dual basis. It allows more flexibility to achieve other outcomes at the cost of energy partitioning property. There are some other "almost orthogonal" systems which are considered by the researchers which gives relaxation on some orthonormal constraints to improve other characteristics. Spectral factorization step is required for the design of orthonormal wavelets which increases the filter length. Classical wavelet filters have these limitations for filter design. These limitations can be avoided by relaxing the condition of orthogonality and hence comes the concept of designing biorthogonal wavelets.

Haar wavelet is the only orthogonal wavelet filter with finite length and symmetric property. However, the major limitation of Haar wavelet is its shorter filter length due to which it is sometimes unable to detect the large variations in input data. Hence, there is a necessity of designing symmetric filters with length greater than two. Smooth biorthogonal wavelets can be constructed with compact support which are either symmetric or antisymmetric which is difficult for orthogonal wavelets, except the case of Haar wavelet particularly. The advantage of symmetric filters is to minimize the edge effect of presentation of a function in discrete wavelet transform [26]. The periodization can be avoided as the larger wavelet coefficients results in false edges.

7.4.1 **Lifting scheme-based wavelet transform**

In this section, lifting scheme-based biorthogonal wavelet is explained for extraction of texture feature. Biorthogonal wavelet is an invertible wavelet transform, which is not essentially orthogonal. Design of biorthogonal wavelets provides more degrees of freedom [26]. One of the degrees of freedom gives an opportunity to design symmetric wavelet function.

Lifting scheme is a technique to carry out discrete wavelet transform and design wavelets [26, 27]. The wavelet transform can be applied independently as various filters to the same input image. In contrast to that, the decomposition based on lifting scheme divides the image like a zipper. Then, a set of convolution operations are used to divide images. In lifting scheme, both predict and update stage coefficients are computed from the corresponding filter for wavelet decomposition.

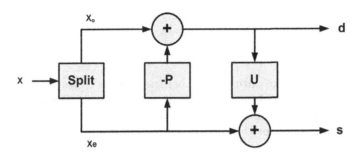

FIG. 7.4

Block diagram of lifting steps.

Fig. 7.4 shows the wavelet decomposition of the lifting scheme. In lifting scheme, there are three major steps for wavelet decomposition.

1. Split: the input image $x[n]$ is divided into two parts, i.e., odd coefficients $x_o[n]$ and even coefficients $x_e[n]$.
2. Predict: This step, using predict filter, generates the wavelet coefficients $d[n]$ as the error in predicting $x_o[n]$ from $x_e[n]$.

$$P : d[n] = x_0[n] - P(x_e[n])$$ (7.8)

3. Update: This step combines the even coefficients $x_e[n]$ and wavelet coefficients $d[n]$ to obtain scaling coefficients $c[n]$ representing an approximation to the original input image $x[n]$. This can be achieved using the update filter.

$$U : c[n] = x_e[n] - U(d[n])$$ (7.9)

Let N_p and N_u be the length of the linear filters P and U. The filters P and U have to satisfy the following conditions to form a biorthogonal wavelet.

$$\sum_{i=1}^{N_p} P_i = 1$$ (7.10)

$$\sum_{i=1}^{N_u} U_i = \frac{1}{2}$$ (7.11)

Hence, there are an undetermined number of $N_p + N_u - 2$ coefficients. The design of wavelets based on lifting scheme has a support length of s/t with s as the support of low pass filter and t as the support of high pass filter.

$$s = 2(N_p + N_u) - 3$$ (7.12)

$$t = 2N_p - 1$$ (7.13)

7.5 **Gabor wavelet transform**

Gabor wavelet filters are popularly used in many applications of image processing such as extraction of edges, texture analysis, object recognition, and many more. Local spatial as well as frequency information can be obtained by the use of Gabor wavelet filters. A two dimensional Gabor wavelet function is defined as a Gaussian function modulated by complex sinusoid [16] and is given as follows.

$$g(x, y) = \frac{1}{2\pi\sigma_x\sigma_y} e^{-\frac{1}{2}\left(\frac{x^2}{\sigma_x^2} + \frac{y^2}{\sigma_y^2}\right)} e^{(j2\pi fx + \phi)} \tag{7.14}$$

where f is the modulation frequency and σ_x and σ_y represent the Gaussian major and minor widths, respectively. The symmetricity of the function is defined by the parameter ϕ and is known as the phase offset of the function. The value of ϕ is either 0 degree or 180 degrees for the function to be symmetric, 90 degrees or 270 degrees to be antisymmetric, and 0, 90, 180, 270 degrees to be asymmetric. Eq. (7.15) generates the Gabor wavelet filter which is given as

$$g_{mn}(x, y) = a^{-m} G(\bar{x}, \bar{y}) \tag{7.15}$$

where m ($m = 0, 1, ..., (M-1)$), n ($n = 0, 1, ..., (N-1)$) are the orientations and $a > 1$ is the scale of the Gabor wavelet. $\bar{x}$ and $\bar{y}$ in (7.15) are expressed by the following equations.

$$\bar{x} = a^{-m}(x \cos\theta + y \sin\theta) \tag{7.16}$$

$$\bar{y} = a^{-m}(-x \sin\theta + y \cos\theta) \tag{7.17}$$

Gabor wavelet filter bank is widely used and is designed with a fixed set of orientations and scales. It is found that it is difficult for these filters to extract the necessary discriminative texture features from the cardiac images. This is due to the design of filter bank with a fixed set of orientations. The number of orientations considered for the design of Gabor wavelet filter bank produces the same number of filters with fixed scales. Considering more number of orientations results in more number of filters, which increases the computational complexity. Hence, a fixed direction set of either six (0, 30, 60, 90, 120, and 150 degrees) or four (0, 45, 90, and 135 degrees) is generally considered to design the Gabor wavelet filter bank to reduce the computational complexity. However, it is found that these fixed directions of the filters do not match with the most dominant directions of the cardiac images due to the heterogeneous nature of the cardiac images.

Samantaray and Rahulkar [20] addressed this issue of Gabor filter bank to design a new adaptive Gabor wavelet filter bank. As per the technique, first, all the images go through some preprocessing techniques such as image enhancement and noise removal to retain the minute details of the cardiac images. Next, the prominent texture orientations of the cardiac images are obtained with the help of analyzing prominent peaks present in the spectrum of cardiac image. Further, to extract the dominant time frequency coefficients, these orientations are utilized to design the Gabor wavelet filter bank for fixed number of scales. Hence, this technique uses different orientation set for different cardiac images as opposed to the same orientation set used in previous Gabor filters. Then, each set of Gabor filtered image gives rise to a set of feature vectors in terms of standard deviation and energy. A match is found between the query image and the images of the database by a similarity measurement metrics between the feature vectors to retrieve the image from the cardiac image database. The authors used maximum likelihood estimation (MLE) as the similarity measurement metrics for the similarity measurement.

7.6 Result analysis

In this chapter, three publicly available cardiac image databases, namely NEMA [28], OASIS [29], and EXACT09 [30] are examined for analysis purpose. There are different size and modalities of cardiac image present in the database. The size of the cardiac images is 512×512, 256×256, and 512×512 for NEMA, OASIS, and EXACT09 databases, respectively. Separate experiments are carried out on three cardiac image databases. The personal computer with R2018a MATLAB software is used for the experimentation on the three databases. It has the additional features such as Intel Core i5-6700 CPU @3.40 3.41 GHz processor, 64-bit operating system, and 8 GB RAM, Windows 10 ultimate operating system with $\times 64$ based processor.

7.6.1 Texture representation

After applying all the above-discussed wavelet transforms on cardiac images, the energy content of cardiac images in different subbands is represented by the wavelet filtered coefficients. Consider $G_{mn}(x, y)$ to be the wavelet filtered coefficients. The magnitude of these filtered coefficients is determined as

$$M(m, n) = \sum_x \sum_y |G_{mn}(x, y)| \tag{7.18}$$

where $m = 0, 1, 2, ..., (M-1)$ and $n = 0, 1, 2, ..., (N-1)$.

The texture-based cardiac image retrieval is based on the key idea of matching the similar texture of the images. It is observed that similar images have analogous texture patterns [31]. These analogous texture patterns of the cardiac images can be represented by certain texture features. In this chapter, standard deviation and energy are considered the texture features to highlight the texture of the wavelet filtered images. Mathematically, these features can be represented by the follow equations.

$$E(m, n) = \sum_x \sum_y |G_{mn}(x, y)|^2 \tag{7.19}$$

$$\sigma_{mn} = \frac{\sqrt{\sum_x \sum_y (|G_{mn}(x, y)| - \mu_{mn})^2}}{M \times N} \tag{7.20}$$

where

$$\mu_{mn} = \frac{E(m, n)}{M \times N}$$

The number of features considered, decides the dimension of the feature vector. Let $G(x, y)$ be the wavelet transformed value for $m \times n$ subband size. In addition to that, standard deviation and energy are the two features computed for each wavelet filtered image. Hence, the dimension of a feature vector to represent one cardiac image is $2 \times (m \times n)$. This feature vector is represented as

$$\bar{f} = \{E_{11}, E_{12}, ..., E_{mn}, \mu_{11}, \mu_{12}, ..., \mu_{mn}\} \tag{7.21}$$

7.6.2 **Similarity measurement**

Distance-based similarity measurement metrics are widely used for the retrieval purpose, among which Manhattan and Euclidean distance measures are popular [32]. Each dimension of Euclidean distance calculates the square before summation. Hence, it gives more importance to the features where the dissimilarity is more. As a result, the retrieval accuracy is less. The more moderate approach is the Manhattan distance which computes the absolute difference in each feature as opposed to computing squares. This distance metric is also known as City block distance which is given by the following equation.

$$D_{Man}(x, y) = \sum_{i=1}^{n} |x_i - y_i| \tag{7.22}$$

A certain number of paths exist between two distance points which are equivalent to Manhattan distance. This distance metric is widely used in frequency distribution, compressed sensing, and regression analysis.

7.6.3 **Evaluation criteria**

The parameters used to evaluate the experiment are presented in this subsection. Manhattan distance is used as the similarity measurement metrics to retrieve the top 10 cardiac images from the database. Average precision (AP) and average recall (AR) are calculated for each category, based on which average retrieval precision (ARP) and average retrieval rate (ARR) are calculated next. The average precisions and recalls are computed for each category after considering the query image from that category. The parameters precision and recall of a query image I_q are determined by the following equations.

$$\text{Precision} : P(I_q) = \frac{\text{Number of relevant images retrieved}}{\text{Total number of images retrieved}} \tag{7.23}$$

$$\text{Recall} : R(I_q) = \frac{\text{Number of relevant images retrieved}}{\text{Total number of relevant images in the database}} \tag{7.24}$$

Similarly, the average retrieval precision (ARP) and average retrieval rate (ARR) can be computed as follows:

$$\text{ARP} = \frac{1}{|DB|} \sum_{i=1}^{|DB|} P(I_i) \tag{7.25}$$

$$\text{ARR} = \frac{1}{|DB|} \sum_{i=1}^{|DB|} R(I_i) \tag{7.26}$$

where the total number of images in a particular database is represented by $|DB|$.

A query image from each category of NEMA, OASIS, and EXACT09 databases is shown in Figs. 7.5A, 7.6A, and 7.7A, respectively. Similarly, the top ten images retrieved by the adaptive Gabor wavelet transform are shown in Figs. 7.5B, 7.6B, and 7.7B for NEMA, OASIS, and EXACT09 databases, respectively. The ARP as well as ARR values for each feature descriptor methods for all cardiac

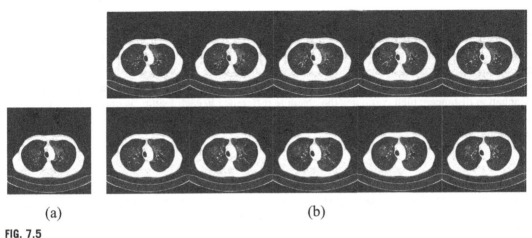

(a)   (b)

FIG. 7.5

(A) Query image, (B) top 10 retrieved images from NEMA database.

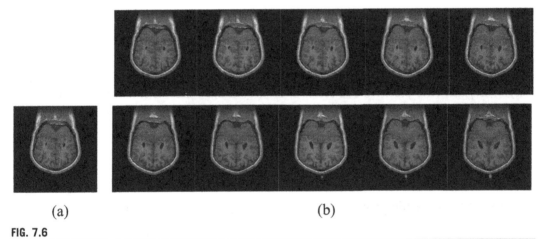

(a)   (b)

FIG. 7.6

(A) Query image, (B) top 10 retrieved images from OASIS database.

image databases is shown in Table 7.1. It is found from Table 7.1 that Haar wavelet shows better performance than Daubechies wavelet. Although both the wavelet transforms belong to the orthogonal wavelet category, Haar wavelet is symmetric in nature. Similarly, biorthogonal wavelets exhibit better result than orthogonal wavelets due to its symmetricity. Though Haar wavelet is symmetric, it does not exhibit satisfactory result because its base functions are discontinuous step functions. Since cardiac images contain smooth regions, Haar wavelet is unable to analyze smooth functions with continuous derivatives. Gabor and Log Gabor wavelet are designed with a set of fixed orientations and scales which do not match with the prominent feature directions of the cardiac images. With this, these techniques are unable to extract the prominent features. However, the adaptive Gabor wavelet is designed

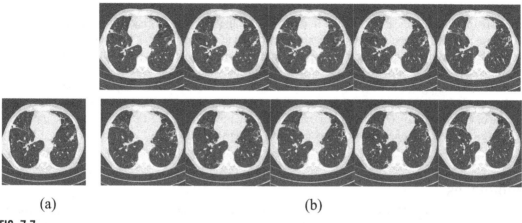

(a)   (b)

FIG. 7.7

(A) Query image, (B) top 10 retrieved images from EXACT09 database.

Table 7.1 **Performance comparison of different wavelet techniques in terms ARP and ARR over all cardiac image databases.**

Methodology	Database					
	NEMA		OASIS		EXACT09	
	Performance parameters					
	ARP%	ARR%	ARP%	ARR%	ARP%	ARR%
Haar	81.92	29.32	77.83	9.93	74.95	19.53
Daub2	80.34	29.66	74.32	9.92	70.53	17.97
Lifting	82.59	29.69	79.89	10.75	73.63	20.45
Gabor	77.00	29.33	73.40	10.77	63.91	18.23
Log Gabor	79.22	30.96	74.69	10.95	73.06	19.91
Adaptive Gabor	85.32	31.33	85.24	14.05	77.00	23.78

with the prominent feature orientations of the images. Hence, this technique gives better result in terms of ARP and ARR than other methods as shown in Table 7.1.

7.7 Conclusion

In this chapter, we reviewed a set of wavelet transforms and their application on cardiac image retrieval. The features are extracted from the heterogeneous cardiac images using these wavelet transforms. To find the match between the query image and the cardiac image from the database, Manhattan distance is used as the similarity measurement metric. Three publicly available databases NEMA,

OASIS, and EXACT09 are used to conduct the experiment using all the wavelet transforms separately. The experimental results are compared in terms of average retrieval precision (ARP) and average retrieval rate (ARR). It is evident from the experimental result comparison that the biorthogonal wavelets exhibit better results than orthogonal wavelets due to their symmetricity. Though all orthogonal and biorthogonal wavelets show better result than Gabor and Log Gabor wavelets, the adaptive Gabor wavelet transform gives better results than all others. This is because the adaptive Gabor wavelet is designed with help of dominant directions of the cardiac image as opposed to the fixed directions in case of Gabor and Log Gabor wavelet transforms. Adaptive Gabor wavelet transform also preserves symmetricity as maintained by biorthogonal wavelet transforms.

References

[1] A.W.M. Smeulders, M. Worring, S. Santini, A. Gupta, R. Jain, Content-based image retrieval at the end of the early years, IEEE Trans. Pattern Anal. Mach. Intell. 22 (12) (2000) 1349–1380, https://doi.org/10.1109/34.895972.

[2] W. Jiang, G. Er, Q. Dai, J. Gu, Similarity-based online feature selection in content-based image retrieval, IEEE Trans. Image Process. 15 (3) (2006) 702–712, https://doi.org/10.1109/TIP.2005.863105.

[3] C.W. Kok, Y. Hui, T.Q. Nguyen, Medical image pseudo coloring by wavelet fusion, in: Proceedings of 18th Annual International Conference of the IEEE Engineering in Medicine and Biology Society, Amsterdam, vol. 2, 1996, pp. 648–649, https://doi.org/10.1109/IEMBS.1996.651909.

[4] G. Zhang, Z.-M. Ma, Texture feature extraction and description using gabor wavelet in content-based medical image retrieval, in: 2007 International Conference on Wavelet Analysis and Pattern Recognition, Beijing, 2007, pp. 169–173, https://doi.org/10.1109/ICWAPR.2007.4420657.

[5] A. Wang, Z. Gu, W. Bo, G. Shen, HMT model and B-spine wavelet based intelligent medical image edge extraction algorithm, in: First International Conference on Intelligent Networks and Intelligent Systems, 2008, pp. 552–555.

[6] A. Wang, X. Zhang, Y. Chen, J. Wu, B spline wavelet and SVM threshold based medical image edge extraction, in: IEEE International Symposium on Industrial Electronics, Vigo, Vol. 2007, 2007, pp. 1628–1632, https://doi.org/10.1109/ISIE.2007.4374848.

[7] G. Zhang, Z.M. Ma, Q. Tong, Y. He, T. Zhao, Shape feature extraction using fourier descriptors with brightness in content-based medical image retrieval, in: 2008 International Conference on Intelligent Information Hiding and Multimedia Signal Processing, Harbin, 2008, pp. 71–74, https://doi.org/10.1109/IIH-MSP.2008.16.

[8] P.K.R. Yelampalli, J. Nayak, V.H. Gaidhane, Daubechies wavelet-based local feature descriptor for multimodal medical image registration, IET Image Process. 12 (10) (2018) 1692–1702, https://doi.org/10.1049/iet-ipr.2017.1305.

[9] P.K.R. Yelampalli, J. Nayak, V.H. Gaidhane, A novel binary feature descriptor to discriminate normal and abnormal chest CT images using dissimilarity measures, Pattern Anal. Appl. 22 (2019) 1517–1526.

[10] S.R. Dubey, S.K. Singh, R.K. Singh, Local wavelet pattern: a new feature descriptor for image retrieval in medical CT databases, IEEE Trans. Image Process. 24 (12) (2015) 5892–5903, https://doi.org/10.1109/TIP.2015.2493446.

[11] M. Idrissa, M. Acheroy, Texture classification using Gabor filters, Pattern Recogn. Lett. 23 (7) (2002) 1095–1102.

[12] T. Andrysiak, M. Choras, Image retrieval based on hierarchical Gabor filters, Int. J. Appl. Math. Comput. Sci. 15 (4) (2005) 471–780.

[13] R. Manthalkar, P.K. Biswas, B.N. Chatterji, Rotation invariant texture classification using even symmetric Gabor filters, Pattern Recogn. Lett. 24 (12) (2003) 2061–2068.

[14] J. Zhang, T. Tan, L. Ma, Invariant texture segmentation via circular Gabor filters, in: Object Recognition Supported by User Interaction for Service Robots, Quebec City, Quebec, Canada, vol. 2, 2002, pp. 901–904, https://doi.org/10.1109/ICPR.2002.1048450.

[15] S. Arivazhagan, L. Ganesan, S.P. Priyal, Texture classification using Gabor wavelets based rotation invariant features, Pattern Recogn. Lett. 27 (16) (2006) 1976–1982.

[16] B.S. Manjunath, W.Y. Ma, Texture features for browsing and retrieval of image data, IEEE Trans. Pattern Anal. Mach. Intell. 18 (8) (1996) 837–842, https://doi.org/10.1109/34.531803.

[17] Y.M. Ro, M. Kim, H.K. Kang, MPEG-7 homogeneous texture descriptor, ETRI J. 23 (2) (2001) 41–51.

[18] X. Gao, F. Sattar, R. Venkateswarlu, Multiscale corner detection of gray level images based on log-gabor wavelet transform, IEEE Trans. Circuits Syst. Video Technol. 17 (7) (July 2007) 868–875, https://doi.org/10.1109/TCSVT.2007.897473.

[19] J. Ilonen, J.K. Kamarainen, H. Kalviainen, Fast extraction of multiresolution gabor features, in: Int. Conf. Image Analysis and Processing (ICIAP), Modena, Italy, 2007, pp. 481–486.

[20] A.K. Samantaray, A.D. Rahulkar, New design of adaptive Gabor wavelet filter bank for medical image retrieval, IET Image Process. 14 (4) (2020) 679–687, https://doi.org/10.1049/iet-ipr.2019.1024.

[21] J.Z. Wang, Wavelets and imaging informatics: a review of the literature, J. Biomed. Inform. 34 (2) (2001) 129–141.

[22] M. Borsotti, P. Campadelli, R. Schettini, Quantitative evaluation of color image segmentation results, Patterns Recogn. Lett. 19 (8) (1998) 741–747.

[23] E.J. Stollnitz, T.D. DeRose, D.H. Salesin, Wavelets for Computer Graphics—Theory and Applications, Morgan Kaufmann Publishers, Inc., San Francisco, CA, 1996.

[24] A. Jensen, A. Cour-Harbo, Ripples in Mathematics: The Discrete Wavelet Transform, Vol. 1st ed., Springer-Verlag, Berlin, Heidelberg, 2001.

[25] I. Daubechies, Ten lectures on wavelet, in: Society for Industrial and Applied Mathematics, Philadelphia, USA, 1992.

[26] G. Quellec, M. Lamard, G. Cazuguel, B. Cochener, C. Roux, Wavelet optimization for content-based image retrieval in medical databases, Med. Image Anal. 14 (2) (2010) 227–241.

[27] G. Quellec, M. Lamard, G. Cazuguel, B. Cochener, C. Roux, Adaptive nonseparable wavelet transform via lifting and its application to content-based image retrieval, IEEE Trans. Image Process. 19 (1) (2010) 25–35, https://doi.org/10.1109/TIP.2009.2030479.

[28] Nema-ct Image Database, Available from: ftp://medical.nema.org/medical/Dicom/Multiframe/.

[29] D.S. Marcus, T.H. Wang, J. Parker, J.G. Csernansky, J.C. Morris, R.L. Buckner, Open access series of imaging studies (OASIS): cross-sectional MRI data in young, middle aged, nondemented, and demented older adults, J. Cogn. Neurosci. 19 (9) (2007) 1498–1507, https://doi.org/10.1162/jocn.2007.19.9.1498.

[30] P. Lo, et al., Extraction of airways from CT (EXACT'09), IEEE Trans. Med. Imag. 31 (11) (2012) 2093–2107, https://doi.org/10.1109/TMI.2012.2209674.

[31] P.A. Freeborough, N.C. Fox, MR image texture analysis applied to the diagnosis and tracking of Alzheimer's disease, IEEE Trans. Med. Imag. 17 (3) (1998) 475–478, https://doi.org/10.1109/42.712137.

[32] A.K. Samantaray, A.D. Rahulkar, Comparison of similarity measurement metrics on medical image data, in: 2019 10th International Conference on Computing, Communication and Networking Technologies (ICCCNT), Kanpur, India, 2019, pp. 1–5, https://doi.org/10.1109/ICCCNT45670.2019.8944781.

AI-based diagnosis techniques for cardiac disease analysis and predictions

M.A. Ansari[a], Rajat Mehrotra[a], Pragati Tripathi[a], and Rajeev Agrawal[b]

Department of Electrical Engineering, Gautam Buddha University, Greater Noida, India[a] Department of Electronics and Communication Engineering, G.L. Bajaj Institute of Technology and Management, Greater Noida, India[b]

Chapter outline

Image Processing for Automated Diagnosis of Cardiac Diseases. https://doi.org/10.1016/B978-0-323-85064-3.00002-9

8.1 Introduction

The field of artificial intelligence (AI) is well acclaimed and widely acknowledged in all domains of technology. This includes computational comprehension which generates curiosity to uncover some conduct [1]. AI strategies and instruments have been utilized in clinical applications for more than four decades with the ultimate target being to improve healthcare services by helping medical experts improve their adequacy, productivity, and cognizance. The persistent improvement in the technology has empowered medical industries to create new incorporated, dependable, and effective techniques for providing quality services. AI is proposed for use in cardiology to improve and expand the effectiveness of cardiologists. AI has begun to penetrate and change the field of cardiovascular medicine. Affecting millions of patients around the world, the weight of cardiovascular ailment is felt in a differing cluster of demography [2, 3]. In the meantime, electronic health records (EHR), multimodal images, portable health gadgets, and so on are amassing a treasure trove of underexploited information for every patient. AI has shown capacity to enhance and impact business via the ability to gain much more information from this big data and apply it to varied situations [4, 5]. With impressive data in every heart pulse, cardiovascular medication will be one of the fields to embrace AI to push toward customized and precision healthcare [6]. Cardiovascular imaging plays a significant role in the identification of cardiovascular ailments. So far, its job has been constrained to the quantitative and visual evaluation of cardiovascular configuration and utility. Nevertheless, with the introduction of machine learning, fresh prospects for fabricating AI-based instruments will legitimately help clinical experts analyze cardiovascular ailments. Despite critical signs of progress in identification and treatment, cardiovascular disease (CVD) remains the most widely recognized cause of mortality and morbidity worldwide, accounting for roughly 33% of yearly deaths [7, 8]. Early and precise identification is vital to treat and cure cardiovascular ailments. Cardiovascular illness gives rise to various medical issues, mostly due to atherosclerosis in which plaque develops in the artery walls [9]. Because of this, the arteries begin contracting, restricting blood flow and causing heart problems.

As per the World Health Organization (WHO), heart disease results in more fatalities per year compared to other diseases [10]. With the expanded enthusiasm for AI research, AI strategies like genetic algorithms, decision trees, artificial neural networks (ANNs), and others are beginning to be used to unravel vague and complex clinical ailments. Clinical experts are additionally making use of computer-aided innovations to enhance the process of diagnosis, as there is a lot of vulnerability in this field [11]. As of late, there have been various investigations into the utilization of AI-based techniques in medicine [12–16]. There has also been a great deal of research on the use of AI strategies in heart disease. A number of these methods is increasingly admired for their appropriateness for intricate analysis. Furthermore, many AI methods have been joined with other methods to increase diagnostic effectiveness. AI has become an inevitable part of our daily lives. From a web engine revealing deceitful credit card usage to email spam and malware separation, AI tends to cater to a person's needs in the domains of business, amusement, and innovation. Sadly, AI has yet to fully penetrate the field of medicine; there is a limited number of AI-based clinical applications. However, AI and deep learning (DL) have witnessed an unprecedented rise in publications related to cardiovascular ailments [17, 18]. These strategies have been pivotal in an assortment of complex fields including translation of echocardiogram diastolic dysfunction grade stratification [19, 20]. The United States Food and Drug Administration (FDA) has granted approval to various medical devices that use AI features [21]. Envision a system that monitors and analyzes every patient, their lab data, imaging outcomes, and so on, to ascertain their risk of CVD and hospitalization, and whether or not drugs need to be prescribed or changed. The framework also presents the clinician with explanations for its proposals that are on a par with those given by the most experienced doctors. This type of system may help the clinician to make shared decisions with patients, both impartially and empathetically. Even though there are a few challenges and difficulties in the clinical implementation of AI, without a doubt AI will drive current medical services toward a progressively individualized and accuracy-based methodology in the coming years. Consequently, general comprehension of AI strategies by clinicians and analysts in cardiovascular medicine is vital. The predominant investigative performance of AI-based analysis of images can significantly mitigate the weight of CVD through quicker and progressively more precise decisions.

8.2 AI-based cardiac disease diagnosis techniques

AI is a technique that actualizes novel ideas to determine intricate difficulties. Since science and medication are quickly becoming information concentrated, DL techniques, which are an assortment of computerized techniques that can separate significant features from extensive data, have been utilized in various domains and have shown unparalleled advantages over existing machine learning (ML) techniques. ML is a part of practical AI that naturally finds samples of information without utilizing precise commands [22]. In AI, the system gains knowledge from the information and executes assignments based on the trained model, while normal computer programs perform undertakings as indicated by the present principles that are dependent on human experience and comprehension. Reinforcement learning (RL), supervised learning (SL), and unsupervised learning (USL) are other terms that depict how a machine gains information (Fig. 8.1). In SL, the algorithm gains knowledge from the information on the result, or ground truth, to build a forecast model. Regression and classification are the tasks handled by SL. The former forecasts the predicted value and the latter outputs the labeled result [3, 18] utilizing known constraints. In contrast, USL does not need the ground truth

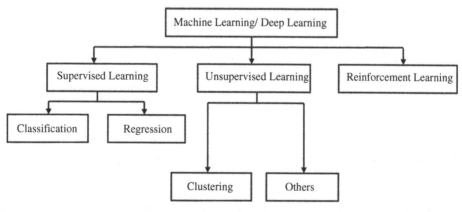

FIG. 8.1

Types of machine learning techniques.

and investigates the information to discover covered features and relations [23]. The most well-known task in USL is grouping and reducing dimensionality. Grouping is an errand to isolate objects into bunches with comparable qualities. Dimensionality diminution, which can likewise be done in an administered way, is an assignment to lessen the dimensionality of information while maintaining the head factors that elucidate the information. Such a task intends to distinguish phenotypes by inducing examples from the informational index without known results. RL is a procedure wherein a parameter is prepared to become familiar with an activity that achieves the highest reward in the circumstance. This procedure is broadly utilized in gaming for decision making [24].

8.2.1 Artificial intelligence in cardiology

Despite its steady infiltration into medicine and science, by and large, many cardiovascular specialists today are bound to relate the term AI with an advanced phenomenon as opposed to a scientific innovation that will improve cardiovascular medicine. Dawes TJW et al. [25] created an algorithm for systolic cardiovascular movement that allowed them to anticipate results in patients with pneumonic hypertension with utmost precision. They used clinical information and investigated on 250 subjects, and the study resulted as 30,000 spots in the hearts contracted with each heart pulse. This developed a virtual 3D heart for every patient, while the algorithm realized which patterns were related to early mortality or cardiovascular breakdown. The author of the paper emphasized that one of the most valuable elements of utilizing AI along these lines is that there is no room for human error. Interpreting these discoveries into clinical implications implies that doctors are given an apparatus that groups patients into explicitly predicted classes without any human interventions. Contrasted with the customary methodology, this technique shields patients from invasive systems, spares time and labor, and limits the hazy area natural to human judgment.

Shah et al. [26] used DL to create another phenotypic categorization of patients with cardiovascular breakdown. This clinical disorder is known to involve heterogeneous substances and despite its pernicious forecast, none of the treatment systems tried in various clinical preliminaries have so far demonstrated success. Normally it is accepted that superior phenotyping of influenced patients may be the way to fruitful restorative methodologies. In the latest research published, the known phenogroups were affirmed by explicit contrasts in repolarization on their electrocardiograms (ECGs) [27]. This was done using USL techniques. Unsurprisingly, the discoveries depicted have inspired the field to seek phenotype-explicit research with clinically exceptional and useful new data [28–30]. Prior to developing an AI system for the estimation of disease based on images, it is important to reasonably characterize the imaging inputs. Imaging sources might include unprocessed data, usual indices of the heart, or extracted features based on radiomics. Fig. 8.2 gives the distribution of input variables in cardiology.

8.2.1.1 AI techniques for detecting cardiovascular disease

Many analysts have utilized distinct AI procedures in their study of CVD. The different methods utilized incorporate support vector machines (SVMs), Naive Bayes systems, ANNs, and so on. In the following subsections, we examine three pivotal AI techniques largely utilized in creating diagnostic frameworks for forecasting cardiac disease. Fig. 8.3 shows different AI technique distribution.

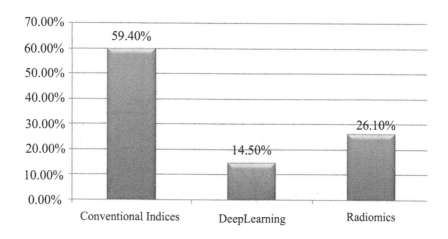

FIG. 8.2

Distribution of input variables.

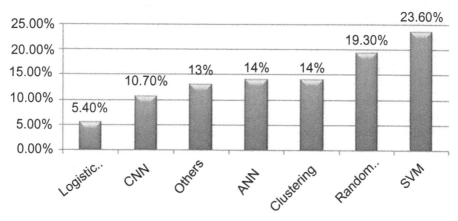

FIG. 8.3

AI techniques distribution.

8.2.2 **ANNs for predicting cardiac disease**

An ANN is a data handling system based on biological neurons like the human brain. The principal feature of this model is a creative framework for handling data derived from different profoundly interconnected cells called neurons that work incongruently for solving a given problem. Fig. 8.4 shows a multilayer ANN structure. Sonawane and Patil [31] developed an ANN-based model for predicting coronary illness. The proposed model was dependent on thirteen input features, and the backpropagation technique was used to train the system with the only outcome, which showed the existence or nonexistence of coronary illness in a patient with specificity of 98%, which is similar to other techniques. Olaniyi and Oyedotun [32] proposed an astute framework dependent on an SVM and a feed-forward

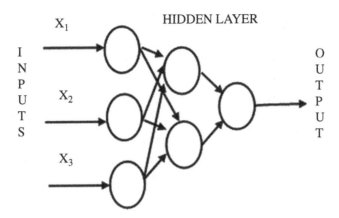

FIG. 8.4

A multilayer ANN network.

ANN. The datasets comprised different heart-related features of patients with heart problems and were acquired from the University of California Irvine (UCI) AI archive. The investigative framework was utilized to determine if patients had coronary disease or not. The ANN was 87.5% accurate and the SVM was 85% accurate.

Samuel et al. [33] utilized an ANN to anticipate cardiovascular breakdown risk. They used thirteen cardiovascular breakdown-related features and derived their consequences via a discussion with an accomplished heart clinician. Fuzzy logic was utilized to find the weights for the features depending on their role. Test results indicated that the proposed technique accomplished a normal prediction precision of 91.10%, which was 4.40% more when contrasted with that of an ordinary ANN. As is obvious, ANNs have been effectively applied in structuring cardiac disease identification frameworks, despite facing significant constraints that need to be addressed. These restrictions include requirement of more time for training, difficulty in manufacturing an ANN-based investigative framework because of the various parameters included, need of an enormous dataset for building an ANN, and trouble deciphering the forecasted outcomes because of the ANN's black box nature. To overcome these issues, significantly more research is required in the field.

8.2.3 Cardiac disease prediction based on genetic algorithms

Jabbar et al. [34] presented an effective identification procedure utilizing the genetic algorithm (GA) method for predicting coronary illness. The investigation was spurred by the fact that a GA uses easy-to-understand principles for finding predicting rules, has high intriguing qualities, and good prescient accuracy. The authors indicated that the rules of classifiers separated from the system assist in the profoundly exact forecasting of cardiac illness supportive to specialists in arriving at conclusion. Niranjana Devi and Anto [35] proposed a transformative and fuzzy logic-based skilled system with the end goal of determining coronary artery disease (CAD). The study utilized a decision tree for identifying the most critical traits, and the yield was then changed over to fuzzy that were then adjusted utilizing GA. The proposed framework's predictions were compared with existing techniques. Long et al. [36] built a diagnostic framework dependent on evolutionary GA and a type-2 fuzzy network. They explored the use of sets-based features diminution utilizing the chaos firefly technique for achieving the best feature diminution useful for decreasing the cost of computation and enhancing the effectiveness of the prediction framework. Exploratory outcomes exhibited that the proposed framework fundamentally outperformed Naive Bayes, SVM, and ANN regarding specificity and precision. Paul et al. [37] proposed a GA-based fuzzy supportive network for estimating the level of risk in coronary disease. The researchers pointed out different issues with this model, including preprocessing of the dataset, efficient feature selection, and evaluation of the fuzzy rules. The viability of the proposed framework was assessed on genuine datasets. Although GA as well as evolutionary algorithms are appropriate for investigating intricate, vast, and multi-dimensional task spaces, they have challenges of high computational complexity and poor prospective for dynamic models.

8.2.4 Neuro-fuzzy technique for predicting cardiac disease

Neuro-fuzzy methods utilize the procedures for learning and adjusting the limits of ANNs for functions of membership resulting from exploratory data to be utilized in a fuzzy inference system. The disadvantages of ANNs and fuzzy frameworks are eliminated with this hybrid approach. Sen et al. [38] developed a two-layered approach dependent on a neuro-fuzzy method of predicting CVD in patients. The primary level deals with the recognition of serious ailments and the subsequent level deals with real disease forecasting. The experimental data for the model was acquired from the UCI repository and was effective in forecasting disease. Abushariah et al. [39] proposed a cardiac disease investigative framework using MATLAB with ANFIS. Additionally, the researchers explored the effect of various estimations of different significant parameters on the neuro-fuzzy based framework for choosing the ideal parameters for acquiring the best outcome. The outcomes from the analyses indicated that the neuro-fuzzy framework outperformed the ANN as far as forecasting accuracy is concerned. Kolus et al. [40] utilized an artificial neuro-fuzzy inference system for locating coronary illness. The pulse rate, which was the outcome of the model, was calculated as extremely light, light, moderate, and heavy. The researchers also took into consideration different unpredictability factors (i.e., physical and physiological contrasts) in patients. The authors [41–43] proposed an analytical tool dependent on the artificial neuro-fuzzy inference system and Levenberg–Marquardt techniques for the identification of cardiac disease in patients. They also demonstrated that the model anticipated the level of patients' cardiac ailments with consistent and progressively exact outcomes. A correlation of results with existing strategies based on investigative precision with the Statlog-Cleveland Heart Disease dataset was accomplished.

8.3 Future of automated diagnosis of cardiac disease

Today's era is an era of stress, which leads to complications in human health, particularly CVD. Heart disease accounts for about 30% of deaths annually [44]. Much progress has been made in this field, which has helped eliminate some CVD trends, but the remaining are very complex and have a disastrous impact on the human race. Fig. 8.5 shows how much capital is continuously invested in managing CVD. Heart disease is mostly related to age, with older adults more commonly affected than younger ones. Those who are obese and/or have diabetes are at greater risk of CVD as well.

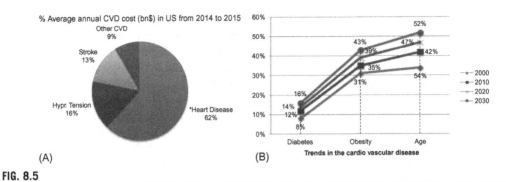

FIG. 8.5

(A) Average annual CVD cost in U.S. [47]. (B) Trends in the cardio vascular disease.

The cost of CVD problems is quite large; related expenses are even greater than those of cancer treatments. The biggest advancement in the field of CVD is the pacemaker, which is a device that replaces the human heart and performs the same functions [45]. A pacemaker requires no new therapy or additional exercise; it is like a heaving a new heart. So the research here is to work in the direction of a method which is somewhat more cheap and slightly more effective. To understand CVD, one must understand the basic functioning of the heart. The heart is a four-chambered organ that pumps blood to every part of the body through arteries and veins [46]. The four chambers include the left ventricle (LV), left atrium (LA), right ventricle (RV), and right atrium (RA). The heart also consists of four valves, including the tricuspid, pulmonary, mitral, and aortic valves.

8.3.1 Clinical applications

Simulation protocols have brought about many advantages to medical providers leading the fight against CVD. Many models are available, one of which is based on Moore's law [47]. This strategy is the most effective for heart problems. Diseases like cardiomyopathies, valvular disease, congenital heart disease, and arrhythmias directly or indirectly affect the functionality of the heart. Cardiovascular health can be examined and analyzed via electrocardiography or magnetic resonance imaging (MRI).

Hypertrophic obstructive cardiomyopathy (HOCM) is a chronic heart disease in which the membrane of the heart thickens, hindering blood flow from the LV [48]. Up to recently, HOCM could only be treated via traditional methods. Nowadays, due to Simulink advancements, surgical methods can also be used for this condition. Both traditional and surgical treatments have their pros and cons, however. Surgery is tricky, subject to human error even by the most accomplished practitioner. In the past, doctors were compelled to perform the same treatment in one disease, but now, due to symmetric modeling, they have additional options depending on the heart rate of the patient. This is an advantage of spending money on a test conducted via Simulink methodology. This system helps in some major heart operations like insertion of ventricular assist devices (VADs), prosthetic valves, cardiac-resynchronization therapy (CRT), and much more. Prior to the availability of simulation, these surgeries were considered too complicated to perform and thus many patients died. Fig. 8.6 shows the type of computation-based therapies that become available with increasing computational speeds [49]. The system here shows the speed of the deterioration of the cell in the heart cavity for counting the functional risk in the Simulink model. The simulated speed can be slowed to 10,000 × and increased to as fast as 100 TFLOPS.

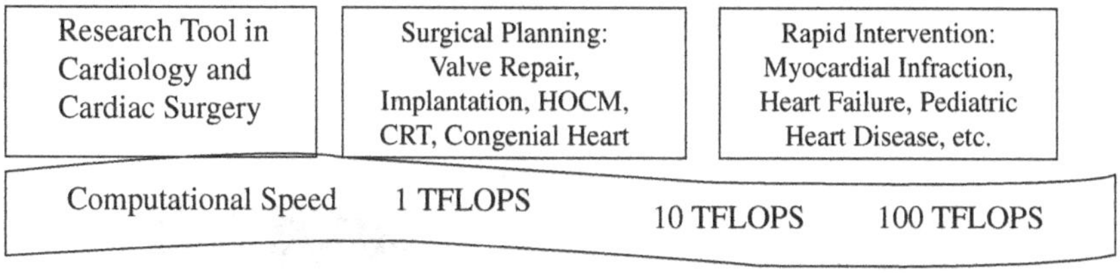

Research Tool in Cardiology and Cardiac Surgery	Surgical Planning: Valve Repair, Implantation, HOCM, CRT, Congenial Heart	Rapid Intervention: Myocardial Infraction, Heart Failure, Pediatric Heart Disease, etc.
Computational Speed	1 TFLOPS	10 TFLOPS	100 TFLOPS

FIG. 8.6

Applications of cardiac simulation for available computational speeds [49].

8.3.2 Challenges and recent advances in cardiac simulation

The recent advancement of simulation-based ideology is helping many heart patients with or without the need for therapy [49], which was compulsory before this discovery. Still, there is a lack of functionality, as the data cannot be processed completely. All the simulation models work on data gained by tests and ECG of the heart. Initially, creating a working graph of heart pump rate was difficult, as there was no system to detect functionality. After the introduction of computerized modeling, it becomes easier to have frequency dependent heart rate using ECHO [50]. This helped in the development of cardiac electromechanics. Simulating the heart helped doctors to determine functionality of contraction and expansion of its four chambers. Blue represents slow speed and white represents fast speed. Fig. 8.7 is a flowchart elaborating the characteristic steps in working on a cardiac imaging-based simulation [51].

8.3.3 Automated diagnosis of coronary artery disease using LDA, PCA, ICA, and DWT

Many people die from coronary artery disease (CAD) every year [52]. In CAD, there is a buildup of plaque in the arteries, which narrows them and thus reduces blood flow [53–55]. The arteries can also harden, restricting their ability to expand when blood demand is high. Such cases are critical. CAD is easily detected via normal lab tests and ECG. Fig. 8.8 is a flowchart of the different optimization techniques.

8.4 Cardiovascular disease and COVID-19

Coronavirus, or COVID-19, has created an exceptional situation for clinical systems throughout the world [56]. It was first recognized on December 8, 2019, in Hubei province, China [57]. It is highly infectious and can progress quickly. In the duration of last one year, the virus spread to 221 countries throughout the world, resulting in 21,621,688 active cases and 2,561,698 deaths (WHO data confirmed on March 03, 2021) [58]. Involvement of the respiratory tract, ranging from mild flulike symptoms to severe cases of pneumonia, is the hallmark of COVID-19 infection [59]. Individuals with CVD are at increased susceptibility to the coronavirus. Additionally, COVID-19 can deteriorate cardiovascular functioning. This section provides information on different cardiovascular complications in persons suffering from COVID-19. It also elaborates the effect of former CVD and the novel inception of

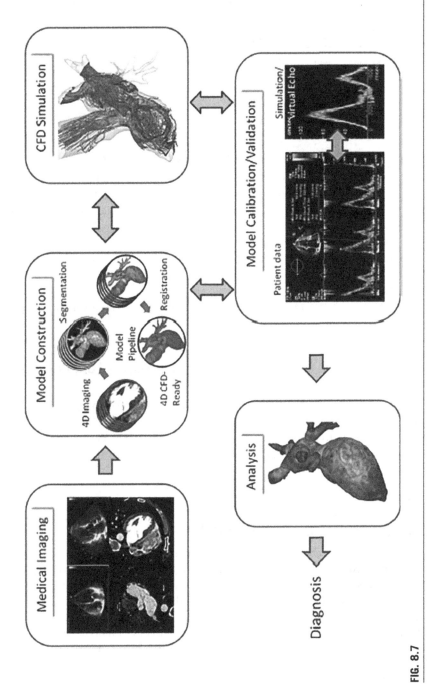

FIG. 8.7

Pipeline for conducting patient-specific cardiac flow simulations [49].

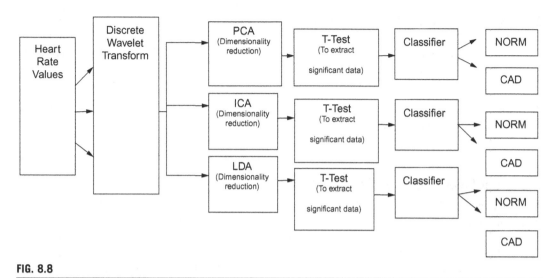

FIG. 8.8

Flow diagram of different optimization techniques.

cardiac issues on medical results in these patients [60]. Although the coronavirus as well as our knowledge of it is constantly changing, this section is based on what we knew about the virus near the beginning of the outbreak in addition to our understanding of Severe Acute Respiratory Syndrome (SARS) and Middle East Respiratory Syndrome (MERS) [61].

8.4.1 Investigation approaches for COVID-19

We completed a literature search using PubMed and Google search engines for novel and appraisal manuscripts, guidelines from specialized groups, and specialist comments available from the inception of the present COVID-19 outbreak [62]. We searched the following terms: "COVID-19" and "coronavirus" plus "cardiac," "cardiovascular," "arrhythmia," and "heart failure" [63]. We also summarized significant, pre-existing citations for SARS and MERS.

8.4.1.1 Contagious contemplation

SARS-CoV-2 is produced by an original covered RNA (i.e., beta coronavirus). The seven genera of these beta coronaviruses are called to root person contamination, with four causing mostly gentle flu-like symptoms. The remaining three are resulting in deadly diseases (SARS, MERS, and the current COVID-19). Even though the respiratory system is the main aim for SARS-CoV-2, the CV scheme might become implicated in several unusual behaviors. The general schemes that are the main cause for cardiovascular risks in COVID-19 [64] include:

1. SARS-CoV-2 penetrates cells employing angiogenesis enzyme 2 (ACE2), a casing vault aminopeptidase that is severely elaborated in the heart as well as lungs. ACE2 acts as a crucial function in neuro-fluid maintenance of the cardiovascular scheme in general health as well as in different illness circumstances.

2. More harsh states of COVID-19 are understood by sensitive universal seditious rejoinder and cytokine tempest that can spread the illness to several organs, potentially resulting in their failure. The literature showed that persons suffering from severe COVID-19 had large circulatory phases of inflammatory cytokines [65].

3. Various antiviral medicines and different types of therapies aimed at curing COVID-19 can also have an injurious impact on the cardiovascular scheme.

8.4.2 Cardiovascular manifestations of COVID-19

A sensitive myocardial wound is the main cardiovascular issue elaborated in COVID-19 (see Table 8.1) [66]. Various types of information give diverse definitions of the myocardial wound, which involves a sudden increase in cardiac enzymes. The sudden enhancement in the sensitivity of cardiac troponin greater than 99% is the most applicable definition. Table 8.1 gives a brief scenario of the different cardiac diseases and their conditions. Some persons with COVID-19 have experienced severe cardiac wounds [67]. These patients are admitted to hospitals suffering from high fever and chest congestion due to a rise in troponin. However, if troponin is low, the patient will likely suffer from a gentle cardiac wound and will not require admission to the hospital. If any of the phenomena follows, then patients with severe cardiac wounds will suffer from the increase in troponin in the case of COVID-19. These statistical data provide a summary of the patients who died of SARS in the SARS epidemic [68]. There is no review of the incidence of ST-segment enhancement of myocardial infarction in COVID-19, but it seems to be low in this case. Heart failure has been observed in patients with COVID-19 and both tachyarrhythmias and bradyarrhythmias can occur. One review reported 138 cases of arrhythmia among COVID-19 patients [69]. COVID-19 patients with arrhythmias living in China have also been reported.

8.4.2.1 Potential long-term consequences

It is too premature to forecast protracted results of patients who recuperate from this disease [70]. However, a few crucial texts could be clarified from preexisting experiences with the SARS epidemic, which resembles SARS-COV-2 [71]. It has been observed that among patients who had recuperated from SARS, 68% sustained disorders of lipid metabolism, 40% have cardiovascular disorders, and 60% have glucose metabolism disorder. Taking this into consideration, there should be continuous tracking of patients who have recuperated from COVID-19 [72].

Table 8.1 Characteristic features of ECG [49].

Wave duration (ms)		Wave amplitude (mv)		Segment retrieval	
P	110 ± 20	P	0.15 ± 0.05	PR	160 ± 40
QRS	100 ± 20	QRS	1.5 ± 0.5	QT_c	400 ± 40
T	180 ± 20	T	0.3 ± 0.2	ST	100 ± 20

8.4.2.2 Organization implications

The general organization ideologies for patients presenting with COVID-19 who are also at risk of CVD or who have former cardiovascular abnormalities are the same for persons without COVID-19. There are certain points that need to be considered: [73].

1. It is crucial to protect clinical providers from becoming infected while taking care of persons with COVID-19. Clinicians must take precautions in using, wearing, and handling personal protective equipment (PPE) [74].
2. The hospital organization should have the necessary infrastructure to handle large numbers of COVID-19 patients, especially those that require ICU facilities. There should also be suitable ideologies in place for sudden analysis and organization of COVID-19 patients with cardiovascular risks [75].
3. Clinicians should not ignore results of unprovoked diagnostic tests (e.g., ECG, troponin elevation, etc.) in patients [76].
4. Medical experts should consider the cardiovascular side effects of different therapies used for treating the coronavirus. In addition to chloroquine/hydroxychloroquine, azathioprine has been put forth as a possible beneficial medication [77].

Summary and future directions for cardiovascular diseases of COVID-19

Though respiratory illness is the dominant clinical presentation of COVID-19, the patients recovered from COVID-19 are more likely to catch cardiovascular situation in future [78]. Taking this into consideration, the present thinking about the interaction among CVD and COVID-19 is glaringly insufficient. Therefore, future research should elaborate on the phenomena, medical proposition, and results of different manifestations of coronavirus in CVD patients.

8.5 Analysis of electrocardiography

Hypothetically, ECG origin is measured in two ways:

1. The first way is to particulate the current sources in the heart by giving space–time distribution and dipole moment per unit volume.
2. The second way is to determine the exterior potentials because of the dipole source. The basic representation of the signal of the heart is described as: the standardized 12-lead ECG signal that records the potential difference between the assumed sites on the body surface during the cycle. The front lobe leads (i.e., leads 1, 2, and 3 and leads AVR, AVL, and AVF) [47].

A typical ECG signal is formed by characteristic waves like P, QRS, and T waves, and sometimes a wave of tiny amplitude called U. Table 8.1 presents the characteristic features of the ECG signal.

Automatic tranquil proposing for cardiac illness requires processor-based detection of a variety of occurrences of uneven movement in the body. An automatic ECG supervisory system uses AI, pattern recognition, and information to analyze cardiac disorders, as shown in Figs. 8.9–9.11.

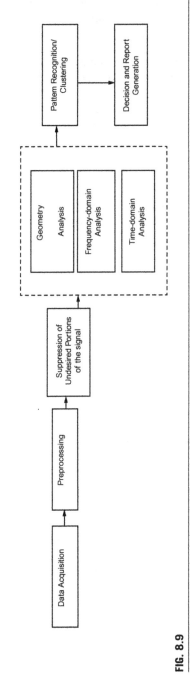

FIG. 8.9

Block diagram of automated ECG analysis system.

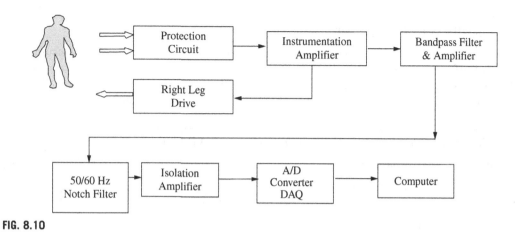

FIG. 8.10

A typical ECG acquisition unit.

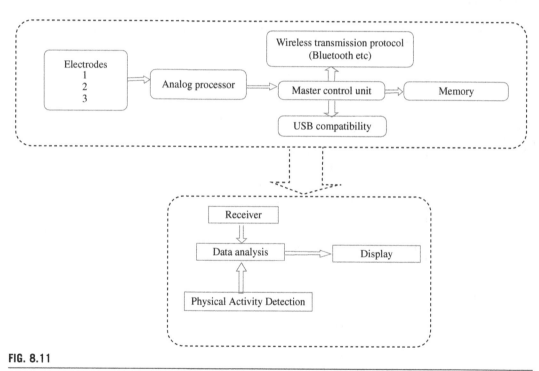

FIG. 8.11

A typical ECG monitoring system using wearable ECG acquisition system.

8.6 Results and discussion

ECG is economical, non-invasive, and widely used in clinical practice applications. As a recording of the body surface's electrical activity, it provides information about heart rhythm abnormalities and helps detect diseases [79]. However, visual inspection of an ECG provides discrete clinically interpreted features that cannot objectively capture the diversity of ECG abnormalities and morphologies.

Table 8.2 State-of-the-art ML techniques for diagnosing CVD [79].

Authors	Techniques	Accuracy
Chazal et al. [80]	LD with QRS-based and time interval features	76%
Llamedo and Martinez [81]	LD (RR intervals and wavelet transform features) with floating feature selection	93%
Yeh et al. [82]	LD	96%
Ubeyli [83]	SVM with error output correction code and discrete wavelet transform	99%
Melgani and Bazi [84]	SVM optimized by particle swarm optimization	90%
Asl et al. [85]	SVM with heart rate variability features and discriminant analysis feature reduction	99%
Nasiri et al.	SVM with principal component analysis and genetic algorithm	93%
Kumaraswamy [86]	Random forest (30 trees) on 150 beats from MIT-BIH	92%
de Oliveira et al. [87]	Bayesian network framework using channel fusion	100%
Coast et al.	HMM with states corresponding to ECG waveforms or intervals	97%
Koski [88]	HMM and broken line approximation (30 states)	100%
Andreao et al. [89]	HMM and rule-based system	100%
Niwas et al. [90]	ANN with heartbeat intervals and spectral entropy features	99%
Inan et al. [91]	Feed-forward MLP with wavelet transform and time intervals features	97%
Ubeyli [92]	RNN with Levenberg–Marquardt training algorithm and eigenvectors	98%
Linh et al. [93]	TSK fuzzy network with Hermite transform	96%
Ozbay et al.	MLP with fuzzy clustering neural network architecture	100%
Mincholé et al.	multivariate discriminant analysis with Wilk's Lambda minimization	88%
Faganeli and Jager	Decision trees with heart rate and Legendre polynomial coefficients features	98% / 85%
Rahman et al.	SVM and random forest with 264 time intervals and waveforms amplitude features	84%
Bailón et al. [94]	Multivariate discriminant analysis with repolarization, depolarization, and heart rate variability features	94% / 92%
Kawazoe et al.	Logistic regression with syncope, R–J interval, QRS duration, and Tpeak–Tend dispersion as features	97% / 63%
Pourbabaee and Lucas	MLP with time interval and morphological waveform features	88%
Colloca et al.	SVM optimized with grid search	85%
Asgari et al. [95]	SVM with stationary wavelet transform	97%

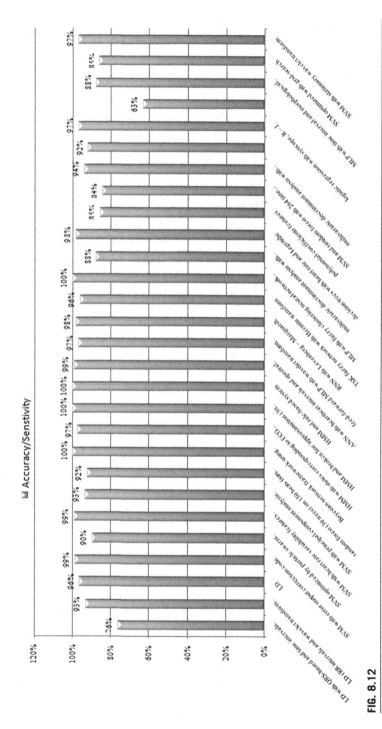

FIG. 8.12

Comparative analysis of various techniques used in CVD.

Therefore computational methods are required, as they can make sense of multivariate complex datasets and detect differences that might be challenging for the human eye. However, analyzing ECG data presents many challenges. Indeed, most large clinical studies still record ECG on paper printouts, requiring manual digitization before computational techniques can be applied. Digital ECG is still yet to be used in many hospitals. Besides, many ECG databases are not publicly available; the research is done on the basis on some publicly available ECG recording. Table 8.2 lists state-of-the-art ML techniques used for diagnosis of cardiac aliments. Fig. 8.12 presents a graphical representation of various techniques used in CVD.

8.7 Conclusion and future scope

This chapter provided a review of computer-aided approaches that have been broadly constructed to evaluate ECG signals and well-built persons to provide enhanced perspectives of clinical challenges. AI techniques give precise and mechanical classifications of heartbeats to identify arrhythmias or unexpected changes in cardiac morphology. AI is also used for automatic syndrome analysis, monitoring, and stratification by managing extended ECG recordings for which diagram and physical investigations can be monotonous and time consuming. AI is flexible and can be practically utilized in wearable ECG devices, assuring competent and dependable monitoring of the heart in both clinical and residential settings. The chapter also examined 3D computer simulations as influential apparatuses for understanding ECG results. Soon, these simulations may be used to produce bulky datasets of artificial data for the exercise of ML classifiers. Even though there are still challenges in the field, these computational approaches to practical medical implementations are likely to become efficient tools for clinical care in the future.

References

[1] D. Mozaffarian, E.J. Benjamin, et al., Executive summary: heart disease and stroke statistics–2016 update: a report from the American Heart Association, Circulation 133 (2016) 447–454.

[2] C.S. Pilkerton, S.S. Singh, T.K. Bias, S.J. Frisbee, Changes in cardiovascular health in the United States, 2003–2011, J. Am. Heart Assoc. 4 (2015), https://doi.org/10.1161/JAHA.114.001650, e001650.

[3] S. Narula, K. Shameer, O.M.A.R.A.M. Salem, J.T. Dudley, P.P. Sengupta, Machine learning algorithms to automate morphological and functional assessments in 2D echocardiography, J. Am. Coll. Cardiol. 68 (2016) 2287–2295.

[4] A. Mayr, H. Binder, O. Gefeller, M. Schmid, The evolution of boosting algorithms. From machine learning to statistical modelling, Methods Inf. Med. 53 (2014) 419–427.

[5] K.W. Johnson, K. Shameer, B.S. Glicksberg, B. Readhead, P.P. Sengupta, J.L.M. Bjorkegren, J.C. Kovacic, J.T. Dudley, Enabling precision cardiology through multiscale biology and systems medicine, JACC Basic Transl. Sci. 2 (2017) 311–327.

[6] E. Wilkins, L. Wilson, K. Wickramasinghe, P. Bhatnagar, J. Leal, R. Luengo-Fernandez, et al., European Cardiovascular Disease Statistics 2017, European Heart Network, Brussels, 2017.

[7] H. Ritchie, M. Roser, Our world in data, in: Causes of Death, 2018. Retrieved from: https://ourworldindata.org/causes-of-death.

[8] O. Opeyemi, E.O. Justice, Development of neuro-fuzzy system for early prediction of heart attack, Int. J. Inf. Technol. Comput. Sci. 9 (9) (2012) 22–28.

[9] World Health Organization. http://www.who.org. (Accessed 9 February 2014).

[10] S. Kumar, G. Sahoo, Classification of heart disease using Naïve Bayes and genetic algorithm, in: Computational Intelligence in Data Mining, 2, Springer, New Delhi, 2015, pp. 269–282.

[11] A. Adeli, M.A. Neshat, Fuzzy expert system for heart disease diagnosis, in: Proceeding of the International Multi Conference of Engineers and Computers Scientists, 2010, p. 656.

[12] N. Allahverdi, S. Torun, İ. Sarıtaş, Design of a fuzzy expert system for determination of coronary heart disease risk, in: International Conference on Computer Systems and Technologies, CompSysTech'07, 2007.

[13] T.M. Nazmy, H. El-Messiry, B. Al-Bokhity, Classification of cardiac arrhythmia based on hybrid system, Int. J. Comput. Appl. 2 (4) (2010) 18–23.

[14] S.S. Sikchi, S. Sikchi, M.S. Ali, Design of fuzzy expert system for diagnosis of cardiac diseases, Int. J. Med. Sci. Public Health 2 (1) (2013) 56–61.

[15] A.V.S. Kumar, Diagnosis of heart disease using advanced fuzzy resolution mechanism, Int. J. Sci. Appl. Inf. Technol. 2 (2013) 22–30.

[16] K. Shameer, K.W. Johnson, B.S. Glicksberg, J.T. Dudley, P.P. Sengupta, Machine learning in cardiovascular medicine: are we there yet? Heart 104 (2018) 1156–1164.

[17] P.P. Sengupta, S. Shrestha, Machine learning for data-driven discovery: the rise and relevance, JACC Cardiovasc. Imaging 12 (2019) 690–692.

[18] M.C. Lancaster, A.M. Salem Omar, S. Narula, H. Kulkarni, J. Narula, P.P. Sengupta, Phenotypic clustering of left ventricular diastolic function parameters: patterns and prognostic relevance, JACC Cardiovasc. Imaging 12 (2019) 1149–1161.

[19] S. Gandhi, W. Mosleh, J. Shen, C.M. Chow, Automation, machine learning, and artificial intelligence in echocardiography: a brave new world, Echocardiography 35 (2018) 1402–1418.

[20] U.S. Food and Drug Administration, FDA News Release: FDA Permits Marketing of Artificial Intelligence-Based Device to Detect Certain Diabetes-Related Eye Problems, 2018. https://www.fda.gov/news-events/pressannouncements/fda-permits-marketing-artificial-intelligence-based-devicedetect-certain-diabetes-related-eye. (Accessed 24 May 2019).

[21] A. Rajkomar, J. Dean, I. Kohane, Machine learning in medicine, N. Engl. J. Med. 380 (2019) 1347–1358.

[22] M. Motwani, D. Dey, D.S. Berman, et al., Machine learning for prediction of all-cause mortality in patients with suspected coronary artery disease: a 5-year multicentre prospective registry analysis, Eur. Heart J. 38 (2017) 500–507.

[23] D. Silver, A. Huang, C.J. Maddison, et al., Mastering the game of go with deep neural networks and tree search, Nature 529 (2016) 484.

[24] T.J.W. Dawes, A. de Marvao, W. Shi, et al., Machine learning of three-dimensional right ventricular motion enables outcome prediction in pulmonary hypertension: a cardiac MR imaging study, Radiology 283 (2) (2017) 381–390.

[25] S.J. Shah, D.H. Katz, S. Selvaraj, M.A. Burke, C.W. Yancy, M. Gheorghiade, R.O. Bonow, C.C. Huang, R.C. Deo, Phenomapping for novel classification of heart failure with preserved ejection fraction, Circulation 131 (3) (2015) 269–279.

[26] S.K. Oskouie, S.B. Prenner, S.J. Shah, A.J. Sauer, Differences in repolarization heterogeneity among heart failure with preserved ejection fraction phenotypic subgroups, Am. J. Cardiol. 120 (4) (2017) 601–606.

[27] M. Obokata, Y.N.V. Reddy, S.V. Pislaru, V. Melenovsky, B.A. Borlaug, Evidence supporting the existence of a distinct obese phenotype of heart failure with preserved ejection fraction, Circulation 136 (1) (2017) 6–19.

[28] D. Dalos, J. Mascherbauer, C. Zotter-Tufaro, F. Duca, A.A. Kammerlander, S. Aschauer, D. Bonderman, Functional status, pulmonary artery pressure, and clinical outcomes in heart failure with preserved ejection fraction, J. Am. Coll. Cardiol. 68 (2) (2016) 189–199.

[29] D.W. Kitzman, S.J. Shah, The HFpEF obesity phenotype: the elephantintheroom, J. Am. Coll. Cardiol. 68 (2) (2016) 200–203.

[30] R. Mehrotra, M.A. Ansari, R. Agrawal, Neural network and wavelet-based study on classification and analysis of brain tumor using MR images, in: 2019 2nd International Conference on Power Energy, Environment and Intelligent Control (PEEIC), 2019, October, pp. 264–269.

[31] J.S. Sonawane, D.R. Patil, Prediction of heart disease using multilayer perceptron neural network, in: IEEE International Conference on Information Communication and Embedded Systems (ICICES), 2014, https://doi.org/10.1109/icices.2014.7033860.

[32] E.O. Olaniyi, O.K. Oyedotun, K. Adnan, Heart diseases diagnosis using neural networks arbitration, Int. J. Intell. Syst. Appl. 7 (12) (2015) 72.

[33] O.W. Samuel, G.M. Asogbona, A.K. Sangaiah, P. Fang, G. Li, An integrated decision support system based on ANN and Fuzzy_AHP for heart failure risk prediction, Expert Syst. Appl. 68 (2017) 163–172.

[34] M.A. Jabbar, P. Chandra, B.L. Deekshatulu, Heart disease prediction system using associative classification and genetic algorithm, in: International Conference on Emerging Trends in Electrical, Electronics and Communication Technologies-ICECIT, 2012.

[35] N. Devi, S. Anto, An evolutionary-fuzzy expert system for the diagnosis of coronary artery disease, An Evol. Fuzzy Expert Syst. Diagnosis Coron. Artery Dis. 3 (4) (2014) 1478–1484.

[36] N.C. Long, P. Meesada, H. Unger, A highly accurate firefly based algorithm for heart disease prediction, Expert Syst. Appl. 42 (21) (2015) 8221–8231.

[37] A.K. Paul, P.C. Shill, R.I. Rabin, M.A.H. Akhand, Genetic algorithm based fuzzy decision support system for the diagnosis of heart disease, in: 5th International conference on informatics, electronics and vision (ICIEV), 2016, https://doi.org/10.1109/iciev.2016.7759984.

[38] A.K. Sen, S.B. Patel, D.P. Shukla, A data mining technique for prediction of coronary heart disease using neuro-fuzzy integrated approach two level, Int. J. Eng.Comput. Sci. 2 (2013) 2663–2671.

[39] A.M. Mohammad Abushariah, A.M. Assal, Y.A. Omar, M.M. Yousef, Automatic heart disease diagnosis system based on artificial neural network (ANN) and adaptive neuro-fuzzy inference systems (ANFIS) approaches, J. Softw. Eng. Appl. 7 (2014) 1055–1064.

[40] A. Kolus, D. Imbeau, P.A. Dubé, D. Dubeau, Classifying work rate from heart rate measurements using an adaptive neuro-fuzzy inference system, Appl. Ergon. 54 (2016) 158–168.

[41] A.M. Sagir, S. Sathasivam, A novel adaptive neuro fuzzy inference system based classification model for heart disease prediction, Pertanika J. Sci. Technol. 25 (2017) 43–56.

[42] M.A. Ansari, R. Mehrotra, R. Agrawal, Detection and classification of brain tumor in MRI images using wavelet transform and support vector machine, J. Interdisc. Math. 23 (2020) 1–12.

[43] A. Kumar, P. Tripathi, M.A. Ansari, A. Ashok, Novel scheme of K-SVM analysis using PCA and NN for detection of MRI brain images, Taylor & Francis, J. Interdisc. Math. 23 (2020) 1–10.

[44] Z. Wu, J.M. McGoogan, Characteristics of and important lessons from the coronavirus disease 2019 (COVID-19) outbreak in China: summary of a report of 72314 cases from the Chinese center for disease control and prevention, JAMA 323 (13) (2020) 1239–1242.

[45] World Health Organization The World Health Organization Corona Virus Disease 2019 (COVID-19) Situation Report e61. Available at: https://www.who.int/docs/default-source/coronavirus/situation-reports/20200321-sitrep-61-covid-19.pdf?sfvrsn¼f201f85c_2. March 2020.

[46] T.Y. Xiong, S. Redwood, B. Prendergast, M. Chen, Corona viruses and the cardiovascular system: acute and -long-term implications, Eur. Heart J. 41 (2020) 1798–1800.

[47] B. Li, J. Yang, F. Zhao, et al., Prevalence and impact of cardiovascular metabolic diseases on COVID-19 in China, Clin. Res. Cardiol. 109 (5) (2020) 531–538.

[48] F. Zhou, T. Yu, R. Du, et al., Clinical course and risk factors for mortality of adult in patients with COVID-19 in Wuhan, China: a retrospective cohort study, Lancet 395 (10229) (2020) 1054–1062.

[49] C. Huang, Y. Wang, X. Li, et al., Clinical features of patients infected with 2019 novel corona virus in Wuhan, China, Lancet 395 (2020) 497–506.

[50] D. Chen, X. Li, Q. Song, C. Hu, F. Su, J. Dai, Hypokalemia and clinical implications in patients with corona virus disease 2019 (COVID-19), medRxiv (2020), https://doi.org/10.1101/2020.02.27.20028530.

[51] D. Wang, B. Hu, C. Hu, et al., Clinical characteristics of 138 hospitalized patients with 2019 novel corona virus-infected pneumonia in Wuhan, China, JAMA 323 (11) (2020) 1061–1069.

[52] M. Arentz, E. Yim, L. Klaff, et al., Characteristics and outcomes of 21 critically ill patients with COVID-19 in Washington state, JAMA 323 (16) (2020) 1612–1614.

[53] G. Lippi, M. Plebani, Laboratory abnormalities in patients with COVID-2019 infection, Clin. Chem. Lab. Med. 58 (7) (2020) 1131–1134.

[54] G.Y. Oudit, Z. Kassiri, C. Jiang, et al., SARS-coronavirus modulation of myocardial ACE2 expression and inflammation in patients with SARS, Eur. J. Clin. Invest. 39 (2009) 618–625.

[55] Q. Wu, L. Zhou, X. Sun, et al., Altered lipid metabolism in recovered SARS patients twelve years after infection, Sci. Rep. 7 (2017) 9110.

[56] V.F. Corrales-Medina, K.N. Alvarez, L.A. Weissfeld, et al., Association between hospitalization for pneumonia and subsequent risk of cardiovascular disease, JAMA 313 (3) (2015) 264–274.

[57] C.F. Tam, K.S. Cheung, S. Lam, et al., Impact of corona virus disease 2019 (COVID-19) outbreak on ST-segment-elevation myocardial infarction care in Hong Kong, China, Circ. Cardiovasc. Qual. Outcomes 13 (4) (2020), e006631.

[58] ACC, ACC Clinical Bulletin Focuses on Cardiac Implications of Corona Virus (COVID-19). https://www.acc.org/latest-in-cardiology/articles/2020/02/13/12/42/acc-clinical-bulletin-focuses-on-cardiac-implications-ofcoronavirus-2019-ncov. (Accessed 22 March 2020).

[59] ASE Statement on COVID-19, https://www.asecho.org/ase-statement-covid-19. (Accessed March 03 2021).

[60] C.M. Ferrario, J. Jessup, M.C. Chappell, et al., Effect of angiotensin-converting enzyme inhibition and angiotensin II receptor blockers on cardiac angiotensin-converting enzyme 2, Circulation 111 (2005) 2605–2610.

[61] ACC, HFSA/ACC/AHA Statement Addresses Concerns Re: Using RAAS Antagonists in COVID-19, 2020. https://www.acc.org/latest-in-cardiology/articles/2020/03/17/08/59/hfsa-acc-aha-statement-addresses-concerns-re-using-raas-antagonists-in-covid-19. (Accessed 22 March 2020).

[62] ESC, Position Statement of the ESC Council on Hypertension on ACE-Inhibitors and Angiotensin Receptor Blockers, 2020. https://www.escardio.org/m Councils/Council-on-Hypertension-(CHT)/News/position-statement-of-theesc- council-on-hypertension-on-ace-inhibitors-and-ang. (Accessed 22 March 2020).

[63] CDC, Information for Clinicians on Therapeutic Options for COVID-19 Patients, 2020. https://www.cdc.gov/coronavirus/2019-ncov/hcp/therapeuticoptions.html. (Accessed 22 March 2020).

[64] U.R. Acharya, N. Kannathal, S.M. Krishnan, Comprehensive analysis of cardiac health using heart rate signals, Physiol. Meas. 25 (2004) 1130–1151.

[65] U.R. Acharya, P.S. Bhat, N. Kannathal, A. Rao, C.M. Lim, Analysis of cardiac health using fractal dimension and wavelet transformation, Innov. Tech. Biol. Med. 26 (2005) 133–139.

[66] S. Arafat, M. Dohrmann, M. Skubic, Classification of coronary artery disease stress ECGs using uncertainty modeling, in: 2005 ICSC Congress On Computational Intelligence Methods and Applications, IEEE, 2005. 4 pp.

[67] I. Babaoglu, O. Findik, E. Ülker, A comparison of feature selection models utilizing binary particle swarm optimization and genetic algorithm in determining coronary artery disease using support vector machine, Exp. Syst. Appl. 37 (2010) 3177–3183.

[68] I. Babaoglu, O. Findik, M. Bayrak, Effects of principle component analysis on assessment of coronary artery diseases using support vector machine, Exp. Syst. Appl. 37 (2010) 2182–2185.

[69] BIOPACTM, 2012. Information available at <http://www.biopac.com/> (Accessed 24 February 2012).

[70] P.H. Brubaker, Coronary Artery Disease: Essentials of Prevention and Rehabilitation Programs, Human Kinetics Publishers, 2002.

[71] CAD, 2012. Information available at <http://www.nhlbi.nih.gov/health/healthtopics/topics/cad/> (Accessed 24 February 2012).

[72] L. Cao, J. Chua, K.S. Chong, W.K. Lee, Q.M. Gu, A comparison of PCA, KPCA and ICA for dimensionality reduction in support vector machine, Neurocomputing 55 (2003) 321–336.

[73] C.K. Chua, V. Chandran, U.R. Acharya, C.M. Lim, Cardiac health diagnosis using higher order spectra and support vector machine, Open Med. Inform. J. 3 (2009) 1–8.

[74] D. Cysarz, H. Bettermann, P. van Leeuwen, Entropies of short binary sequences in heart period dynamics, Am. J. Physiol. Heart Circ. Physiol. 278 (2000) H2163–H2172.

[75] V. David, A. Sanchez, Advanced support vector machines and kernel methods, Neurocomputing 55 (2003) 5–20.

[76] S. Dua, U.R. Acharya, P. Chowriappa, S. VinithaSree, Wavelet-based energy features for glaucomatous image classification, IEEE Trans. Inf. Technol. Biomed. 16 (2012) 80–87.

[77] R.O. Duda, P.E. Hart, D.G. Stork, Pattern Classification, second ed., Wiley, 2001.

[78] Task Force of the European Society of Cardiology and North American Society of Pacing and electrophysiology Heart Rate Variability: Standards of measurement, physiological interpretation and clinical use, Eur. Heart J. 17 (1996) 354–381.

[79] A. Lyon, A. Mincholé, J.P. Martínez, P. Laguna, B. Rodriguez, Computational techniques for ECG analysis and interpretation in light of their contribution to medical advances, J. R. Soc. Interface 15 (2018), https://doi.org/10.1098/rsif.2017.0821, 20170821.

[80] P. De Chazal, M. O'Dwyer, R.B. Reilly, Automatic classification of heartbeats using ECG morphology and heartbeat interval features, I.E.E.E. Trans. Biomed. Eng. 51 (2004) 1196–1206, https://doi.org/10.1109/TBME.2004.827359.

[81] M. Llamedo, J.P. Martinez, Heartbeat classification using feature selection driven by database generalization criteria, I.E.E.E. Trans. Biomed. Eng. 58 (2011) 616–625, https://doi.org/10.1109/TBME.2010.2068048.

[82] Y.-C. Yeh, W.-J. Wang, C.W. Chiou, Cardiac arrhythmia diagnosis method using linear discriminant analysis on ECG signals, Measurement 42 (5) (2009) 778–789.

[83] E.D. Übeyli, ECG beats classification using multiclass support vector machines with error correcting output codes, Digit. Signal Process. 17 (2007) 675–684, https://doi.org/10.1016/j.dsp.2006.11.009.

[84] F. Melgani, Y. Bazi, Classification of electrocardiogram signals with support vector machines and particle swarm optimization, IEEE Trans. Inf. Technol. Biomed. 12 (2008) 667–677, https://doi.org/10.1109/TITB.2008.923147.

[85] B.M. Asl, S.K. Setarehdan, M. Mohebbi, Support vector machine-based arrhythmia classification using reduced features of heart rate variability signal, Artif. Intell. Med. 44 (2008) 51–64, https://doi.org/10.1016/j.artmed.2008.04.007.

[86] R. Ganeshkumar, Y.S. Kumaraswamy, Investigating cardiac arrhythmia in ECG using random forest classification, Int. J. Comput. Appl. 37 (2012) 31–34, https://doi.org/10.5120/4599-6557.

[87] L.S.C. De Oliveira, R.V. Andreão, M. Sarcinelli-Filho, The use of Bayesian networks for heart beat classification, Adv. Exp. Med. Biol. 657 (2010) 217–231, https://doi.org/10.1007/978-0-387-79100-5_12.

[88] A. Koski, Modelling ECG signals with hidden Markov models, Artif. Intell. Med. 8 (1996) 453–471, https://doi.org/10.1016/S0933-3657(96)00352-1.

[89] R.V. Andreao, B. Dorizzi, J. Boudy, ECG signal analysis through hidden Markov models, I.E.E.E. Trans. Biomed. Eng. 53 (2006) 1541–1549, https://doi.org/10.1109/TBME.2006.877103.

[90] S. Issac Niwas, R. Shantha Selva Kumari, V. Sadasivam, Artificial neural network based automatic cardiac abnormalities classification, in: Sixth International Conference on Computational Intelligence and Multimedia Applications, 2005. 16–18 August, IEEE, Las Vegas, NV. Piscataway, NJ, 2005, pp. 41–46, https://doi.org/10.1109/ICCIMA.2005.13.

[91] O.T. Inan, L. Giovangrandi, G.T.A. Kovacs, Robust neural-network-based classification of premature ventricular contractions using wavelet transform and timing interval features, I.E.E.E. Trans. Biomed. Eng. 53 (2006) 2507–2515, https://doi.org/10.1109/TBME.2006.880879.

[92] E.D. Übeyli, Combining recurrent neural networks with eigenvector methods for classification of ECG beats. Digit, Signal Process. 19 (2009) 320–329, https://doi.org/10.1016/j.dsp.2008.09.002.

[93] T.H. Linh, S. Osowski, M. Stodolski, On-line heart beat recognition using Hermite polynomials and neuro-fuzzy network, IEEE Trans. Instrum. Meas. 52 (2003) 1224–1231, https://doi.org/10.1109/TIM.2003.816841.

[94] R. Bailón, J. Mateo, S. Olmos, P. Serrano, J. García, A. del Río, I.J. Ferreria, P. Laguna, Coronary artery disease diagnosis based on exercise electrocardiogram indexes from repolarisation, depolarisation and heart rate variability, Med. Biol. Eng. Comput. 41 (2003) 561–571, https://doi.org/10.1007/BF02345319.

[95] S. Asgari, A. Mehrnia, M. Moussavi, Automatic detection of atrial fibrillation using stationary wavelet transform and support vector machine, Comput. Biol. Med. 60 (2015) 132–142, https://doi.org/10.1016/j.compbiomed.2015.03.005.

An improved regularization and fitting-based segmentation method for echocardiographic images

Kalpana Chauhan[a] and Rajeev Kumar Chauhan[b]

Department of Electrical Engineering, Central University of Haryana, Mahendragarh, India[a] Department of Electrical Engineering, Dayalbagh Educational Institute, Agra, India[b]

Chapter outline

9.1 Introduction

The details obtained from echocardiography are important for determining extent of disease in heart patients. The closed curves approaching the boundaries help to differentiate the different sections of the heart. Echocardiography machines can show good views of the internal structure of the heart, but their capability for automatic segmentation for specific diagnostic purposes is limited. These limitations are due to the high noise that usually covers many parts inside echocardiographic images. The boundaries that need to be segmented are uncertain due to speckle noise and low resolution. Many segmentation methods for ultrasound images have been proposed in the literature, among which deformable models [1–3] are most suitable. Achim et al. [4] applied a deformable model called the active appearance motion model to echocardiographic images to segment them. This method is based on training stages. Ahn et al. [5] used another technique called active contour for segmenting the left ventricle.

There are many studies done for segmentation of ultrasound imaging. There are various approaches proposed for the segmentation of echocardiographic images, like for volume change in left ventricle [6–12], and so on. However, in conventional contour-based segmentation techniques, the curves have difficulty approaching the desired boundaries via basic regularization techniques because of the presence of high signal-to-noise ratio, speckle noise, and comparatively low-contrast echocardiographic images.

The solution for segmenting ultrasound images like echocardiographic images is curve evolution. The idea behind the curve evolution technique is minimization of the energy function with the level set method. The energy function ($E(\varphi)$) with a level set (φ) is the combination of two terms. The first term is the regularization term ($R(\varphi)$), which maintains the smoothness of the contour ($C\_\varphi := (\varphi = 0)$). The second term is the fitting term ($\lambda F(\varphi)$), which helps the zero level set contour (C_φ) to approach the desired object.

The parameter (λ) with the fitting term is called the local binary fitting model [13, 14]. Different kinds of fitting models are available, including edge-based methods [15–20], region-based methods [21–23], and those based on prior information [24–27]. However, these methods are less capable of handling high speckle noise and poor, low-contrast ultrasound images.

High speckle noise and poor contrast in ultrasound images creates difficulty for the regularization model in smoothing contour lines while approaching the object under the fitting force. In addition, intensity inhomogeneity and speckle noise create problems for determining the right fitting energy. The improved regularization and fitting-based segmentation (IRFS) technique is a new regularization and fitting model. The regularization model focuses on closed curves with smoothness and fitting energy based on the speckle noise density present in the echocardiographic images. This segmentation method has been tested for echocardiographic images that suffer from poor contrast and high speckle noise. The method has been analyzed for checking the quality of the segmentation by calculating similarity-, error-, and sensitivity-based parameters. The IRFS method also increases the speed of the convergence to boundary.

This chapter begins with an introduction to deformable models, related literature, and the IRFS segmentation method. The second section deals with the formulation of speckle noise and the third section presents an overview of the energy minimization of active contour models. The fourth section is devoted to IRFS method formulation, energy minimization, and implementation of the IRFS method. The fifth section presents the results of the analysis of the quality (errors and overlapping regions) of the segmentation methods. The chapter concludes with a discussion of the outcomes of the IRFS method.

9.2 Materials and method

Speckle noise should be properly analyzed before choosing a segmentation technique. There is not yet a standardized definition of speckle noise in ultrasound images. However, the most acceptable formulation for speckle noise is to consider it as multiplicative noise, which is different from additive noise. A coherent system is formed when the image system undergoes coherent illumination (i.e., there is no matter the source points of the illumination they are having the fixed phase and tried to synchronized for getting fixed when their phase get fluctuated). These fluctuation tunings create constructive and destructive interference patterns to form a fixed phase. The reflection of the coherent ultrasonic radiation on the surface of same size radiant wavelength, an interference between two waves occurs, which generates a multiplicative noise called speckle noise [28].

The multiplicative approximation model of speckle noise is defined as:

$$\zeta_{l,p} = \chi_{l,p} z_{l,p} + a_{l,p}; \quad l,p \in N \tag{9.1}$$

where $\zeta_{l,p}$ is the middle pixel that has noise in the middle of the moving window, $\chi_{l,p}$ is the pixel that is free from noise, $z_{l,p}$ is the multiplicative noise, and $a_{l,p}$, is the additive noise, which is independent of mean 0, $z_{l,p}$. The l and p indicate the spatial locations and belong to the real numbers in space (i.e., $l,p \epsilon R^2$).

The speckle noise variance (σ_n^2) may be computed from the image, which is compressed logarithmically, by considering the dimensions of many windows larger than the filtering window and taking the average noise variance over them. The noise variance in each window is computed as [29–32]:

$$\sigma_n^2 = \sum_{i=1}^{p} \sigma_p^2 \Big/ \vartheta_p \tag{9.2}$$

where σ_p^2 is the variance, ϑ_p is the mean of the noise in the windows selected for the work, and index p is used to cover all pixels in the image [28–32].

The image characteristics for noise (ϑ_p and σ_p^2) can be used to calculate the speckle noise variance σ_n^2. This variance is used as a part of an operator for despeckling filters. When the nonlinear processing approaches employed on ultrasound echo images, for example logarithmic compression, affect the speckle statistics in such a way that the local mean is not proportional to the standard deviation but the local variance. The applied logarithmic compression has greater effect on the high-intensity tail of the Rayleigh and Rician PDFs compared to the low-intensity part. This results in turning the speckle noise corresponding to the uncompressed Rayleigh signal to white Gaussian noise [28–32].

The multiplicative noise component is having comparatively high effect and significance then to additive noise [33] such that:

$$\left(\|a_{l,p}\|^2 \ll \|z_{l,p}\|^2 \right) \tag{9.3}$$

The filters for such noises can be modeled by utilizing first order statistics (means and the variance) of the middle pixels and its neighborhood from Eq. (9.1) and represented by following multiplicative noise:

$$\zeta_{l,p} \approx \chi_{l,p} z_{l,p} \tag{9.4}$$

The model in Eq. (9.4) can be simplified by applying the logarithmic amplification transforms and converted to the following algebraic equation:

$$\log(\zeta_{l,p}) = \log(\chi_{l,p}) + \log(z_{l,p}) \tag{9.5}$$

$$\delta_{l,p} = \Upsilon_{l,p} + \nu_{l,p} \tag{9.6}$$

In Eq. (9.5), term $\log(\zeta_{l,p})$ is the pixel observed after compression on the display of the ultrasound, denoted by $\delta_{l,p}$ in Eq. (9.6), and term $\log(\chi_{l,p})$ and term $\log(z_{l,p})$ are the noise component and noise-free pixel, represented in Eq. (9.6) by $\Upsilon_{l,p}$ and $\nu_{l,p}$, respectively, after logarithmic compression.

9.3 Theory and calculation

9.3.1 Energy minimization formulation and level set method of active contour models

The curve evolution of an image to be segmented $I{:}\Omega \to R$ can be done using techniques from the level-set method by setting the target curve C_φ to a zero level set $C_\varphi := \{x \in \Omega \mid \varphi(x) = 0\}$, where φ is the level-set function. The energy function with two energies is used to segment the desired object with contour C_φ. These two energies are regularization term and fitting term. The regularization is the internal energy that keeps the contour C_φ smooth and prevents it from noise that may generate undesired segmentation, thus the dependency of regularization is on φ. The fitting term is associated with the external energies, which help the contour C_φ to attract toward the object boundary and depend both on φ and the image I. The CV model proposed by Chan-Vese is a famous active contour model [12] based on the solution of piecewise constant segmentation problem and given as:

$$F(c_1, c_2, \phi) = \mu \cdot \Lambda(\varphi) + \nu \cdot \aleph(inside(\varphi)) + \lambda_1 \int_{inside(C)} |I(x, y) - c_1|^2 dxdy + \lambda_2 \int_{outside(C)} |I(x, y) - c_2|^2 dxdy \quad (9.7)$$

where the fixed parameters μ, $\nu > 0$ are added to give the weight to the different terms in the energy. The Λ (length) and $\aleph$ (area) used for regularization in Eq. (9.7) can be expressed in terms of energy as follows:

$$\Lambda\{\varphi = 0\} = \int_\Omega |\nabla H(\varphi(x, y))| dxdy = \int_\Omega \delta_0(\varphi(x, y)) |\nabla \varphi(x, y)| dxdy \quad (9.8)$$

$$\aleph\{\varphi \geq 0\} = \int_\Omega H(\varphi(x, y)) dxdy \quad (9.9)$$

where $H(.)$ is the Heaviside function and δ_0 is the one-dimensional Dirac measure. These are defined, respectively, as:

$$H(z) = \begin{cases} 1, & \text{if } z \geq 0 \\ 0, & \text{if } z < 0 \end{cases}, \quad \delta_0(z) = \frac{d}{dz} H(z) \quad (9.10)$$

The constants c_1 and c_2 in the fitting terms are represented as:

$$c_1(\phi) = \frac{\int_\Omega I(x, y) H(\varphi(x, y)) dxdy}{\int_\Omega H(\varphi(x, y)) dxdy} \quad (9.11)$$

and

$$c_2(\phi) = \frac{\int_\Omega I(x, y)(1 - H(\varphi(x, y))) dxdy}{\int_\Omega (1 - H(\varphi(x, y))) dxdy} \quad (9.12)$$

In conventional active contour methods of segmentation, the curve fails to draw the desired boundary due to lack of controlling the fitting parameter to smooth the curve without dividing it into many segments.

9.3.2 IRFS method

The selection of improved regularization and fitting leads to a perfect curve for the desired boundary even in a high-noise image. For this purpose, we propose the model with improved regularization and fitting terms.

9.3.2.1 Model for IRFS regularization

The conventional regularization models are not able to draw boundaries, however, regularization as used in [14], has shown better results. Like the CV model, the arc length and area inside the curve are considered the regularization term, but a better balancing between length and area improves the smoothness of the curve. Meanwhile, the regularization proposed in [25] takes the distance term to avoid re-initialization. As echocardiographic images have too much noise and are low contrast, both terms are important.

The regularization used in [15] shows a balancing between the length of the arc, which is done with the area inside the curve. The regularization (R_{Chi}) is represented as the ratio of the arc length and square root of the area.

$$R_{Chi}(\varphi) = \int_{C_\varphi} \frac{\Lambda_r(X(s))}{\sqrt{\aleph_r(X(s))}} ds \tag{9.13}$$

Level set can be rewritten using Eqs. (10.8) and (10.9) as:

$$R_{Chi}(\varphi) = \int_{\Omega} \left(\frac{\int \delta(\varphi(x,y))|\nabla\varphi(x,y)|dxdy}{\sqrt{\int H(\varphi(x,y))dxdy}} \right) dxdy \tag{9.14}$$

The regularization is improved by modifying the length term including the potential effect proposed in [25] to give a distance regularization to stop the re-initialization. The proposed regularization ($R_k(\varphi)$) is formulated as:

$$R_k(\varphi) = \int_{\Omega} \left(\frac{\int \delta(\varphi(x,y))|\nabla\varphi(x,y)|dxdy}{\sqrt{\int H(\varphi(x,y))dxdy}} \right) dxdy$$
$$+ \frac{1}{2}\int_{\Omega} (|\nabla\varphi(x,y)| - 1)^2 dxdy \tag{9.15}$$

where the potential term for distance regularization (P_{DR}) can be represented as:

$$P_{DR} = \frac{1}{2}\int_{\Omega} (|\nabla\varphi(x,y)| - 1)^2 dxdy \tag{9.16}$$

The dual effect distance regularization helps to converge the curve to draw the echocardiographic image boundaries affected by high noise.

9.3.2.2 Model for proposed fitting function

A region-based fitting function is modeled by taking the advantage of speckle present in the images. The proposed fitting function $(F_k(\varphi))$ is formulated as:

$$F_k(\varphi) = \lambda \int I(x-y)|\Upsilon * S|^2 H(\varphi(y)) dxdy \tag{9.17}$$

where λ is the positive constant.

The speckle region intensity is given in the second term by convolving the speckle component given in Eq. (9.6) with a speckle weight S. The self-speckle component (Υ) of the image helps to select the desired region that should be inside the boundary. The fitting energy with the speckle noise component can be decided by assuming that the area inside the boundary has the most speckle noise compared to other additive noise, and the outside desired boundary has less speckle noise or high additive noise. This is because the inner area includes the chambers of the heart, which have blood flow, and papillary muscles, while the region outside the chambers may be affected by other additive noises due to heart walls, muscles, and other factors. Therefore, the energy function $(\varepsilon_k(\varphi))$ for the proposed active contour model is given as:

$$\varepsilon_k(\varphi) = \mu R_k(\varphi) + \nu F_k(\varphi) \tag{9.18}$$

or

$$\varepsilon_k(\varphi) = \int_\Omega \left(\frac{\mu \int \delta(\varphi(x,y))|\nabla\varphi(x,y)|dxdy}{\sqrt{\int H(\varphi(x,y))dxdy}} \right) dxdy + \frac{1}{2}\int_\Omega (|\nabla\varphi(x,y)|-1)^2 dxdy$$
$$+ \nu \left\{ \lambda \int I(x-y)|\Upsilon * S|^2 H(\varphi(y)) dxdy \right\} \tag{9.19}$$

where ν is a positive constant handling the balancing of fitting function with the regularization.

9.3.2.3 Energy minimization

The energy minimization has been done by the Newton Raphson method as done in our previous method proposed in [34]. The method differs from the steepest descent, in form that the information of the second derivative is used to locate the minimum of the function. The significance of using the Newton Raphson method is faster convergence of the curve. When applying the method in Eq. (9.19), the evolution equation is obtained as follows:

$$\frac{\partial(\varphi)}{\partial t} = \left[\delta_e \left\{ \mu \left(\text{div}\left(\frac{\nabla\varphi}{|\nabla\varphi|} \right) - \frac{1}{2}(\delta_e(\varphi))^{-3/2} \right) \right\} + \left\{ (|\nabla\varphi|-1)\left(\text{div}\left(\frac{\nabla\varphi}{|\nabla\varphi|} \right) \right) \right\} + 2\nu\lambda_n I |\Upsilon_n S|]^{-1} \bullet \varepsilon_e(\varphi) \tag{9.20}$$

The artificial time $(t \geq 0)$ decides the flow direction. The suffix e represents the form of Eular–Lagrange parameters. The equation evolves for $(0,\infty) \times \Omega$ and the condition for the zero level set is:

$$\varphi(0,x,y) = \varphi_0(x,y) \text{ in } \Omega, \quad \text{while } \frac{\delta_e(\varphi)}{\nabla\varphi} \frac{\partial\varphi}{\partial\vec{n}} = 0 \text{ on } \partial\Omega$$

where $\vec{n}$ is the normalization of the exterior and normal derivative $\left(\partial\varphi / \partial n \right)$ at the boundary.

9.3.2.4 Implementation

For implementation purposes, all the partial derivatives in Eq. (9.20) are converted in discrete form by finite differences. For this discretize Eq. (9.20) by taking h as the space step and Δt as the time step as in Eq. (9.21). The initialization of the level set is done by a binary step function as it has the advantage of being able to emerge new contours with faster curve evolution. The step function takes the positive constant values inside the boundary and negative constant values inside the boundary. The truncation mask for the kernel K_σ is selected as $\omega \times \omega;\; \omega > 4\sigma$.

$$
\begin{aligned}
\frac{\varphi_{i,j}^{n+1} - \varphi_{i,j}^{n}}{\Delta t} =& \left[\delta_h\left(\varphi_{i,j}^{n}\right)\cdot\left\{\frac{\mu}{2h^2}\Delta_{-}^{x}\left(\frac{2\Delta_{+}^{x}\varphi_{i,j}^{n} - \left(\delta_h\left(\Delta_{+}^{x}\varphi_{i,j}^{n}\right)\right)^{-3/2}}{\sqrt{\frac{\left(\Delta^x{}_+\varphi_{i,j}^{n}\right)^2}{(h)^2} + \frac{\left(\varphi_{i,j+1}^{n} - \varphi_{i,j-1}^{n}\right)^2}{(2h)^2}}}\right)\right. + \frac{\mu}{2h^2}\Delta_{-}^{y}\left(\frac{2\Delta_{+}^{y}\varphi_{i,j}^{n+1} - \left(\delta_h\Delta_{+}^{y}\left(\varphi_{i,j}^{n}\right)\right)^{-3/2}}{\sqrt{\frac{\left(\varphi_{i+1,j}^{n} - \varphi_{i-1,j}^{n}\right)^2}{(2h)^2} + \frac{\left(\Delta^y{}_+\varphi_{i,j}^{n}\right)^2}{(h)^2}}}\right) \\
&- \left(\frac{\Delta^x{}_{-}\varphi_{i,j}^{n+1}}{h^2} - 1\right)\frac{\Delta_{+}^{x}\varphi_{i,j}^{n}}{\sqrt{\frac{\left(\Delta^x{}_+\varphi_{i,j}^{n}\right)^2}{(h)^2} + \frac{\left(\varphi_{i,j+1}^{n} - \varphi_{i,j-1}^{n}\right)}{(2h)^2}}} + \left(\frac{\Delta^y{}_{-}\varphi_{i,j}^{n+1}}{h^2} - 1\right)\frac{\Delta_{+}^{y}\varphi_{i,j}^{n+1}}{\sqrt{\frac{\left(\varphi_{i+1,j}^{n} - \varphi_{i-1,j}^{n}\right)^2}{(2h)^2} + \frac{\left(\Delta^y{}_+\varphi_{i,j}^{n}\right)^2}{h^2}}} \\
&\left. + 2\frac{\nu}{h^2}\lambda I_{i,j}\left(\Upsilon_{i,j}S\right)\right]^{-1} \bullet F_h\left(\varphi_{i,j}^{n}\right)
\end{aligned}
\tag{9.21}
$$

9.4 Results

We applied the IRFS method of segmentation on echocardiographic images taken from the Advanced Cardiac Center of the Postgraduate Institute of Medical Education and Research (PGIMER), Chandigarh, India. The experiment is done by applying conventional segmentation methods along with IRFS with improved regularization and fitting function. It is important to find the position of the initial contour in the case of a heart image taken in original form to draw the boundary of the particular chamber (atrium or ventricle). The active contour is implemented in a MATLAB environment. The parameters used are $\lambda = 1.0$ and $\nu = 1.0$, however, the value of μ and area of the curvature are selected depending on the size of the desired object (the organ, in case of echocardiographic images). The initial contour and its position are free to select in the image. The size of the testing images is 440×396 pixels. Fig. 9.1A–E shows the curve evolution using conventional methods of CV, modified CV (MCV), distance regularized level set (DRLS), and regularized signed force (RSF), as well as the IRFS method.

The original image is the apical four-chamber view of the heart in the diastolic condition. Starting from the initial contour, the curve grows with each iteration. It is noticeable that starting from the same contour size and position, the curve in the IRFS method grows much faster and is bounded with lesser iterations as compared to the conventional methods. Fig. 9.1 shows the curve evolution after 80, 160, 240, 320, and 400 iterations. The contour starts leaking with the disturbed boundary with many spurious areas. The desired boundary of the organ is evaluated after 200 iterations only and with lesser disturbance in boundary and without leakage from the boundary.

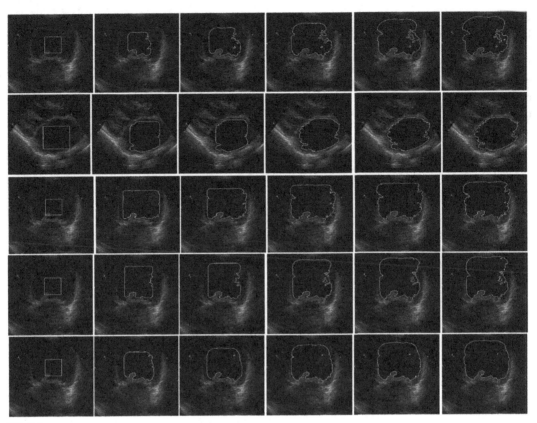

FIG. 9.1

(A) Contour evolution with conventional regularization with CV model with fitting parameters $\lambda = 1$. Initial contour, contour after 80, 160, 240, 320, and 400 iteration steps (left to right). (B) Contour evolution with MCV model with fitting parameters $\lambda = 1$. Initial contour, contour after 80, 150, 200, 300, and 350 iteration steps (left to right). (C) Contour evolution with DRLS model with fitting parameters $\lambda = 1$. Initial contour, contour after 80, 130, 180, 250, and 300 iteration steps (left to right). (D) Contour evolution with RSF model with fitting parameters $\lambda = 1$. Initial contour, contour after 80, 130, 165, 180, and 250 iteration steps (left to right). (E) Contour evolution with IRFS model with fitting function with fitting parameters $\lambda = 1$. Initial contour, contour after 80, 120, 160, 180, and 200 iteration steps (left to right).

The iteration values increased and the quality of the contour decreased with the conventional methods, as shown in Fig. 9.2, which is the parasternal long-axis view of the heart.

Figs. 9.3 and 10.4 show the final contours obtained from all five methods with boundaries drawn by the clinician (taken as the ground truth). The images show the apical four-chamber view of the heart and the organs that have to be drawn are the left ventricle (Fig. 9.3) and left atrium (Fig. 9.4). The dotted-line contour is the ground truth boundary and the solid line contours are the boundaries obtained from the conventional (Fig. 9.3A–D) and IRFS methods (Fig. 9.3E), respectively..

In Fig. 9.4, the dotted-line contour is the ground truth boundary and the solid line contours are the boundaries obtained from the conventional (Fig. 9.4A–D) and IRFS methods (Fig. 9.4E), respectively.

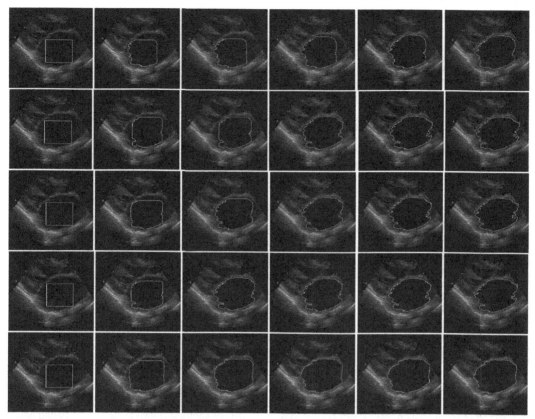

FIG. 9.2

(A). Contour evolution with conventional regularization with CV model with fitting parameters $\lambda = 1$. Initial contour, contour after 80, 180, 260, 350, and 450 iteration steps (left to right). (B) Contour evolution with MCV model with fitting parameters $\lambda = 1$. Initial contour, contour after 80, 150, 200, 300, and 400 iteration steps (left to right). (C) Contour evolution with DRLS model with fitting parameters $\lambda = 1$. Initial contour, contour after 80, 130, 180, 280, and 350 iteration steps (left to right). (D) Contour evolution with RSF model with fitting parameters $\lambda = 1$. Initial contour, contour after 80, 120, 140, 200, and 300 iteration steps (left to right). (E) Contour evolution with IRFS model with fitting function with fitting parameters $\lambda = 1$. Initial contour, contour after 80, 100, 120, 160, and 200 iteration steps (left to right).

Visual prescriptions of these two images reflect that the contour obtained with the IRFS method is approaching the ground truth contour, but the contour obtained with conventional methods (CV, MCV, DRLS, and RSF) is not. The error calculated with the conventional methods is around 38 pixels, however, the error value becomes less in case of the IRFS method at around 16 pixels. MATLAB codes for contour evolution are run in MATLAB 7.6 with Windows 7 on a Dell Vostro laptop with an Intel Core i-33,110M processor with 2.24 GHz, 4 GB, and a 32-bit operating system. As shown in Fig. 9.3, the CPU time taken by conventional CV, MCV, DRLS, and RSF methods to evolve the contour is 58.19 s, 55.43 s, 53.87 s, and 49.91 s, respectively, whereas the IRFS method takes only 36.18 s.

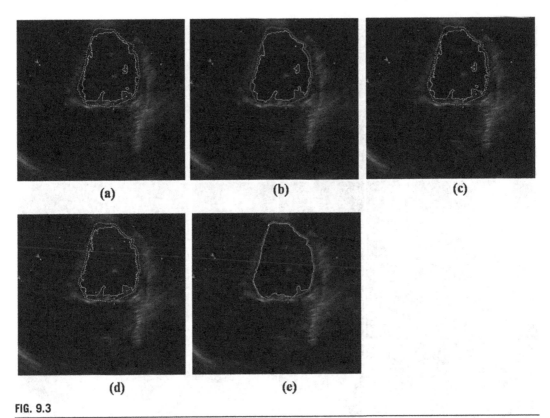

(a)   (b)   (c)

(d)   (e)

FIG. 9.3

Comparison of segmentation results with ground truth (boundary of ventricle drawn by clinician). Dotted line is the boundary drawn by clinicians, while the solid line is drawn with (A) conventional CV, (B) MCV, (C) DRLS, (D) RSF, and (E) IRFS method.

As shown in Fig. 9.4, the CPU time taken by conventional CV, MCV, DRLS, and RSF methods to evolve the contour is 56.20 s, 48.5 s, 45.2 s, and 42.6 s, respectively, whereas the IRFS method takes only 34 s.

9.5 Discussions

We analyze the quality of the segmentation by calculating several parameters, including similarity coefficient (Jaccard and Dice coefficients), distance (Hausdorff error), and sensitivity. The Jaccard coefficient shows the similarity between two boundaries, and the largest value can be assumed as 1. If the ground truth image is (I_g) and the simulated image is (I_s), the Jaccard coefficient (J_c) can be calculated as:

$$J_c = \frac{|I_g \cap I_s|}{|I_g \cap I_s|} = \frac{|I_g \cap I_s|}{|I_g| + |I_s| - |I_g \cap I_s|} \tag{9.22}$$

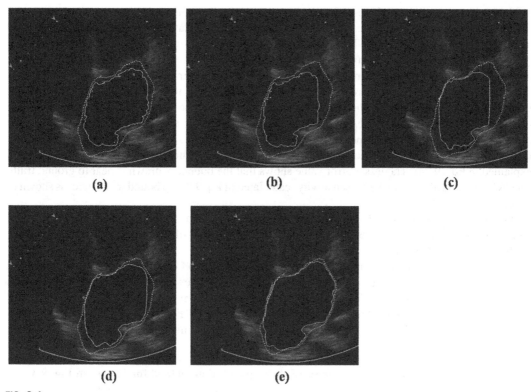

FIG. 9.4

Comparison of segmentation results with ground truth (boundary of atrium drawn by clinician). Dotted line is the boundary drawn by clinicians, while the solid line is drawn with (A) conventional CV, (B) MCV, (C) DRLS, (D) RSF, and (E) IRFS method.

The Dice coefficient (D_c) is a static also used for similarity between two images and can be calculated as:

$$D_c = \frac{2 \times |I_g \cap I_s|}{|I_g| + |I_s|} \tag{9.23}$$

The Dice coefficient evaluates similarity better than the Jaccard coefficient.

The Hausdorff error (H_e) is the longest distance between two boundaries and can be calculated as:

$$H_e = \max_x [\min_z \|c_x - c_z\|](c_x \in g, c_z \in s) \tag{9.24}$$

where s and g are the simulated pixel data and ground truth data, respectively, and c_x and c_z are the pixels related with two images (ground truth and simulated).

The sensitivity (S_s) is given by

$$S_s = \frac{|I_g \cap I_s|}{I_g} \tag{9.25}$$

Table 9.1 lists the values of these segmentation performance parameters.

The lesser CPU time indicates that the IRFS method works faster to converge the contour for achieving the desired boundary. There is a significant CPU time difference with the IRFS method (22, 19.3, 17.69, and 13.73 s, as shown in Fig. 9.3) when compared with CV, MCV, DRLS, and RSF, respectively. This difference is also seen when another image is operated in the same conditions. The time difference is around 21.4, 13.7, 10.2, and 7.8 s when compared with CV, MCV, DRLS, and RSF, respectively. The IRFS segmentation method also shows better performance when testing the region similarity parameters as in Eqs. (10.24) and (10.25). The high values of J_c and D_c show that the segmented images showing the very same result as those obtained by the ground truth. The IRFS method shows a lesser value of H_e, which is an error-based comparison explained in Eq. (9.24). The lesser error value shows that the boundary drawn is near to ground truth. The IRFS method also shows better sensitivity (calculated in Eq. 9.25) to boundary change, as shown in Tables 10.1 and 10.2.

Fig. 9.5A and B shows the Hausdorff error for different values of λ. The curves related to the errors when applying conventional methods increase when the value of λ increases. The conventional methods are unstable with the change in λ.

The curve related to the error when applying the IRFS method does not increase too much as λ increases, showing a minor effect from changing the value of λ. However, when the value of λ is less, the error is not too high and remains stable up to a value of $\lambda = 1$. Beyond this value, the error becomes too large in case of conventional methods. While the errors in the IRFS method are not too great, whatever the value of λ, i.e., it is less affected with λ. For testing the similarity region between the ground

Table 9.1 Statistical comparison analysis of the segmentation method for images in Fig. 9.3.

Parameters	Conventional methods				IRFS method
	CV	MCV	DRLS	RSF	
Jaccard coefficient (%)	68.43	73.12	76.09	81.33	89.56
Dice coefficient (%)	40.63	42.56	45.03	50.09	68.43
Hausdorff error (pixels)	38	36	31	30	16
Sensitivity	0.6343	0.6425	0.6902	0.7123	0.8456
CPU time (s)	58.19	55.43	53.87	49.91	36.18

Table 9.2 Statistical comparison analysis of the segmentation method for images in Fig. 9.4.

Parameters	Conventional methods				IRFS method
	CV	MCV	DRLS	RSF	
Jaccard coefficient (%)	64.13	72.26	75.45	80.99	88.96
Dice coefficient (%)	37.83	40.16	43.98	49.9	67.13
Hausdorff error (pixels)	41	39	36	31	18
Sensitivity	0.6553	0.6751	0.6882	0.7023	0.8369
CPU time (s)	56.20	48.5	45	42.6	34.8

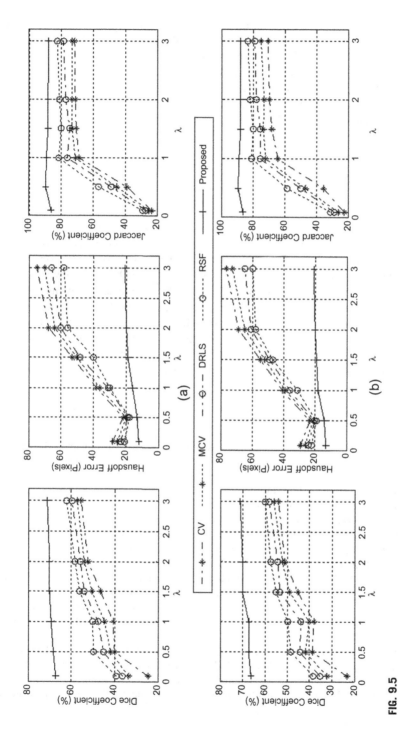

FIG. 9.5

Change in Dice coefficient with the different values of λ. Change in Hausdorff error with the different values of λ, and the change in Jaccard coefficient with the different values of λ. (A) Statistics related to image from Fig. 9.3 and (B) statistics related to image from Fig. 9.4.

truth image and simulated image, the two coefficients (Jaccard and Dice coefficients) were also tested for different values of λ. In both cases, the curve related to the IRFS method has large values and is stable. Greater or lesser values of λ do not affect the quality of the segmentation done by the IRFS method. However, segmentation is greatly affected by change in the value of λ in conventional methods. The similarity in conventional methods is less when the values of λ are less because the contour shrinks with lesser values of λ. At greater values, however, the similarity become slightly greater with compromising contour leakage. Similarity is stable and significantly high in case of the IRFS method.

9.6 Conclusions

The IRFS method is developed by formulating a new regularization model and fitting function. The new regularization model has the capability to bind the curve by retaining its smoothness. This is proven in the resultant images and statistical parameters. The IRFS regularization also protects the segmentation from leaking at the boundary. The fitting function proposed here is a new idea specifically for echocardiographic image segmentation, as it takes speckle noise as an advantageous feature for detecting image boundary regions. Segmentation methods suffer due to speckle noise in images, but the IRFS method has the capability to work with such images. In our experiment, we took real images with high noise, and results show that the IRFS method is successful in drawing the boundaries of these images. Statistical analysis proves the quality of the IRFS segmentation method. In addition, the IRFS method is faster than conventional methods in terms of CPU time.

References

[1] K.Z. Abd-Elmoniem, A.B.M. Youssef, Y.M. Kadah, Real-time speckle reduction and coherence enhancement in ultrasound imaging via nonlinear anisotropic diffusion, I.E.E.E. Trans. Biomed. Eng. 49 (2002) 997–1014.
[2] K. Saini, M. Rohit, A modified hybrid filter for echocardiographic image noise removal, Int. J. Sig. Proc. Image Proc. Pattern Recogn. 5 (2) (2012) 61–72.
[3] K. Chauhan, R.K. Chauhan, A. Saini, Enhancement and despeckling of echocardiographic images, in: Soft Computing Based Medical Image Analysis, Academic Press, 2018, pp. 61–79.
[4] A. Achim, A. Bezerianos, P. Tsakalides, Novel Bayesian multiscale method for speckle removal in medical ultrasound Images, IEEE Trans. Med. Imaging 20 (2001) 772–783.
[5] C.Y. Ahn, Y.M. Jung, O.I. Kwon, J.K. Seo, A regularization technique for closed contour segmentation in ultrasound images, IEEE Trans. Ultrason. Ferroelectr. Freq. Control 58 (2011) 1577–1589.
[6] E. Angelini, S. Homma, G. Pearson, J. Holmes, A. Laine, Segmentation of real-time three-dimensional ultrasound for quantification of ventricular function: a clinical study on right and left ventricles, Ultrasound Med. Biol. 31 (1143) (2005) 1158.
[7] M. Avendi, A. Kheradvar, H. Jafarkhani, A combined deep-learning and deformable-model approach to fully automatic segmentation of the leftventricle in cardiac MRI, Med. Image Anal. 30 (2016) 108–119.
[8] A. Belaid, D. Boukerroui, Y. Maingourd, J.F. Lerallut, Phase based level set segmentation of ultrasound images, in: IEEE International Conference on Information Technology and Applications in Biomedicine, 2009, pp. 1–4.

[9] V. Caselles, F.V. Caselles, F. Catte, T. Coll, F. Dibos, A geometric model for active contours in image processing, Num. Math. 66 (1993) 1–31.

[10] V. Caselles, R. Kimmel, G. Sapiro, Geodesic active contours, Int. J. Comput. Vis. 22 (1997) 61–79.

[11] T.F. Chan, L.A. Vese, Active contours without edges, IEEE Trans. Image Process. 10 (2001) 266–277.

[12] K. Chauhan, R.K. Chauhan, Boundary detection of echocardiographic images during mitral regurgitation, in: Recent Advances in Computer Vision, Springer, Cham, 2019, pp. 281–303.

[13] Y. Chen, H.D. Tagare, S. Thiruvenkadam, F. Huang, D. Wilson, K.S. Gopinath, R.W. Briggs, E.A. Geiser, Using prior shapes in geometric active contours in a variational framework, Int. J. Comput. Vis. 50 (2001) 315–328.

[14] C. Corsi, G. Saracino, A. Sarti, C. Lamberti, Left ventricular volume estimation for real-time three-dimensional echocardiography, IEEE Trans. Med. Imaging 21 (2002) 1202–1208.

[15] V. Dutt, Statistical Analysis of Ultrasound Echo Envelope, Ph.D. dissertation, Mayo Graduate School, Rochester, MN, 1995.

[16] R. Goldenberg, R. Kimmel, E. Rivlin, M. Rudzsky, Fast geodesic active contours, IEEE Trans. Image Process. 10 (2001) 1467–1475.

[17] X. Hao, S. Gao, X. Gao, A novel multiscale nonlinear thresholding method for ultrasonic speckle suppressing, IEEE Trans. Med. Imaging 18 (1999) 87–794.

[18] L. Heucke, M. Knaak, R. Orglmeister, A new image segmentation method based on human brightness perception and foveal adaptation, IEEE Signal Process. Lett. 7 (2000) 129–131.

[19] S. Kichenassamy, A. Kumar, P. Olver, A. Tannenbaum, A. Yezzi, Gradient flows and geometric active contour models, in: Proceedings of IEEE International Conference on Computer Vision, 1995, 1995, pp. 810–815.

[20] S.G. Lacerda, A.F. da Rocha, D.F. Vasconcelos, J.L. de Carvalho, I.G. Sene, J.F. Camapum, Left ventricle segmentation in echocardiography using a radial-search-based image processing algorithm, in: International Conference of the IEEE Engineering in Medicine and Biology Society, 2008, pp. 222–225.

[21] M. Leventon, O. Faugeras, E. Grimson, W. Wells, Level set based segmentation with intensity and curvature priors, in: Proceedings IEEE Workshop on Mathematical Methods in Biomedical Image Analysis, 2000, pp. 4–11.

[22] C. Li, Active contours with local binary fitting energy, in: Presented at the IMA Workshop on New Mathematics and Algorithms for 3-D Image Analysis, 2006.

[23] C. Li, C. Xu, C. Gui, M.D. Fox, Distance regularized level set evolution and its application to image segmentation, IEEE Trans. Image Process. 19 (2010) 3243–3254.

[24] C. Li, C. Kao, J. Gore, Z. Ding, Implicit active contours driven by local binary fitting energy, in: Presented at the IEEE Conference on Computer Vision and Pattern Recognition, 2007.

[25] R. Malladi, J.A. Sethian, B.C. Vemuri, Shape modeling with front propagation: a level set approach, IEEE Trans. Pattern Anal. Mach. Intell. 17 (1995) 158–175.

[26] T. McInerney, D. Terzopoulos, Deformable models in medical image analysis: a survey, Med. Image Anal. 1 (1996) 91–108.

[27] J. Nascimento, J.S. Marques, J. Sanches, Estimation of cardiac phases in echographic images using multiple models, in: Proceeding of the IEEE International Conference on Image Processing, vol. 2, 2001, pp. 149–152.

[28] S.K. Pal, D.D. Madjumadar, Fuzzy Mathematical Approach to Pattern Recognition, Wiley, New York, 1986.

[29] N. Paragios, R. Deriche, A PDE-based level set approach for detection and tracking of moving objects, in: IEEE International Conference on Computer Vision, 1998, pp. 1139–1145.

[30] K. Saini, M.L. Dewal, M. Rohit, Level set based on new signed pressure force function for echocardiographic image segmentation, Int. J. Innov. Appl. Stud. 3 (2) (2013) 560–569.

[31] K. Saini, M.L. Dewal, M.K. Rohit, Segmentation of mitral regurgitant jet using the combination of wavelet and watershed transformation, in: 2012 IEEE 8th International Colloquium on Signal Processing and its Applications, 2012, March, pp. 74–79.

[32] N. Paragios, O. Mellina-Gottardo, V. Ramesh, Gradient vector flow fast geodesic active contours, in: Proceedings of the IEEE International Conference on Computer Vision, 2001, pp. 67–73.

[33] K. Saini, M.L. Dewal, M. Rohit, A fast region-based active contour model for boundary detection of echocardiographic images, J. Digit. Imaging 25 (2012) 71–278.

[34] J. Simpson, L. Lopez, P. Acar, M.K. Friedberg, N.S. Khoo, H.H. Ko, et al., Three-dimensional echocardiography in congenital heart disease: an expert consensus document from the European association of cardiovascular imaging and the American society of echocardiography, J. Am. Soc. Echocardiogr. 30 (2017) 1–27.

Identification of heart failure from cine-MRI images using pattern-based features

10

Megha Agarwal[a] and Amit Singhal[b]

Department of Electronics and Communication Engineering, Jaypee Institute of Information Technology, Noida, India[a]
Department of Electronics and Communication Engineering, Bennett University, Greater Noida, India[b]

Chapter outline

10.1 Introduction

There has been a significant advancement in the field of medicine and diagnostics. Despite this, heart diseases comprise one of the major causes of mortality globally, accounting for more than 30% of deaths annually [1]. An early diagnosis can help in proper treatment leading to a faster recovery. Radiology techniques, such as magnetic resonance imaging (MRI), computed tomography (CT) and echocardiography, are employed by doctors to diagnose various heart diseases [2]. While most of these techniques hold their importance, cardiac MRI provides more detailed images.

The left side of the heart is responsible for pumping oxygen-rich blood to all parts of the body. Heart failure refers to a condition where the heart is not able to maintain enough blood flow as required by the body. There is an increased pressure on the heart muscles to pump more blood. Ejection fraction (EF) measures the fraction of blood ejected from the heart chamber in each contraction and lies between 50% and 75% for normal persons [3]. The symptoms for heart failure include excessive fatigue, swelling of legs, and short breath, thereby, limiting the ability of the person to engage in any strenuous activity [4]. It can be caused by high blood pressure, a previous heart attack, excessive alcohol consumption, atrial fibrillation, or coronary heart disease. In mild cases, treatment could include lifestyle changes to quit smoking and alcohol consumption, increase physical exercise, and adoption of a healthy diet to reduce salt intake and lower cholesterol levels.

Cine-MRI [5] is performed for capturing cardiac images sequentially for a complete assessment. Our focus lies on the problem of detecting heart failure from cine-MRI images using texture features based on local patterns. Intensity variations in the local neighborhood of any pixel can be captured by using pattern-based features. These features are able to represent textural information present in local regions of any image. Many such features [6–13] have been proposed in the literature and have shown promising results in biomedical applications [12–15]. Local binary pattern (LBP) [6] is the first feature to be proposed in the family of features denoting local patterns in an image. Instead of using a binary coding scheme, authors in the study cited herein [7] consider a ternary code to form local ternary pattern (LTP). Further, difference of two Gaussian-filtered images is considered in the reference study [8] to construct difference of Gaussian LTP (DoGLTP). After computing the ternary patterns in an image, cooccurrence computed over different neighborhood distances yields local ternary cooccurrence pattern (LTCoP) [9]. Considering five different Gaussian-filtered images, a 3-dimensional (3D) structure is created in [10] to form 3DLTCoP feature. LTP is extracted across various channels in [11] to construct multi-channel LTP. On the contrary, authors in [12] propose local directional extrema pattern by finding relation between diagonal neighbors of pixels. Relationship among the different neighbors of a reference pixel are considered in [13] to form local mesh patterns.

In this chapter, we compute different pattern-based features from cine-MRI images, evaluate classification results for four machine learning-based classifiers and compare their performance in terms of popular performance metrics. The results highlight the efficacy of these features in automatic detection of heart failure.

10.2 Pattern-based features

Extraction of appropriate features is pertinent to obtain a consolidated representation of an image. Various pattern-based features have been explored for applications in diverse domains. To differentiate images for patients with heart failure from healthy ones, we consider four different features as discussed in the following sections.

10.2.1 Local binary pattern (LBP)

LBP is a well-known and widely used feature for many applications, including face recognition, fingerprint identification, and other classification problems [6]. It is computed as a binary encoding of difference in pixel intensities in the local neighborhood. Let I_o denote the intensity of a pixel and its neighbors are represented as I_{rn}, where r denotes the radius of neighborhood and n refers to the

24	15	40
31	**31**	57
25	14	19

0	0	1
1		1
0	0	0

	19	

Example image   LBP   LBP value

FIG. 10.1

Illustration of LBP calculation for $r=1$.

position of the neighbor, $1 \leq n \leq 8$, with $n=1$ denoting the pixel to the right of the center pixel, and n increasing in the anticlockwise direction. Considering $r=1$ neighborhood for any pixel, LBP is computed as

$$\text{LBP}_{rn} = \begin{cases} 1, & I_{rn} \geq I_o \\ 0, & I_{rn} < I_o \end{cases}$$

After computing the pattern, LBP value is obtained by considering this pattern as a binary number with $n=8$ representing the most significant bit (MSB) and converting this 8-bit binary to a decimal value in the range 0–255, as shown in Fig. 10.1. Such decimal values are computed for every pixel in the image and a histogram of these values is created to form the LBP feature.

10.2.2 Local ternary pattern (LTP)

LTP is considered for face recognition problem in [7]. It is constructed in a way similar to that discussed above, but ternary coding is used instead of binary coding, i.e.,

$$\text{LTP}_{rn} = \begin{cases} 1, & I_{rn} > I_o \\ 0, & I_{rn} = I_o \\ -1, & I_{rn} < I_o \end{cases}$$

To deal with the negative values obtained herein, the LTP are separated into two binary patterns, referred as upper and lower LTP, corresponding to -1 and 1, respectively. The binary numbers thus obtained are converted to decimal and lastly, histograms are computed to represent the LTP feature for the image. Fig. 10.2 illustrates the calculation of LTP values.

10.2.3 Difference of Gaussian LTP (DoGLTP)

DoGLTP is explored for classification of natural images in [8]. Firstly, two Gaussian filters G_1 and G_2 are constructed with zero mean and standard deviations σ_1 and σ_2, respectively. The input image is filtered using DoG filter $(G_1 - G_2)$. In the second step, edges in four different orientations, i.e., horizontal, vertical, diagonal, and off-diagonal, are extracted. Next, LTP are computed over both $r=1$ and $r=2$ neighborhoods, where

$$\text{LTP}_{2n} = \begin{cases} 1, & I_{2n} > I_{1n} \\ 0, & I_{2n} = I_{1n} \\ -1, & I_{2n} < I_{1n} \end{cases}$$

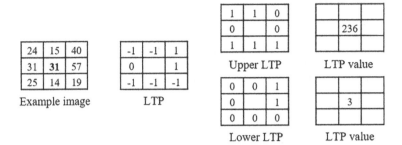

FIG. 10.2

Example for calculation of LTP values for $r=1$.

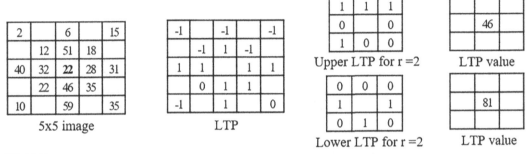

FIG. 10.3

LTP calculation for $r=2$.

Calculation of LTP for $r=2$ is depicted in Fig. 10.3. Lastly, LTP corresponding to both the neighborhoods are converted to upper and lower patterns. Histograms are computed from the decimal equivalents of the binary numbers obtained in the previous step.

10.2.4 3D local ternary cooccurrence pattern (3DLTCoP)

This feature proposed in [10] obtains high accuracy in identifying categories of images belonging to datasets of various kinds. While DoGLTP considers two Gaussian filters, a filter bank of five Gaussian filters is considered here. The filtered images are arranged in a 3D structure. 5×5 image matrices are obtained by scanning this structure in horizontal, vertical, center, diagonal, and off-diagonal directions. For each of these 5×5 matrices, center pixel is considered as reference and LTCoP is computed as

$$LTCoP_n = \begin{cases} 1 & LTP_{2n} = LTP_{1n} = 1 \\ -1 & LTP_{2n} = LTP_{1n} = -1 \\ 0 & \text{otherwise} \end{cases}$$

Thereafter, LTCoP is separated into two binary patterns for -1 and 1, referred as upper and lower LTCoP, respectively. Decimal equivalents are computed for the binary patterns and histograms are constructed for the entire image. Fig. 10.4 shows an example for calculation of LTCoP values from 5×5 image matrix.

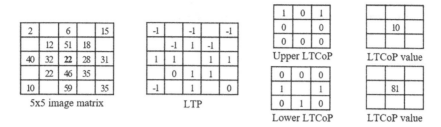

FIG. 10.4

Example for calculation of LTCoP values.

10.3 System overview

Block diagram of the system is shown in Fig. 10.5. The first step is extraction of pattern-based features from the input dataset image followed by computation of histograms to obtain a representation of the image, thereby, helping in comparison of different images. Then, the classification is performed using machine learning-based classifiers to identify input image as heart failure or healthy.

10.3.1 Dataset

In this work, publicly available Sunnybrook cardiac data (SCD) are used [16]. The data consist of cine-MRI images of 45 patients with four different pathologies, namely, heart failure (HF) with infarction, HF without infarction, left ventricular (LV) hypertrophy, and healthy. Infarction refers to death of a tissue caused by obstruction of blood flow. On the other hand, hypertrophy is the enlargement of a tissue or an organ. Contrast agents such as gadolinium complexes are administered intravenously before MRI to achieve higher contrast between infarcted muscles or normal heart.

The description of dataset is provided in Table 10.1. Images in this database are preclassified into above-mentioned four pathologies based on different parameters [17]. Table 10.2 comprises average and standard deviation of end-diastolic volume, end-systolic volume, ejection fraction, and LV mass for each pathology. In Table 10.2, 244.92 (86.02) signifies an average value of 244.92 and a standard deviation of 86.02. End-diastolic volume refers to the blood volume in ventricle prior to the contraction and end-systolic volume is the amount of blood remaining in the ventricle after the heart has contracted,

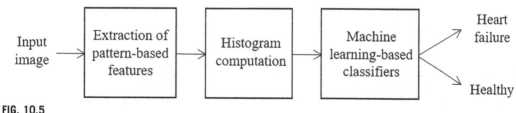

FIG. 10.5

Block diagram of the system.

Table 10.1 Sunnybrook cardiac data (SCD) description.

Pathology	Number of patients	Ejection fraction (EF)	Evidence
HF (with infarction)	12	<40%	Late gadolinium enhancement
HF (without infarction)	12	<40%	No late gadolinium enhancement
LV hypertrophy	12	>55%	Ratio of LV mass over body surface area is $>83\,\text{g/m}^2$
Healthy	9	>55%	No hypertrophy

Table 10.2 Pathology-wise group statistics in terms of average and standard deviation.

	HF (with infarction)	HF (without infarction)	LV hypertrophy	Healthy
End-diastolic volume (mL)	244.92 (86.02)	233.67 (63.21)	114.39 (50.46)	115.69 (36.89)
End-systolic volume (mL)	174.34 (90.64)	158.28 (56.34)	43.11 (24.50)	43.10 (14.74)
Ejection fraction (%)	32.01 (12.27)	33.09 (13.07)	62.72 (9.22)	62.93 (3.65)
LV mass (g)	201.32 (45.24)	193.69 (39.01)	175.87 (85.70)	130.27 (32.69)

i.e., at the end of systole. An average-sized man has end-diastolic and systolic volumes of about 120 and 50 mL, respectively. A female has slightly lower values of these volumes as compared to a male. Stroke volume is equal to the difference between the end-diastolic and systolic volumes.

A subset of this dataset is used for classification in this work by considering images of HF with (or without) infarction and healthy patients. Sample images of the dataset are shown in Fig. 10.6. The first, second, and third row represent HF (with infarction), HF (without infarction), and healthy images, respectively.

10.3.2 Classification

There are many classification techniques available in the literature. In this chapter, four different techniques, support vector machine (SVM), linear discriminant analysis (LDA), k-nearest neighbors (kNN), and ensemble bagged trees (EBT) are used for performance comparison. All these classifiers are applied to each of the pattern-based features individually and their classification performance is evaluated. A brief description of the classifiers is provided as follows:

(i) **Support vector machine (SVM):** SVM is proposed by Vapnik et al. in 1992 [18]. It is a widely used supervised learning model for classification and regression. In the case of classification, SVM model is trained using the given set of labeled images. These images are represented as data

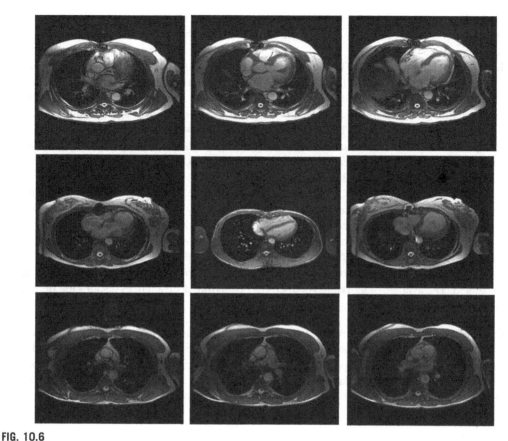

FIG. 10.6

Sample images of the SCD dataset.

points in high-dimensional space. Further, hyperplanes are drawn to separate images such that there is sufficient margin between images of different classes. The testing images are then mapped to this space and their class is predicted based on the distance to the hyperplanes. Along with the linear classification, SVM also works well for the nonlinear classification using kernel functions, and hence becomes suitable for practical problems as well. Many extensions and variants of SVM are available in the literature.

(ii) **Linear discriminant analysis (LDA):** LDA is proposed by Fisher in 1936 [19]. It is a type of dimensionality reduction technique and is also being used as a supervised learning classifier. SVM works mainly upon the support vectors, which means that the data points which are close to the decision boundary are considered more important. On the other hand, LDA assumes that all the data points are having the same covariance and normally distributed. LDA computes the statistical properties (mean and variance) of each class for modeling. By using Bayes theorem, the probability of new data belonging to each class is estimated. The discriminant function predicts the class of the input data based on these probabilities. Other than LDA, there also exists nonlinear discriminant analysis [20].

(iii) k-nearest neighbors (kNN): This supervised learning technique was proposed by Cover et al. for classification purpose in 1967 [21]. It requires a labeled training dataset. The class of the testing data is predicted based on the most frequent class of its k nearest neighbors. k is a user-defined constant value selected by heuristic techniques. If $k = 1$, then the class of that kth neighbor is assigned to the testing data. When k is more than one, then weights are assigned to k neighbors. The nearest neighbor contributes more by assigning the highest weightage. Common distance metrics being used are Euclidean, Manhattan and Minkowski. Classification by this algorithm becomes difficult if the class distribution is nonuniform.

(iv) Ensemble bagged trees (EBT): In the ensemble techniques, many decision trees are trained rather than a single one for better prediction [22]. Thus, many weak learners (or base models) are combined together to get a stronger one. Actually, base models have high bias and variance. Hence, they are less robust. Bagging or bootstrap aggregation reduces the variance of decision trees. For a classification problem, subsets of random data are chosen from training data. Now, each of these subsets is used to train their decision tree. Hence, a set of ensemble models are generated. The average of individual predictions made from decision trees decides the final class of the testing sample. Hence, it is a more robust classifier.

For all these classifiers, m-fold cross validation is done for prediction (for $m = 10$). In this method, total data are partitioned into m subsamples. $(m - 1)$ subsamples are used to train the model. mth subsample is used for testing. This process is iterated m times by considering each subsample as testing data once and rest as training data. Results obtained from these m iterations are averaged to get the final prediction. The main advantage of using this method is that every sample is used as training and testing both.

10.3.3 Performance measures

In this chapter, pathologies are predicted by using machine learning classifiers. It can assist doctors in prescreening and provide faster diagnosis with more accurate identification. But accuracy alone is not sufficient to rate a classifier output. There exist many factors to evaluate the performance of a classifier. Some important terms like true positive (TP), true negative (TN), false positive (FP) and false negative (FN) need to be introduced before the classification parameters like sensitivity, specificity, accuracy, area under curve (AUC), and F-Measure are discussed [23].

Let us consider a binary classification problem of gender identification: male (positive class) and female (negative class). TP represents correct identification of positive class by the classifier, i.e., predicting a case as male and the prediction is correct. Similarly, TN represents correct prediction of negative class by the classifier. It means correctly predicting a case as female. On the contrary, FP means predicting a negative class as a positive class. It means, classifying a case as male where actually it was female. Similarly, FN means predicting a positive class as a negative class, i.e., classifying a case as female where actually it was male. Since all these terms are little confusing, a matrix is defined from these four terms and is called as confusion matrix. These parameters are arranged as shown in Fig. 10.7.

Now, let us discuss the classifier performance parameters derived from this confusion matrix.

	Predicted positive class	Predicted negative class
True positive class	TP	FN
True negative class	FP	TN

FIG. 10.7

Confusion matrix.

(i) Sensitivity: It is also called as a true-positive rate (TPR) or recall. It represents the ratio of true positive with respect to all positive cases.

$$\text{Sensitivity} = \frac{TP}{TP + FN}$$

(ii) Specificity: It is also called as true-negative rate (TNR). It represents the ratio of true negative with respect to all negative cases.

$$\text{Specificity} = \frac{TN}{TN + FP}$$

(iii) False-positive rate (FPR): It depicts the proportion of false positive with respect to all negative cases.

$$FPR = (1 - \text{specificity}) = \frac{FP}{TN + FP}$$

(iv) Accuracy: It is the proportion of correct classification made with respect to the total cases.

$$\text{Accuracy} = \frac{TP + TN}{TP + TN + FP + FN}$$

(v) Precision: It is the measure of true positive with respect to the total cases classified as positive.

$$\text{Precision} = \frac{TP}{TP + FP}$$

(vi) Receiver operating characteristics (ROC): It is a graphical presentation of TPR versus FPR at different classification thresholds. TPR and FPR both lie in the range [0,1].

(vii) Area under curve (AUC): AUC is independent of classification thresholds. It reflects the probability that the classifier will rank a random positive case more highly than a random negative case. AUC is extracted by the total area under the ROC curve. The value of AUC lies within [0,1]. Higher value of AUC means a better prediction by the classifier.

(viii) F1-score: It is also called dice similarity coefficient (DSC). It also lies in the range [0,1]. Higher value of F1-score means a better classifier performance. It includes both precision and recall by computing their harmonic mean and hence, it is a more balanced parameter.

$$F1 - \text{score} = 2 \times \frac{1}{\frac{1}{\text{precision}} + \frac{1}{\text{recall}}}$$

10.4 Results and discussion

Two experiments are conducted for the pathology classification, HF (with infarction) versus healthy and HF (without infarction) versus healthy. To solve this purpose, performance is analyzed on the SCD database [21]. Combinations of four different features, LBP, LTP, DoGLTP, and 3DLTCoP along with the four different classifiers, SVM, LDA, kNN (with $k = 1$), and EBT are used. It gives total sixteen distinct combinations. The notation LBP-kNN indicates the feature-classifier combination, i.e., LBP feature is used and classification is performed using kNN. Similar notation has been used throughout this chapter.

Performance measures discussed in the above section are computed for each of these combinations and are summarized in Table 10.3 for HF (with infarction) versus healthy. It is observed from the table that kNN classifier is producing best results for all features under consideration by giving accuracy of 99.1%, 100%, 98.2%, and 95.5% for LBP, LTP, DoGLTP, and 3DLTCoP, respectively. Highest accuracy is achieved for the combination LTP-kNN.

For the computation of AUC, first ROC is drawn for TPR versus FPR. In the following figures, confusion matrices and ROCs are shown for all the features with kNN as a classifier for discrimination between HF (with infarction) and healthy cases.

It is clear from the Figs. 10.8 and 11.9 that TP, FN, FP, and TN are 99%, 1%, 0%, and 100%, respectively, for LBP-kNN. Also, AUC is 0.99.

It is observed from the confusion matrix shown in Fig. 10.10 that TP, FN, FP, and TN are 100%, 0%, 0%, and 100%, respectively, for LTP-kNN. Fig. 10.11 illustrates that AUC is highest, i.e., 1, which makes it the best feature-classifier combination.

Table 10.3 Classification performance measures for HF (with infarction) versus healthy with respect to different combinations of pattern features and classifiers.

Feature	Classifier	Sensitivity (%)	Specificity (%)	Accuracy (%)	AUC	F1-score
LBP	SVM	96	93	94	0.98	0.96
LBP	LDA	81	74	78.2	0.78	0.82
LBP	kNN	**99**	**100**	**99.1**	**0.99**	**0.99**
LBP	EBT	96	77	88.2	0.97	0.91
LTP	SVM	96	94.4	95.5	0.99	0.96
LTP	LDA	87	77	82.7	0.82	0.86
LTP	kNN	**100**	**100**	**100**	**1.00**	**1**
LTP	EBT	93	77	86.4	0.96	0.89
DoGLTP	SVM	90	98	92.7	0.96	0.94
DoGLTP	LDA	49	86	63.6	0.61	0.62
DoGLTP	kNN	**99**	**98**	**98.2**	**0.98**	**0.98**
DoGLTP	EBT	91	65	80.9	0.92	0.85
3DLTCoP	SVM	100	81	92.7	0.98	0.94
3DLTCoP	LDA	90	70	81.8	0.77	0.86
3DLTCoP	kNN	**94**	**98**	**95.5**	**0.96**	**0.96**
3DLTCoP	EBT	97	79	90.0	0.95	0.92

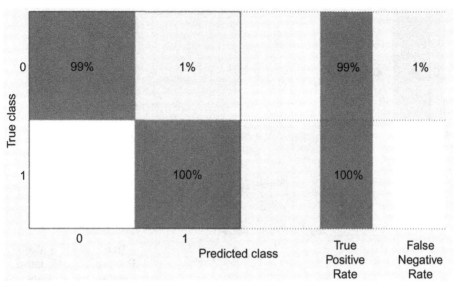

FIG. 10.8

Confusion matrix of LBP-kNN for HF (with infarction) versus healthy.

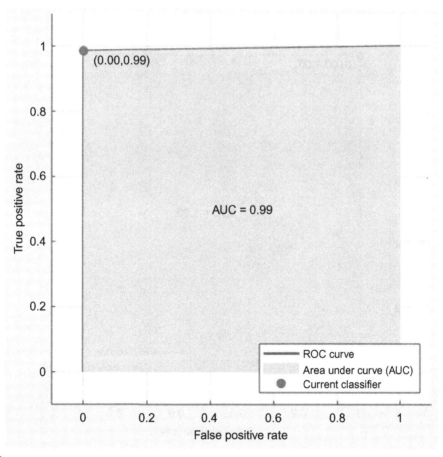

FIG. 10.9

ROC of LBP-kNN for HF (with infarction) versus healthy.

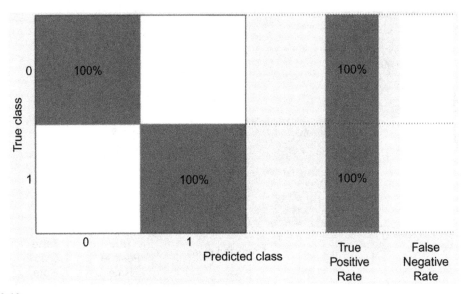

FIG. 10.10

Confusion matrix of LTP-kNN for HF (with infarction) versus healthy.

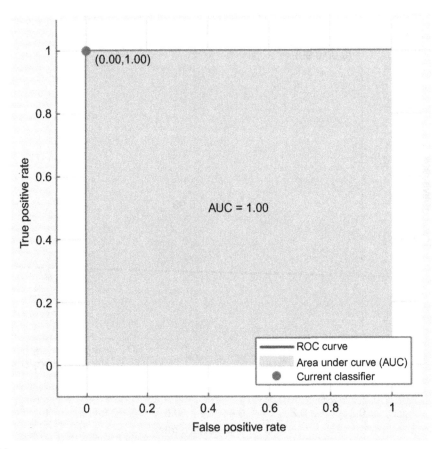

FIG. 10.11

ROC of LTP-kNN for HF (with infarction) versus healthy.

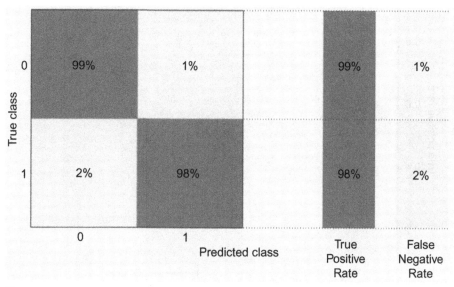

FIG. 10.12

Confusion matrix of DoGLTP-kNN for HF (with infarction) versus healthy.

From the confusion matrix of DOGLTP-kNN depicted in Fig. 10.12, it is figured out that TP, FN, FP, and TN values are 99%, 1%, 2%, and 98%, respectively, and AUC is 0.98, as observed from Fig. 10.13.

Figs. 10.14 and 11.15 indicate that the combination of 3DLTCoP feature with the kNN classifier has TP, FN, FP, and TN values of 94%, 6%, 2%, and 98%, respectively, and this combination achieves AUC of 0.96.

Table 10.4 is drawn corresponding to the classification of HF (without infarction) versus healthy pathologies. It is evident from the table that kNN classifier is performing the best among all classifiers under consideration by giving accuracy of 91%, 91%, 97%, and 87% for LBP, LTP, DoGLTP, and 3DLTCoP pattern features, respectively. The highest accuracy is obtained for the combination DoGLTP-kNN. In the following figures, confusion matrices and ROCs are shown for all the features with kNN as a classifier for the prediction of HF (without infarction) and healthy patients.

Fig. 10.16 illustrates that for LBP-kNN combination, TP, FN, FP, and TN values are 91%, 9%, 9%, and 91%, respectively. Also, from Fig. 10.17, it is observed that AUC is 0.91 for LBP-kNN.

It is clear from Figs. 10.18 and 11.19 that TP, FN, FP and TN values are 93%, 7%, 12% and 88%, respectively, for LTP-kNN and the observed AUC is 0.91.

TP, FN, FP, and TN values observed in Fig. 10.20 are 96%, 4%, 2%, and 98% respectively, for DoGLTP-kNN. Fig. 10.21 illustrates that kNN is achieving the best AUC of 0.97.

Figs. 10.22 and 11.23 show that TP, FN, FP and TN values are 84%, 16%, 9%, and 91%, respectively, for 3DLTCoP-kNN and AUC is 0.87.

Another observation from these two experiments is that although pattern features are performing very well, better classification performance is obtained for HF (with infarction) versus healthy prediction as compared to HF (without infarction) versus healthy.

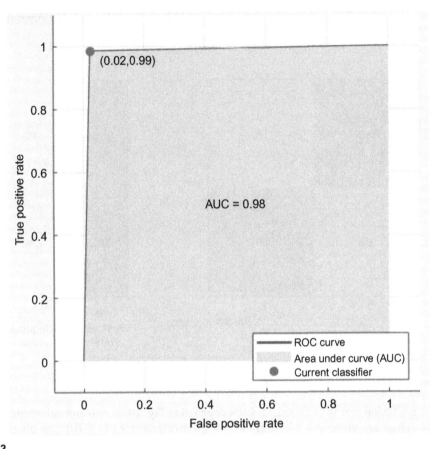

FIG. 10.13

ROC of DoGLTP-kNN for HF (with infarction) versus healthy.

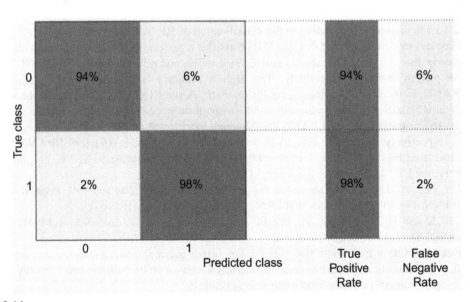

FIG. 10.14

Confusion matrix of 3DLTCoP-kNN for HF (with infarction) versus healthy.

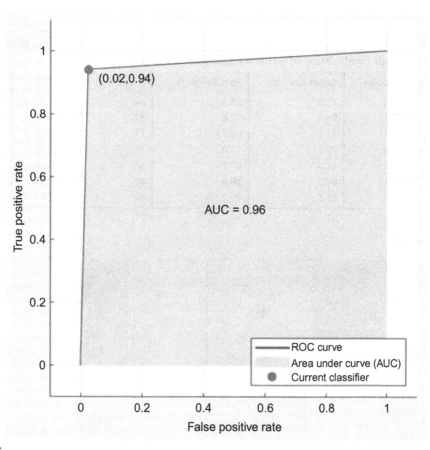

FIG. 10.15

ROC of 3DLTCoP-kNN for HF (with infarction) versus healthy.

Table 10.4 Classification performance measures for HF (without infarction) versus healthy with respect to different combination of pattern features and classifiers.

Feature	Classifier	Sensitivity (%)	Specificity (%)	Accuracy (%)	AUC	F1-score
LBP	SVM	89.4	83.7	87	0.92	0.89
LBP	LDA	75.4	74.4	75	0.75	0.77
LBP	kNN	**91.2**	**90.6**	**91**	**0.91**	**0.92**
LBP	EBT	87.7	67.4	79	0.88	0.83
LTP	SVM	82.4	86.0	84	0.92	0.85
LTP	LDA	80.7	74.4	78	0.78	0.81
LTP	kNN	**92.9**	**88.3**	**91**	**0.91**	**0.92**
LTP	EBT	87.7	72.0	81	0.89	0.84
DoGLTP	SVM	89.4	79.0	85	0.94	0.87

Continued

Table 10.4 Classification performance measures for HF (without infarction) versus healthy with respect to different combination of pattern features and classifiers—cont'd

Feature	Classifier	Sensitivity (%)	Specificity (%)	Accuracy (%)	AUC	F1-score
DoGLTP	LDA	45.6	88.3	64	0.73	0.59
DoGLTP	kNN	**96.4**	**97.6**	**97**	**0.97**	**0.97**
DoGLTP	EBT	87.7	62.7	77	0.9	0.81
3DLTCoP	SVM	89.4	72.0	82	0.93	0.85
3DLTCoP	LDA	61.4	62.7	62	0.66	0.65
3DLTCoP	kNN	**84.2**	**90.6**	**87**	**0.87**	**0.88**
3DLTCoP	EBT	91.2	69.7	82	0.94	0.85

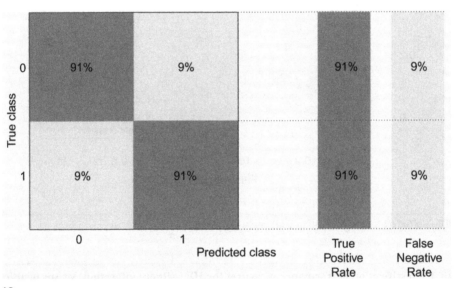

FIG. 10.16

Confusion matrix of LBP-kNN for HF (without infarction) versus healthy.

10.5 Conclusions

In this chapter, prediction of three classes HF (with infarction), HF (without infarction), and healthy is done by using combination of four different pattern features (LBP, LTP, DoGLTP, and 3DLTCoP) along with four different machine learning classifiers (SVM, LDA, kNN, and EBT). Pattern-based features capture fine details of the cine-MRI images by operating on the local neighborhoods. It helps to differentiate different pathologies. Experiments are conducted on benchmark dataset and classification

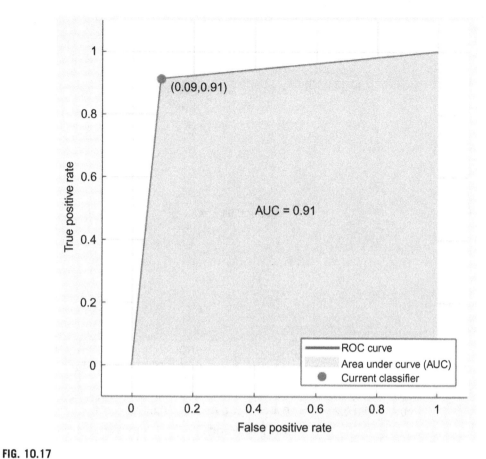

FIG. 10.17

ROC of LBP-kNN for HF (without infarction) versus healthy.

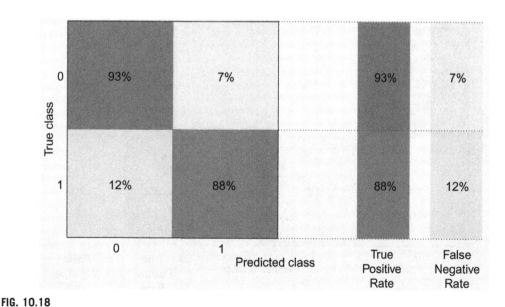

FIG. 10.18

Confusion matrix of LTP-kNN for HF (without infarction) versus healthy.

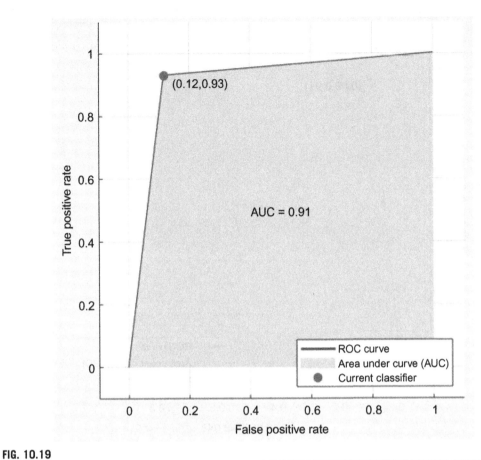

FIG. 10.19

ROC of LTP-kNN for HF (without infarction) versus healthy.

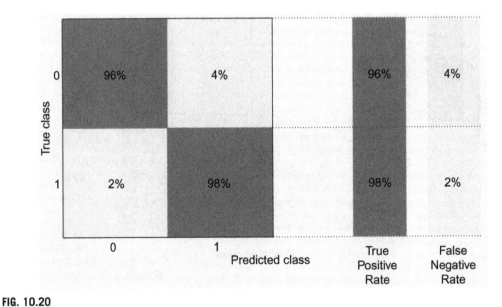

FIG. 10.20

Confusion matrix of DoGLTP-kNN for HF (without infarction) versus healthy.

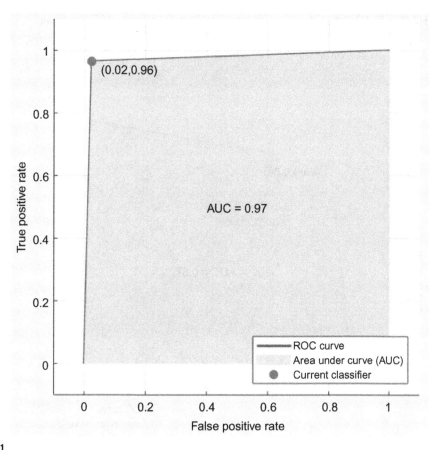

FIG. 10.21

ROC of DoGLTP-kNN for HF (without infarction) versus healthy.

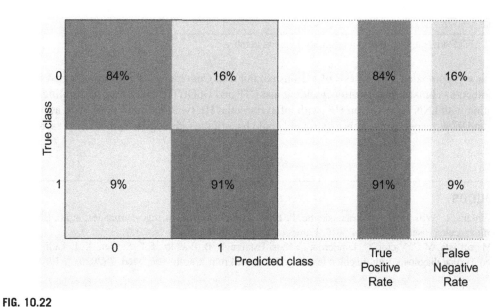

FIG. 10.22

Confusion matrix of 3DLTCoP-kNN for HF (without infarction) versus healthy.

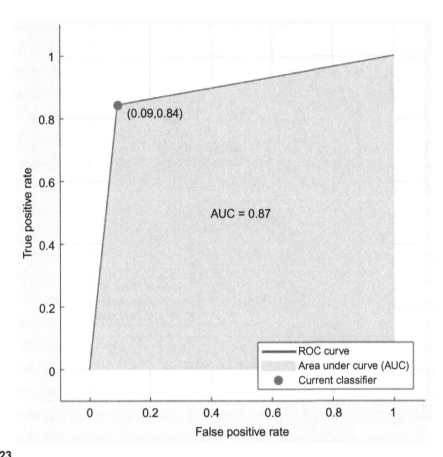

FIG. 10.23

ROC of 3DLTCoP-kNN for HF (without infarction) versus healthy.

performance is compared on the basis of various parameters. Convincing results are obtained in both the experiments of binary classification, yielding that LTP and DoGLTP features are performing best in combination with kNN classifier on HF (with infarction) and HF (without infarction), with accuracies of 100% and 97%, respectively. This experiment could benefit the radiologists with faster prescreening of HF.

References

[1] E. Wilkins, L. Wilson, K. Wickramasinghe, P. Bhatnagar, J. Leal, R. Luengo-Fernandez, et al., European Cardiovascular Disease Statistics 2017, European Heart Network, Brussels, 2017.
[2] C. Martin-Isla, M.C. Victor, C. Izquierdo, Z. Raisi-Estabragh, B. Baebler, E.P. Steffen, K. Lekadir, Image based cardiac diagnosis with machine learning: a review, Front. Cardiovasc. Med. 7 (2020) 1–19.

[3] G.T. Krishnamurthy, V.R. Bobba, E. Kingston, Radionuclide ejection fraction: a technique for quantitative analysis of motor function of the human gallbladder, Gastroenterology 80 (3) (1981) 482–490.

[4] National Clinical Guideline Centre (UK), Chronic Heart Failure: National Clinical Guideline for Diagnosis and Management in Primary and Secondary Care: Partial Update, National Clinical Guideline Centre, 2010, pp. 19–24.

[5] C.M. Kramer, J. Barkhausen, S.D. Flamm, R.J. Kim, E. Nagel, Standardized cardiovascular magnetic resonance (CMR) protocols 2013 update, J. Cardiovasc. Magn. Reson. 15 (91) (2013) 1–10.

[6] T. Ojala, M. Pietikainen, D. Harwood, A comparative study of texture measures with classification based on feature distributions, Pattern Recogn. 29 (1996) 51–59.

[7] X. Tan, B. Triggs, Enhanced local texture feature sets for face recognition under difficult lighting conditions, IEEE Trans. Image Process. 19 (6) (2010) 1635–1650.

[8] M. Agarwal, A. Singhal, DoG based local ternary pattern for image retrieval, in: 2019 International Conference on Signal Processing and Communication, 2019, pp. 1–4.

[9] S. Murala, Q.M.J. Wu, Local ternary co-occurrence patterns: a new feature descriptor for MRI and CT image retrieval, Neurocomputing 119 (2013) 399–412.

[10] M. Agarwal, A. Singhal, B. Lall, 3D local ternary co-occurrence patterns for natural, texture, face and bio medical image retrieval, Neurocomputing 313 (2018) 333–345.

[11] M. Agarwal, A. Singhal, B. Lall, Multi-channel local ternary pattern for content based image retrieval, Pattern. Anal. Applic. 22 (4) (2019) 1585–1596.

[12] S.R. Dubey, S.K. Singh, R.K. Singh, Local diagonal Extrema pattern: a new and efficient feature descriptor for CT image retrieval, IEEE Signal Process. Lett. 22 (9) (2015) 1215–1219.

[13] S. Murala, Q.M.J. Wu, Local mesh patterns versus local binary patterns: biomedical image indexing and retrieval, IEEE J. Biomed. Health Inform. 18 (3) (2014) 929–938.

[14] L. Sorensen, S.B. Shaker, M. de Bruijne, Quantitative analysis of pulmonary emphysema using local binary patterns, 300 IEEE Trans. Med. Imaging 29 (2) (2010) 559–569.

[15] S. Peng, D. Kim, S. Lee, M. Lim, Texture feature extraction on uniformity estimation for local brightness and structure in chest CT images, Comput. Biol. Med. 40 (2010) 931–942.

[16] P. Radau, Y. Lu, K. Connelly, G. Paul, A.J. Dick, G.A. Wright, Evaluation Framework for Algorithms Segmenting Short axis Cardiac MRI, MIDAS J. Cardiac MR Left Ventricle Segment. Challenge (2009) 1–7.

[17] K. Alfakih, S. Plein, H. Thiele, T. Jones, J.P. Ridgway, M.U. Sivananthan, Normal human left and right ventricular dimensions for MRI as assessed by turbo gradient echo and steady-state free precession imaging sequences, J. Magn. Reson. Imaging 17 (3) (2003) 323–329.

[18] B. Boser, I. Guyon, V. Vapnik, A training algorithm for optimal margin classifiers, in: 1992 Fifth Annual Workshop on Computational Learning Theory, 1992, pp. 144–152.

[19] R.A. Fisher, The use of multiple measurements in taxonomic problems, Ann. Eugenics 7 (2) (1936) 179–188.

[20] C.R. Rao, The utilization of multiple measurements in problems of biological classification, J. R. Stat. Soc. Ser. B Methodol. 10 (2) (1948) 159–203.

[21] T. Cover, P. Hart, Nearest neighbor pattern classification, IEEE Trans. Inf. Theory 13 (1) (2006) 21–27.

[22] L. Rokach, Ensemble-based classifiers, Artif. Intell. Rev. 33 (2010) 1–39.

[23] V. Kotu, B. Deshpande, Chapter 8—Model evaluation, in: Predictive Analytics and Data Mining, Concepts and Practice with Rapidminer, 2015, pp. 257–273.

Medical image fusion methods: Review and application in cardiac diagnosis

11

Kalpana Chauhan[a], Rajeev Kumar Chauhan[b], and Anju Saini[c]

Department of Electrical Engineering, Central University of Haryana, Mahendragarh, India[a] Department of Electrical Engineering, Dayalbagh Educational Institute, Agra, India[b] Department of Mathematics, Graphic Era University, Dehradun, India[c]

Chapter outline

11.1 Introduction

There are many imaging modalities available for diagnosing diseases, including echocardiography, magnetic resonance imaging (MRI), computed tomography (CT), ultrasound and magnetic resonance angiography (MRA), position emission tomography (PET), angiography, electrocardiogram (ECG), single-photon emission computed tomography (SPECT), and functional MRI (fMRI). Although these techniques work well enough, sometimes more valuable information is required or unwanted information needs to be removed. This is not possible using only a single modality. To obtain the relevant

Image Processing for Automated Diagnosis of Cardiac Diseases. https://doi.org/10.1016/B978-0-323-85064-3.00004-2

information, one medical image modality must be correlated to another. In addition, the manual method of integrating multiple medical imaging modalities is comprehensive, time consuming, expensive, prone to human error, and requires years of experience. The automated combination of multimodal medical images is possible by fusing the images and has thus become a main subject of research in medical image processing [1]. Fusion of images requires the incorporation of complementary knowledge present in multiple captured images into a single image with greater interpretative reliability and data quality. Photo fusion blends multiple source images using improved image processing tools unable to use a single fusion methodology for different applications.

11.1.1 Medical image fusion process

The process of medical image fusion involves several steps, the first and most important of which is registration. Some researchers have dealt with multi-channel type image registration for these issues. There are many techniques proposed for cardiac image registration. Legg et al. [2] extracted several features from input or reference images and then integrated these feature images into a regional, shared image registration dissimilarity measure. Staring et al. [3] adopted a k-nearest neighbor graph (KNNG) for the implementation of multifunctional mutual information (α-MI) to record cervical MRI data. Rivaz et al. [4] implemented the α-MI weighted self-similarity using local structural information to capture multiple images of features. In Ref. [5] an objective feature has been developed which relies on local structure autocorrelation (ALOST) for intra-image registration with signal fluctuations. In Ref. [6] multi-channel registration has been developed as a question of group-specific image registration, using the modality independent neighborhood descriptor (MIND) as the function images.

Selecting discriminative features that can create exact correlation in terms of anatomy between two images is important for these methods. To achieve good performance, most multi-channel image registrations use handcrafted technologies, such as multi-scale derivatives engineering. Handcrafted features usually require intense manual effort to develop the model to fit unique needs. Learning-based methods were developed to pick the best collection of features that can be tailored to the data at hand from a wide feature pool [7]. Additionally, deep learning can automatically and hierarchically learn from the data to effectively represent features. Shin et al. [8] applied stacked auto-encoders in MRI images to identify organs. Chmelik et al. [9] identified a convolutional neural network (CNN) with lesions in spinal 3D CT images. In Ref. [10] convolutionary stacked auto-encoder has been used to classify intrinsic representations of deep features for multi-channel image recording.

The second step of medical image fusion is feature extraction, which may be gray-level based (local binary pattern, gray level co-occurrence matrix (GLCM), Haralick texture features, grey level run length method (GLRLM) filter based (Gabor feature extraction, symbolic dynamic filtering, learning vector and quantization), and component-based analysis (principal component analysis (PCA), and Independent component analysis (ICA)). Image labels are annotations from experts in medicine, such as radiologists. Where imagery is the reference norm, such annotations may be considered ground reality. Choosing the right label for a given image AI framework involves a compromise between choosing the best distinguishing categories (i.e., standard vs. emerging) and clinically specific granularity (i.e., liver lesion subtype) according to the desired mission. The function of semantic image segmentation (medical) consists of classifying each pixel of an image (or only several) into an instance where each instance (or category) corresponds to a class. This role is part of the idea of understanding the environment or better describing an image's global meaning. Image segmentation can be used for image-guided interventions in the medical image analysis domain (Fig. 11.1).

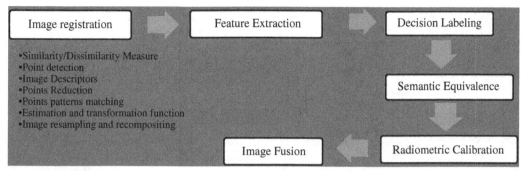

FIG. 11.1

Step of medical image fusion.

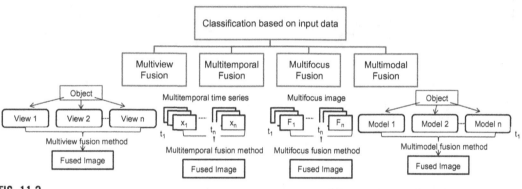

FIG. 11.2

Classification of image fusion methods based on the input data.

11.1.2 Classification of image fusion

Image fusion can be classified based on the purpose for which it is used, the input data, methods and techniques, and domain. Images can be fused from a single modality or multiple modalities. Multimodal imaging is used for fusing an image in various applications. It can be classified into the following: multi-view fusion, in which more than one view is taken from the same object with the same or different sensor; multitemporal fusion, in which different spatial time series are used for the fusion; multi-focus fusion, in which more than one image taken at different focus is used; and multimodal fusion, in which more than one modality is used to collect the images and the fusion method is applied after preprocessing of various data separately. Fig. 11.2 presents the categories of fusion imaging based on input data.

Fig. 11.3 presents the classification of fusion methods based on the domain. There are two main domains: spatial and transform. In spatial domain fusion, there is direct work on the pixels of the input image. In transform domain fusion, the image must be converted in the frequency domain before continuing further in the process.

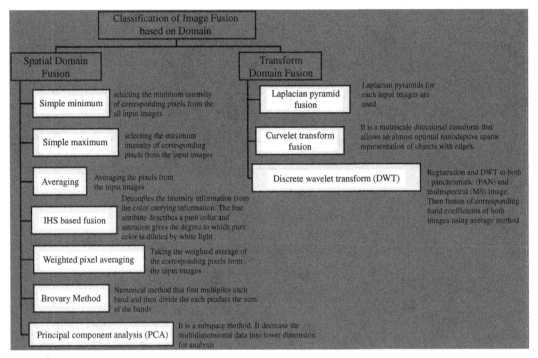

FIG. 11.3

Classification of image fusion methods based on domain.

There are many methods of **spatial domain** fusion. Some of them are **simple minimum** (used for low-brightness images), as they involve pixels with extremely low resolution. This method is expressed as:

$$
\begin{aligned}
&If\, I_1(i,j) \leq I_2(i,j) \\
&\quad I_F(i,j) = I_1(i,j) \\
&else\, I_F(i,j) = I_2(i,j)
\end{aligned}
\tag{11.1}
$$

where $I_1(i,j)$ and $I_1(i,j)$ are the input images and $I_F(i,j)$ is the fused image.

The **simple maximum** method works based on the selection of the highest pixel. The maximum intensity pixel is selected from the input image and used to create the fused image as:

$$
\begin{aligned}
&If\, I_1(i,j) \geq I_2(i,j) \\
&\quad I_F(i,j) = I_1(i,j) \\
&else\, I_F(i,j) = I_2(i,j)
\end{aligned}
\tag{11.2}
$$

Image averaging is the most used method of fusion based on arithmetic pixels, in which the fused image can be get by the pixel-by-pixel average of the input images. Images with high contrast are considered for simple averaging fusion.

$$
I_F = \frac{I_1(i,j) + I_2(i,j)}{2}
\tag{11.3}
$$

The fusion-based **intensity hue saturation (IHS)** technique transforms an image with RGB space into an IHS color space image. In the IHS space, the intensity band (I) is replaced by a high-resolution image and then converted back into the original RGB space along hue and saturation bands. This results in an IHS image fused in. HIS uses three bands [b] for fusion as follows:

$$
\begin{bmatrix} I \\ x_1 \\ x_1 \end{bmatrix} = \begin{bmatrix} \frac{1}{\sqrt{3}} & \frac{1}{\sqrt{3}} & \frac{1}{\sqrt{3}} \\ \frac{-1}{\sqrt{6}} & \frac{-1}{\sqrt{6}} & \frac{2}{\sqrt{6}} \\ \frac{-1}{\sqrt{2}} & \frac{1}{\sqrt{2}} & 0 \end{bmatrix} \begin{bmatrix} R \\ G \\ B \end{bmatrix}
$$

(11.4)

Hue is calculated as:

$$
H = \tan^{-1}\left(\frac{x_2}{x_1}\right)
$$

(11.5)

Saturation is calculated as:

$$
S = \sqrt{x_1^2 + x_2^2}
$$

(11.6)

The x_1 and x_2 are two values which comes in intermediate. The corresponding inverse transformation is defined as:

$$
x_1 = S\cos(H) \, \text{and} \, x_2 = S\sin(H)
$$

(11.7)

$$
\begin{bmatrix} R' \\ G' \\ B' \end{bmatrix} = \begin{bmatrix} \frac{1}{\sqrt{3}} & \frac{-1}{\sqrt{6}} & \frac{1}{\sqrt{2}} \\ \frac{1}{\sqrt{3}} & \frac{-1}{\sqrt{6}} & \frac{1}{\sqrt{2}} \\ \frac{1}{\sqrt{3}} & \frac{2}{\sqrt{6}} & 0 \end{bmatrix} \begin{bmatrix} I \\ x_1 \\ x_1 \end{bmatrix}
$$

(11.8)

The resulting fused picture is obtained via the **weighted average method** by taking the weighted average strength of the corresponding pixels from both the image to input, as follows:

$$
I_F(x, y) = \sum_{x=0}^{m} \sum_{y=0}^{n} WI_1(xy) + (1 - W)I_2(x, y)
$$

(11.9)

where W is the weight factor.

The **Brovey transform method** is the standard color transform fusion method and is used for multi-spectral color normalization RGB image display, high-resolution images, and maximum fusion. This method can sharpen the image while preserving the original image spectral information effect. Brovey transformation produces clear edges and contours of the fused image, helping to extract boundary features, textures, and ground feature information.

$$
\begin{aligned}
R &= r_1 \times (r/(r+g+b)) \times I_2^r \\
G &= g_1 \times (g/(r+g+b)) \times I_2^g \\
B &= b_1 \times (b/(r+g+b)) \times I_2^b
\end{aligned}
$$

(11.10)

where $r_1, r_2, g_1, g_2, b_1,$ and b_2 are the red, green, and blue coefficients of transformation of one image; r, g, and b are the red, green, and blue bands of the multi-spectral image; and I_2 is the brightness image with high spatial resolution.

Principal component analysis (PCA) is a sub-space approach that reduces the multidimensional data sets for analyzing lower dimensions. The weights for each source are determined in this method. The picture uses the own vector corresponding to the covariance matrix with the largest value of each source image. The vectors of two input images are $I_1 = \left[I_1{}^1, I_1{}^2, ...I_1{}^n\right]^T$ and $I_2 = \left[I_2{}^1, I_2{}^2, ...I_2{}^n\right]^T$, respectively. The mean values of I_1 and I_1 are as in Eqs. (12.11) and (12.12), respectively.

$$\mu_1 = \frac{1}{pq} \sum_{i=1}^{p,q} I_1^i \tag{11.11}$$

$$\mu_2 = \frac{1}{pq} \sum_{i=1}^{p,q} I_2^i \tag{11.12}$$

Covariance is calculated as follows:

$$\sum_{I_1, I_2} = \frac{1}{N} \sum_{i=1}^{p,q} \left(I_1^i - \mu_1\right) * \left(I_2^i - \mu_2\right) \tag{11.13}$$

where N is the complete image. The covariance matrix is:

$$M = \begin{bmatrix} \sum_{I_1, I_1} & \sum_{I_1, I_2} \\ \sum_{I_2, I_1} & \sum_{I_2, I_2} \end{bmatrix} \tag{11.14}$$

The eigenmatrix λ and eigenvector V (used to determine the fusion weights) can be calculated by separating M using eigenvalue dissociation. Fusion weights can be calculated as follows:

$$\alpha_1 = \frac{V(1, 1)}{\sum V(1)} \tag{11.15}$$

$$\alpha_2 = \frac{V(2, 1)}{\sum V(2)} \tag{11.16}$$

The fused image with PCA is generated as:

$$I_F = \alpha_1 * I_1 + \alpha_2 * I_2 \tag{11.17}$$

Transform domain methods include **Laplacian pyramid fusion**, curvelet transform fusion, and discrete wavelet transform (DWT). The concept of multi-resolution image representation is known as the Gaussian Laplacian pyramid [11, 12]. In this pyramid, an image is decomposed into a series of filtered component band-passed images, each representing a different band of spatial frequency. Transformation of a pyramid resolution decomposes an image at various scales into multiple resolutions. The pyramid's lowest level has the same scale as the input image and includes the details with higher resolution. The Laplacian pyramid is developed from the Gaussian pyramid, which is a series of images in which every image is formed by passing the previous image through a low-pass filter, reducing sample resolution as well as density. Usually, the reduction is by a factor of 2 such that in both spatial densities every successive representation of the image is halved. It is described as:

$$[t]I_R = \sum_{m=-2}^{2} \sum_{n=-2}^{2} w(m, n)I_{k-1}(2i+m, 2j+n) \tag{11.18}$$

where $k = 1, \ldots, N$; $I_0 = I$ is the original image, and w is the filter kernel.

This is the REDUCE process for 2D images and is expressed as:

$$I_k = \text{REDUCE}\,(I_{k-1}) \tag{11.19}$$

The Laplacian pyramid is produced by subtracting from the Gaussian pyramid two successive layers and thus forming a band-pass filter. There is need to expand the image because the sizes of Gaussian pyramid levels are different.

$$M_k = I_k - \text{EXPAND}\,(I_{k+1}) \tag{11.20}$$

The Laplacian pyramid must have one lower level than the Gaussian one. Gaussian pyramids are generated in our implementation, with three levels above the base image. Very small-sized output images can be obtained, which may not be useful at higher levels, and the edge effects of successive convolutions with the generating kernel will become detrimental. Fusion with less than four pyramid levels can be performed, but the algorithm's ability to differentiate features from various size images. The fused image is then implemented using a decision mechanism for selection of features for each level of the pyramid. This can be done using several combination modes, such as selection or averaging.

Curvelet transform is essentially a nonadaptive method that represents the images with multi-scale details. It is a generalized version of the Fourier transform. The generalization which is rendered consists of two. Additional features include [13, 14] spatial frequency and position of the objects in the images. The curvelet method is typically used in the domain when the objects contain the minimum scale length within the images. Examples include text and geometric figures.

Curvelet functions are characterized by parameters of size, orientation, and translation, the values of which are described in an adaptable way. There are four steps to the curvelet transformation [10]:

11.1.2.1 Sub-band decomposition
The image is divided into individual frequencies of the sub-bands. It is given as:

$$La(P_0L, \Delta_1L, \Delta_2L, K) \tag{11.21}$$

where L is the image matrix, P_0 is the low-pass filter, and $\Delta_1, \Delta_2, \ldots$ are the band-pass filters.

11.1.2.2 Smooth partitioning
The grid of a dyadic square is given as:

$$Q_{(s, k_1, k_2)} = \left[\frac{k_1}{2}, \frac{k_1+1}{2}\right] \times \left[\frac{k_2}{2}, \frac{k_2+1}{2}\right] \in Q_s \tag{11.22}$$

where Q_s is all the dyadic squares of the grid. Now, let us consider w (size $2^{-s} \times 2^{-s}$) to be a smooth windowing function. w_Q is a displacement of w localized near Q. Multiplying $\Delta_s f$ with w_Q ($\forall Q \in Q_s$) results in a function of smooth dissection into the squares. w is the positive function.

11.1.2.3 Re-normalization

Re-normalization is the process of centering every dyadic square into a unit square. For each Q, the operator G_Q is defined as:

$$(G_Q f)(y_1, y_2) = 2^s f(2^s y_1 - k_1, 2^s y_2 - k_2) \tag{11.23}$$

Each square can be renormalized as:

$$g_Q = T_Q^{-1} h_Q \tag{11.24}$$

11.1.2.4 Ridgelet analysis

In the orthonormal ridgelet analysis, each grid is analyzed. This means that if there is an entity (say, f) representing the boundary, once the filtering is done in each sub-band, each phase yields a sub-band of fine scale, which should have a border that is thickened by a factor of 2^{-2s} (Fig. 11.4).

Wavelets are used to locate time frequencies and perform multi-scale and multi-resolution operations. **Discrete wavelet transform (DWT)** converts a single time signal into a discrete representation of the wavelet. It transforms a series of inputs $i_0, i_1, \ldots, i_m$ into one series of high-pass wavelet coefficients and one series of low-pass wavelet coefficients (of length $n/2$ each) given by:

$$H_j = \sum_{m=0}^{k-1} i_{2j-m} s_m(z)$$
$$L_j = \sum_{m=0}^{k-1} i_{2j-m} t_m(z) \tag{11.25}$$

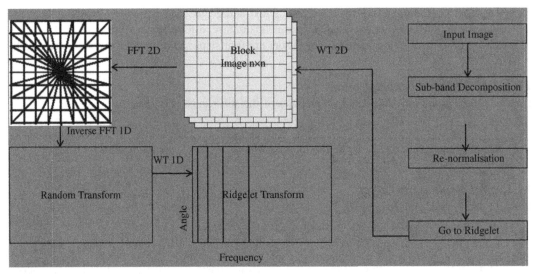

FIG. 11.4

Curvelet transform block diagram.

where $s_m(z)$ and $t_m(z)$ are the wavelet filters, k is the length of the filter, and $j = 0, ..., [n/2]-1$. In practice, such a transformation will be implemented on the low-pass sequence recursively until the desired number of iterations is reached.

The classification given in Fig. 11.5 is based on the different techniques or methods adopted for the fusion. Fuzzy logic is implemented either as a transformer function or as an image fusion decision operator [15–31]. Artificial neural networks (ANNs) are a potential method with its processing features. The ANN models involve a set of input data to define the set of parameters, which are known as weights. The neural network models can predict, interpret, and infer data information without complex mathematical solutions. This makes ANNs a good solution for image fusion since the nature of difference between the images is subject to change every time. Neural networks are having the training property so to follow the improvements, which are required in many medical image fusion applications, such as classification, feature generation problems, data fusion, breast cancer detection, microcalcification diagnosis. On the other hand ANN is having property in terms of training methods. Some of examples of these are neural-fuzzy, wavelet-neural network, fuzzy-genetic-neural network-rough set and SVM-ANN-GMM [32–34]. The feasibility of combinations of all the various imaging modalities is technically difficult to prove, as these methods are biased towards the nature of the images chosen for testing, which may vary greatly from one imaging condition to another.

The primary principle used in wavelet image fusion [35–39] is removal of detailed features from one image and insertion of those features into another image. The detailed information in images is typically high frequency, so wavelets will be able to choose frequencies in both time and space. The resulting fused image has the "right" features, meaning it has features from both images, which improves image quality. Many versions are available for injection, the easiest of which is substitution. Many mathematical injection models exist, such as basic addition process and aggregator as well as more complex mathematical models. Regardless of the models used, the image resolution remains the same before and after the fusion, for functional purposes. Moreover, the reference image resolution enforces the minimum number of multiple levels of decomposition, so a high-resolution image will need more levels of decomposition than a low-resolution image. Contourlet transform is a new,

Computation Intelligence	Wavelet based fusion methods	Contourlet transform	Curvelet transform	Combined approach
• Duzzy Logic	• Traditional Wavelet transform	• Traditional Cotourlet transform	• Wrapping based curvelet	• Wavelet and Neuro-fuzzy
• Neuro Fuzzy			• Simple curvelet	• Wavelet and Contourlet
• Genetic Algorithm	• Lifting Wavelet transform	• Non-Sampled Contourlet		
	• Discrete Wavelet transform			• Multiwavelet and curvelet

FIG. 11.5

Classification of image fusion methods based on the techniques.

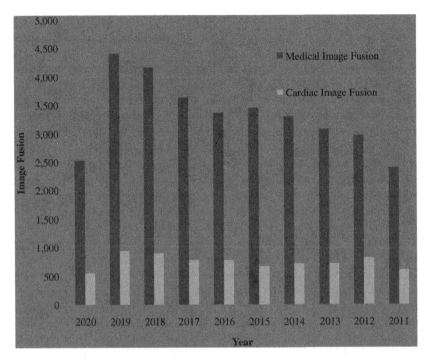

FIG. 11.6

Classification of image fusion methods based on the input data.

anisotropic image analysis method that has strong directional selectivity. Thus, it can accurately represent the information on the image edges in different scale and direction frequency sub-bands. In recent years, several fusion algorithms based on contourlet transformation have been proposed. Contourlet transform is a discrete image multi-scale and multi-directional structure. The multi-scale analysis and the multidirectional analysis are split serially in the transform. The Laplacian pyramid is first used to catch point discontinuities and then to link point discontinuities into linear structures using a directional filter bank (DFB). A double filter bank structure is the combination of a directional filter bank and Laplacian pyramid. The contourlet transform base function has twenty-one directions and a versatile ratio of length to width [40, 41].

Fig. 11.6 presents a year-wise analysis of medical image fusion methods along with the evolution in cardiac image fusion. The data from 2020 is current up to June.

11.2 Cardiac image fusion

Echocardiography imaging is a common technique for acquiring cardiac images, but it suffers from glitches, high noise, and a small field of view. The images generated are distorted by an implied distortion called "speckle," which comes from the disruptive and coherent summation of ultrasonic echoes. Speckle distortion can be characterized as multiplicative noise in that it results in a granular look,

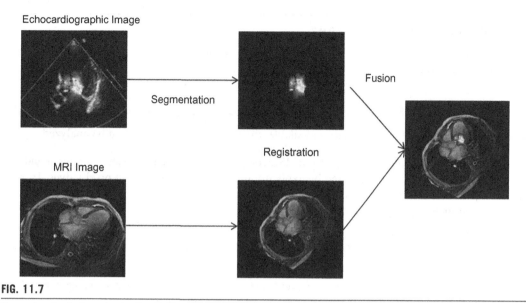

FIG. 11.7

Example of a fusion of an echocardiography and MRI image [42].

degraded image contrast, and decreased ability to find information within the images. A strategy for coping with these constraints is to use multiple images, choosing the best part from each image to produce a better-quality image. Some essential criteria for the fusion process should be considered, including: (1) the fusion process should hold all the related details stored in the source images, (2) the fusion process should not create any deviations or anomalies that could lead to a misdiagnosis, and (3) the fusion process should cover irrelevant characteristics and noise. Medical imaging fusion aims to merge information from the same view of different images (or various imaging sensors) to create a fused image that provides the best possible data. The fused image is a better picture compared to any one of the input images. Attempts at segmenting and tracking heart ventricles using echocardiography is problematic because of low-contract images, resulting in speckle noise, restricted field of view, and missed anatomy. The simplest medical image fusion is to assume pixel by pixel the mean of the input gray-level images. Using this technique on echocardiographic images [42–48], however, creates some undesired effects and reduces the contrast between features. One more thing can be done to fuse different modality images. Fig. 11.7 shows an example of cardiac image fusion using echocardiography and MRI images. Echocardiography shows poor resolution compared to MRI; it also suffers from a poor field of view. MRI also has drawbacks, particularly in calculating hemodynamic behaviors and alterations in real time. The fusion of a Doppler color picture and MRI image is a potential solution to these problems. Such limitations are expressed simultaneously in the moving heart by both anatomical and hemodynamic details. It is possible with the aid of computer-based technologies. Fuse images using various approaches, like ultrasonic and MRI [49–51] proposed a method for fusion of 3D ultrasonic images with MRI in the liver.

11.3 Analysis of fused images

The sections that follow present two cases of analyzing fused images: (1) when the reference image is available and (2) when the reference image is not available.

11.3.1 Analysis of the quality of the fused image when reference image is available

In the case where the reference image is available, the following parameters can be analyzed.

(a) *Root Mean Square Error (RMSE)*: RMSE compares the difference between the input and the fused images. It is widely used by explicitly measuring the variance in pixel values. If the RMSE value is zero, the fused image is near the input image. RMSE is a good predictor for fused image spectral efficiency.

$$RMSE = \sqrt{\frac{1}{mn}\sum_{i=1}^{m}\sum_{j=1}^{n}(I_I(i,j) - I_F(i,j))^2} \tag{11.26}$$

where $I_I(i,j)$ and $I_F(i,j)$ are the input and fused images, respectively, and mn is the image size. The small value of RMSE shows the good quality of the fused image.

(b) *Signal-to-Noise Ratio (SNR)*: SNR is used for calculating the ratio of fused image information to noise. The larger value shows the similarity of both the reference and fused images.

$$SNR = 10\log_{10}\left(\frac{\sum_{i=1}^{m}\sum_{j=1}^{n}(I_I(i,j))^2}{\sum_{i=1}^{m}\sum_{j=1}^{n}(I_I(i,j) - I_F(i,j))^2}\right) \tag{11.27}$$

(c) *Peak Signal-to-Noise Ratio (PSNR)*: PSNR is the most used parameter and it is measured by finding gray levels in the image separated by the input image and the fused image. The fused and input images are identical when the value is small. A larger value indicates a greater merger.

$$PSNR = 10\log_{10}\left(\frac{mn}{RMSE^2}\right) \tag{11.28}$$

(d) *Spectral Angle Mapper (SAM)*: SAM is the measure of angle of spectrum between pixel, reference signal vector, and fused image. It is executed either in degrees or in radians. This is achieved on a pixel-by-pixel basis. Its zero value shows lack of spectral distortion.

$$\alpha = \cos^{-1}\left(\frac{\sum_{k=1}^{N}A_kB_k}{\sqrt{\sum_{k=1}^{N}A_kA_k}\sqrt{\sum_{k=1}^{N}B_kB_k}}\right) \tag{11.29}$$

where N is the number of bands (i.e., dimension of the spectral space), $A = (A_1, A_2, A_3, ..., A_N)$ re the multispectral and $B = (B_1, B_2, B_3, ..., B_N)$ are merged signals. Both are of the same wavelength. For each individual pixel, the measured α is the spectral angle that ranges from 0 to 90.

(e) *Mean Bias (MB)*: MB is the difference between reference image mean and fused image mean. The required value is zero, which implies consistency between the input image and the fused image. Mean value refers to gray pixels in an image.

$$MB = \frac{I_{Imean} - I_{Fmean}}{I_{mean}} \tag{11.30}$$

(f) *Percentage fit error (PFE)*: PFE measures the difference between the input image pixels and fused image pixels. The zero value shows that the input and the fused images are identical. As the value increases from zero, variation occurs between the two images.

$$PFE = \frac{norm(I_I - I_F)}{norm(I_I)} \times 100 \tag{11.31}$$

(g) *Correlation coefficient (CC)*: CC is used to measure the spectral similarity between the input image and the fused image. CC value equal or near to +1 shows that the input image and the fused image are the same. The variation in both images occurs as this value decreases to less than +1.

$$CC = \frac{2C_{IF}}{C_I + C_F} \tag{11.32}$$

where C_{IF} is input and fused image and C_I and C_F are for the input and fused images, respectively.

(h) *Mutual information (MI)*: MI is used for calculating the image strength similarity between the fused image and the reference image. The larger MI value shows the better quality of the fused image.

$$MI = \sum_{i=1}^{m} \sum_{j=1}^{m} h I_I I_F(i,j) \log_2 \left(\frac{h I_I I_F(i,j)}{h I_I(i,j) h I_F(i,j)} \right) \tag{11.33}$$

where h indicates the intensity component.

(i) *Universal quality index (UQI)*: UQI is used to measure the sum of transformation from the reference image into a fused image of the related data. This metric scale is -1 to 1. A value of 1 shows similarity between the reference and fused images.

$$UQI = \frac{4\sigma_{I_I I_F} \left(\mu_{I_I} + \mu_{I_F} \right)}{(\sigma^2 I_I + \sigma^2 I_F)(\mu^2 I_I + \mu^2 I_F)} \tag{11.34}$$

where σ and μ are the standard deviation and means, respectively.

(j) *Structural similarity index measure (SSIM)*: SSIM is the parameter that compares the pixel intensity patterns between the input and the fused images locally. The scale ranges from -1 to 1. A value of 1 shows that input image and the fused image are identical.

$$SSIM = \frac{\left(2\mu_{I_I}\mu_{I_F} + C_1 \right)\left(2\sigma_{I_I I_F} + C_2 \right)}{(\mu^2 I_I + \mu^2 I_F + C_1)(\sigma^2 I_I + \sigma^2 I_F + C_2)} \tag{11.35}$$

(k) *Quality Index (QI)*: QI is used to model loss of correlation, distortion of luminance, and distortion of contrast. The *QI* scale is -1 to 1. A value of 1 indicates that the reference and fused images are identical.

$$UQI = \frac{4\sigma_{I_I I_F} \overline{I_I} \overline{I_F}}{\left(\sigma_{I_I}^2 + \sigma_{I_F}^2\right)\left(\left(\overline{I_I}\right)^2 + \left(\overline{I_F}\right)^2\right)} \tag{11.36}$$

11.3.2 Analysis of the quality of the fused image when reference image is not available

(a) *Standard deviation (σ)*: This is measure of the contrast in the image; in this case, this image is a fused image. The large value of σ shows a high-contrast fused image, and it is a required feature.

$$\sigma = \sqrt{\frac{1}{mn-1}\sum_{i=1}^{m}\sum_{j=1}^{n}\left(I_I(i,j) - \overline{I_I}\right)^2} \tag{11.37}$$

(b) *Entropy (H)*: This shows the information content in the output image. If the value of entropy is greater, that is, there is more information in the fused image. It does not test fused image and source image similarity. The larger the entropy value, the better the effects of the fusion.

$$H = -\sum_{k=1}^{z} P_k \log(P_k) \tag{11.38}$$

where P_k is the probability of the occurrence of k.

(c) *Spatial frequency (SF)*: SF is determined by measuring the frequency of the fused image in the row and in the column. The larger SF value suggests the input image and the fused image are identical.

$$SF = \sqrt{r_f^2 + c_f^2} \tag{11.39}$$

where r_f is the row frequency and c_f is the column frequency.

(d) *Fusion mutual information (FMI)*: FMI is used for calculating the dependencies in the input image and the fused image.

$$FMI = MI_{I_{t_1}}I_F + MI_{I_{t_2}}I_F \tag{11.40}$$

(e) *Fusion quality index (FQI)*: FQI is used to measure the fused image quality index. The range of this metric is between 0 and 1. A value of 1 means the fused image contains all the input image information.

$$FMI = MI_{I_{t_1}}I_F + MI_{I_{t_2}}I_F \tag{11.41}$$

11.4 **Results and analysis of fusion**

We tested the performance of fusion techniques on echocardiographic images taken at different times but from the same view.

11.4.1 **Visual analysis**

Here, we chose DWT for changing the echocardiographic images from the spatial domain to the frequency domain using two-level decomposition. The original image is divided into horizontal and vertical outlines, showing DWT first order, and then the image is projected to four levels: LL1, LH1, HL1, and HH1 (Figs. 11.8 and 12.9).

For analysis purposes, the two echocardiography images I_1 and I_2 were taken at slightly different time instants. First, we took the DWT of both images separately to decompose them into high- and low-frequency levels. After, we fused both image components and applied inverse discrete wavelet transform (IDWT) to obtain the final fused image.

Fig. 11.10 shows the decomposition of the echocardiographic images using DWT and their fusion. We used IDWT to obtain the fused image. Fig. 11.11 shows the results obtained with PCA fusion.

In the first column there are two echocardiographic images to be fused. The second row is the 2-level DWT. In Fig. 11.11, the first column contains the original images to be fused, and the second column contains the principal component images. We fused the components to obtain the final fused image.

11.4.2 **Statistical analysis**

We performed a statistical or qualitative analysis to check the quality of the fused image obtained from different methods (as discussed Section 11.2). Table 11.1 lists the parameter values obtained with different fusion techniques.

Table 11.1 presents the performance of simple averaging, maximum, minimum, PCA, and DWT methods based on the qualitative analysis of RMSE, PSNR, Entropy, Mean, and standard deviation (SD). Fig. 11.12A shows that DWT has the minimum value of RMSE (i.e., less error), whereas the minimum method has the maximum RMSE. Ranking of methods from high to low error values is: Minimum > Average > Maximum > PCA > DWT. Fig. 11.12B shows that the minimum method has

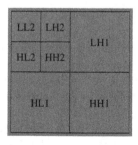

FIG. 11.8

Wavelet decomposition on levels 2.

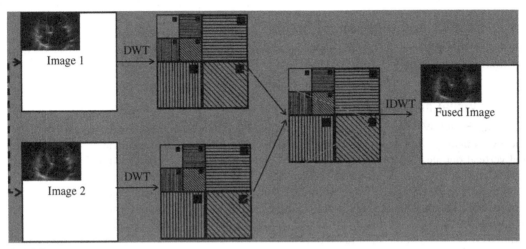

FIG. 11.9

Wavelet decomposition on levels 2.

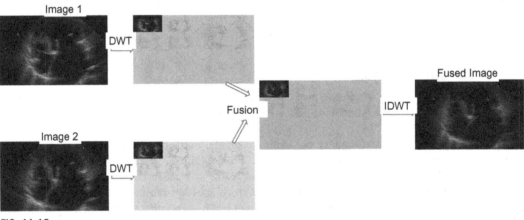

FIG. 11.10

DWT (on level 2) fusion.

the lowest value of PSNR, whereas the maximum method has the highest value of PSNR. Ranking of methods from high to low PSNR is: Maximum > DWT > Average > PCA > Minimum. Fig. 11.12C shows that the minimum method has the lowest value of entropy, whereas the DWT has the highest value of entropy. Ranking of methods from high to low entropy is: DWT > Maximum > Average > PCA > Minimum. Fig. 11.12D shows that the minimum method has the lowest value of mean, whereas DWT has the highest value of mean. Ranking of methods from high to low mean is: DWT > Maximum > Average > PCA > Minimum. Fig. 11.12E shows that the minimum method has the

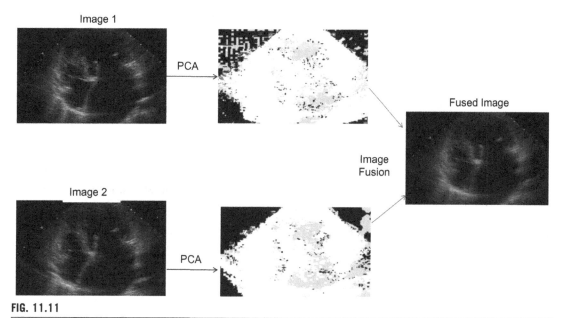

FIG. 11.11

PCA-based fusion of echocardiography images.

lowest value of SD, whereas PCA has the highest value of SD. Ranking of methods from high to low mean is: PCA > DWT > Maximum > Average > Minimum.

It is clear from these results that the maximum method and DWT result in less error and images with good contrast and features. Therefore, these methods are best suited for echocardiographic images. PCA may be used, but the minimum method should be avoided due to low performance.

11.5 Conclusions

There are many challenges in cardiac imaging. Advances in imaging technology and methods have resulted in increased accuracy and reliability, however, there are still some problems. The big issue is that different modality images have different features and limitations. The organ and tissue type to be imaged also affect the parameters. Image fusion is helpful for maintaining consistency

Table 11.1 Comparison of RMSE, PSNR, Entropy, Mean, and SD.					
Methods	**RMSE**	**PSNR**	**Entropy**	**Mean**	**SD**
Average	41.0026	36.0229	5.3732	30.0987	33.5467
Maximum	26.5436	44.9456	6.8765	57.0984	60.7654
Minimum	73.6749	30.4828	1.9967	4.5432	17.5578
PCA	45.9876	31.8765	3.9764	41.8766	81.4532
DWT	23.7543	43.5434	7.6549	58.9874	60.6543

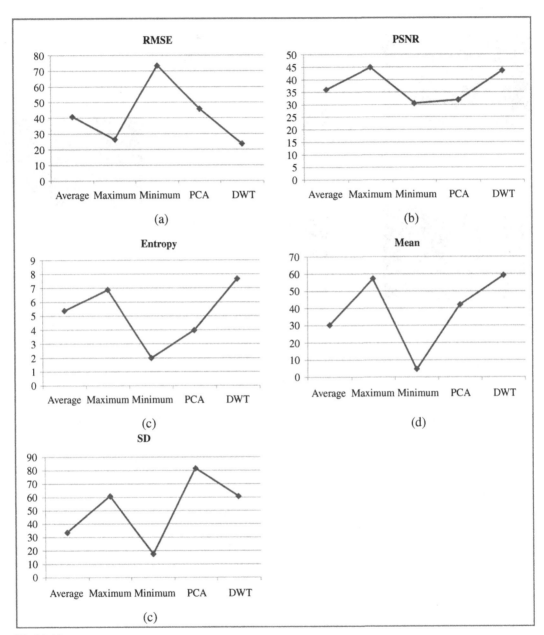

FIG. 11.12

Statistical analysis of the methods based on the quantitative parameters.

and enhancing image quality. The development and growth of a wide variety of imaging modalities has made it possible for medical image fusion to be used in clinical applications. Although substantial progress has been made in the field, the implementation of general fusion algorithms is constrained by realistic clinical consequences placed by medical experts based on particular requirements. Some algorithms that can improve cardiac image quality include discrete wavelet transform (DWT), principle component analysis (PCA), and maximum model. It is also found that the combination of one or more methods of image fusion is effective in cardiac image analysis.

References

[1] B. Solaiman, R. Debon, F. Pipelier, J.M. Cauvin, C. Roux, Information fusion: application to data and model fusion for ultrasound image segmentation, IEEE TBME 46 (10) (1999) 1171–1175.

[2] P.A. Legg, P.L. Rosin, D. Marshall, J.E. Morgan, A robust solution to multi-modal image registration by combining mutual information with multi-scale derivatives, in: G.-Z. Yang, D. Hawkes, D. Rueckert, A. Noble, C. Taylor (Eds.), Medical Image Computing and Computer-Assisted Intervention-MICCAI 2009. LNCS, 5761, Springer, Berlin, Heidelberg, 2009, pp. 616–623, https://doi.org/10.1007/978-3-642-04268-3_76.

[3] M. Staring, U.A.V.D. Heide, S. Klein, M.A. Viergever, J.P.W. Pluim, Registration of cervical MRI using multifeature mutual information, IEEE Trans. Med. Imaging 28 (9) (2009) 1412–1421.

[4] H. Rivaz, Z. Karimaghaloo, D.L. Collins, Self-similarity weighted mutual information: a new nonrigid image registration metric, Med. Image Anal. 18 (2) (2014) 343–358.

[5] Z. Li, D. Mahapatra, J.A.W. Tielbeek, J. Stoker, L.J. Vliet, F.M. Vos, Image registration based on autocorrelation of local structure, IEEE Trans. Med. Imaging 35 (1) (2016) 63–75.

[6] J.M. Guyader, W. Huizinga, V. Fortunati, D.H.J. Poot, J.F. Veenland, M.M. Paulides, W.J. Niessen, S. Klein, Groupwise multichannel image registration, IEEE J. Biomed. Health Inform. 23 (3) (2019) 1171–1180.

[7] Y. Bengio, A. Courville, P. Vincent, Representation learning: a review and new perspectives, IEEE Trans. Pattern Anal. Mach. Intell. 35 (8) (2013) 1798–1828.

[8] H. Shin, M.R. Orton, D.J. Collins, S.J. Doran, M.O. Leach, Stacked autoencoders for unsupervised feature learning and multiple organ detection in a pilot study using 4D patient data, IEEE Trans. Pattern Anal. Mach. Intell. 35 (8) (2013) 1930–1943.

[9] J. Chmelik, R. Jakubicek, P. Walek, J. Jan, P. Ourednicek, L. Lambert, E. Amadori, G. GavellieChmelik, et al., Deep convolutional neural network-based segmentation and classification of difficult to define metastatic spinal lesions in 3D CT data, Med. Image Anal. 49 (2018) 76–88.

[10] G.R. Wu, M.J. Kim, Q. Wang, B.C. Munsell, D.G. Shen, Scalable high-performance image registration framework by unsupervised deep feature representations learning, IEEE Trans. Biomed. Eng. 63 (7) (2016) 505–1516.

[11] E.H. Adelson, C.H. Anderson, J.R. Bergen, P.J. Burt, J.M. Ogden, Pyramid methods in image processing, RCA Eng. 29 (6) (1984) 33–41.

[12] P.J. Burt, E.H. Adelson, The laplacian parymidas a compact image code, IEEE Trans. Commun. 31 (4) (1983) 532–540.

[13] J.L. King, M.P. Lowe, N.A. Crowder, Contrast adaptation is spatial frequency specific in mouse primary visual cortex, Neuroscience 310 (2015) 198–205.

[14] J.M. Pérez, M. Jofre, P. Martínez, M.A. Yáñez, V. Catalan, V. Pruneri, An image cytometer based on angular spatial frequency processing and its validation for rapid detection and quantification of waterborne microorganisms, Analyst 22 (2015).

[15] W. Dou, S. Ruan, Y. Chen, D. Bloyet, J.M. Constans, A framework of fuzzy information fusion for the segmentation of brain tumor tissues on MR images, Image Vis. Comput. 25 (2) (2007) 164–171.

[16] R. Wasserman, R. Acharya, C. Sibata, K. Shin, A data fusion approach to tumor delineation, in: Proceedings: IEEE International Conference on Image Processing, Vol. 2, 1995, pp. 476–479.

[17] V. Barra, J.Y. Boire, Automatic segmentation of subcortical brain structures in MR images using information fusion, IEEE Trans. Med. Imaging 20 (7) (2001) 549–558.

[18] C.H. Huang, J.D. Lee, Improving MMI with enhanced-FCM for the fusion of brain MR and SPECT images, in: Proceedings 17th IEEE International Conference on Pattern Recognition, vol. 3, 2004, pp. 562–565.

[19] A. Villeger, L. Ouchchane, J.J. Lemaire, J.Y. Boire, Data fusion and fuzzy spatial relationships for locating deep brain stimulation targets in magnetic resonance images, in: J. Blanc-Talon, W. Philips, D. Popescu, P. Scheunders (Eds.), Advanced Concepts for Intelligent Vision Systems. ACIVS, Lecture Notes in Computer Science, vol. 4179, Springer, Berlin, Heidelberg, 2006, https://doi.org/10.1007/11864349_83.

[20] W. Dou, S. Ruan, Q. Liao, D. Bloyet, J.M. Constans, Y. Chen, Fuzzy information fusion scheme used to segment brain tumor from MR images, in: V. Di Gesú, F. Masulli, A. Petrosino (Eds.), Fuzzy Logic and Applications. WILF, Lecture Notes in Computer Science, vol. 2955, Springer, Berlin, Heidelberg, 2003, https://doi.org/10.1007/10983652_26.

[21] X. Tai, W. Song, An improved approach based on FCM using feature fusion for medical image retrieval, in: Proceedings IEEE Fourth International Conference on Fuzzy Systems and Knowledge Discovery (FSKD 2007), vol. 2, 2007, pp. 336–342.

[22] W. Song, T. Hua, Analytic implementation for medical image retrieval based on FCM using feature fusion with relevance feedback, in: Proceedings IEEE Second International Bioinformatics and Biomedical Engineering, 2008, pp. 2590–2595.

[23] Y. Na, H. Lu, Y. Zhang, Content analysis based medical images fusion with fuzzy inference, in: Proceedings IEEE Fifth International Conference on Fuzzy Systems and Knowledge Discovery, vol. 3, 2008, pp. 37–41.

[24] A. Das, M. Bhattacharya, Evolutionary algorithm based automated medical image fusion technique: comparative study with fuzzy fusion approach, in: Proceedings IEEE World Congress on Nature and Biologically Inspired Computing, 2009, pp. 269–274.

[25] A. Assareh, L.G. Volkert, Fuzzy rule base classifier fusion for protein mass spectra based ovarian cancer diagnosis, in: Proceedings IEEE Symposium on Computational Intelligence in Bioinformatics and Computational Biology, 2009, pp. 193–199.

[26] F. Masulli, S. Mitra, Natural computing methods in bioinformatics: a survey, Inform. Fusion 10 (3) (2009) 211–216.

[27] J.K. Avor, T. Sarkodie-Gyan, An approach to sensor fusion in medical robots, in: Proceedings IEEE International Conference on Rehabilitation Robotics, 2009, pp. 818–822.

[28] G.N. Brock, W.D. Beavis, L.S. Kubatko, Fuzzy logic and related methods as a screening tool for detecting gene regulatory networks, Inform. Fusion 10 (3) (2009) 250–259.

[29] R.K. De, A. Ghosh, Linguistic recognition system for identification of some possible genes mediating the development of lung adenocarcinoma, Inform. Fusion 10 (3) (2009) 260–269.

[30] J. Teng, S. Wang, J. Zhang, X. Wang, Fusion algorithm of medical images based on fuzzy logic, in: Proceedings IEEE Seventh International Conference on Fuzzy Systems and Knowledge Discovery, vol. 2, 2010, pp. 546–550.

[31] M. Bhattacharya, A. Das, Multimodality medical image registration and fusion techniques using mutual information and genetic algorithm-based approaches, in: H. Arabnia, Q.N. Tran (Eds.), Software Tools and Algorithms for Biological Systems, Advances in Experimental Medicine and Biology, vol. 696, Springer, New York, NY, 2011, pp. 441–449, https://doi.org/10.1007/978-1-4419-7046-6_44.

[32] Y.P. Wang, J.W. Dang, Q. Li, S. Li, Multimodal medical image fusion using fuzzy radial basis function neural networks, in: Proceedings IEEE International Conference on Wavelet Analysis and Pattern Recognition, vol. 2, 2007, pp. 778–782.

[33] J. Teng, S. Wang, J. Zhang, X. Wang, Neuro-fuzzy logic based fusion algorithm of medical images, in: Proceedings IEEE 3rd International Congress on Image and Signal Processing, vol. 4, 2010, pp. 1552–1556.

[34] D. Lederman, B. Zheng, X. Wang, X.H. Wang, D. Gur, Improving breast cancer risk stratification using resonance-frequency electrical impedance spectroscopy through fusion of multiple classifiers, Ann. Biomed. Eng. 39 (3) (2011) 931–945.

[35] W. Xue-jun, M. Ying, A medical image fusion algorithm based on lifting wavelet transform, in: Proceeding IEEE International Conference on Artificial Intelligence and Computational Intelligence, vol. 3, 2010, pp. 474–476.

[36] S. Rajkumar, S. Kavitha, Redundancy discrete wavelet transform and contourlet transform for multimodality medical image fusion with quantitative analysis, in: Proceedings IEEE 3rdInternational Conference on Emerging Trends in Engineering and Technology, 2010, pp. 134–139.

[37] C. Kavitha, C. Chellamuthu, Multimodal medical image fusion based on integer wavelet transform and - neuro-fuzzy, in: Proceedings International Conference on Signal and Image Processing, 2010, pp. 296–300.

[38] S. Vekkot, Wavelet based medical image fusion using filter masks, in: P. Vadakkepat, et al. (Eds.), Trends in Intelligent Robotics. FIRA, Communications in Computer and Information Science, vol. 103, Springer, Berlin, Heidelberg, 2010, pp. 298–305, https://doi.org/10.1007/978-3-642-15810-0_38.

[39] M.N. Do, M. Vetterli, The contourlet transform: an efficient directional multiresolution image representation, IEEE Trans. Image Process. 14 (12) (2005) 2091–2106.

[40] X.B. Qu, J.W. Yan, G.D. Yang, Multifocus image fusion method of sharp frequency localized Contourlet transform domain based on sum-modified-Laplacian, Opt. Precis. Eng. 17 (5) (2009) 1203–1212.

[41] M.A. Cimmino, W. Grassi, What is new in ultrasound and magnetic resonance imaging for musculoskeletal disorders? Best Pract. Res. Clin. Rheumatol. 22 (2008) 1141–1148.

[42] K. Saini, M.L. Dewal, M.K. Rohit, A fast region-based active contour model for boundary detection of echocardiographic images, J. Digit. Imaging 25 (2) (2012) 271–278.

[43] K. Chauhan, R.K. Chauhan, A. Saini, Enhancement and de-speckling of echocardiographic images, in: N. Dey, A.S. Ashour, F. Shi, V.E. Balas (Eds.), Soft Computing Based Medical Image Analysis, Elsevier, 2018, pp. 61–79.

[44] K. Chauhan, R.K. Chauhan, Boundary detection of echocardiographic images during mitral regurgitation, in: M. Hassaballah, K. Hosny (Eds.), Recent Advances in Computer Vision: Theories and Applications, vol. 804, Springer, 2018, pp. 281–303, https://doi.org/10.1007/978-3-030-03000-1_12.

[45] M.L. Dewal, K. Saini, M.K. Rohit, Assessment of mitral regurgitation severity with intensity based region growing, Int. J. Hybrid Inform. Technol. 8 (6) (2015) 45–56.

[46] K. Saini, M.L. Dewal, M.K. Rohit, Level set based on new signed pressure force function for echocardiographic image segmentation, Int. J. Innov. Appl. Stud. 3 (2) (2013) 560–569.

[47] K. Saini, M.L. Dewal, M.K. Rohit, Statistical analysis of speckle noise reduction techniques for echocardiographic images, in: Proceedings International Conference on Methods and Models in Science and Technology, vol. 1414, 2011, pp. 95–99.

[48] K. Saini, M.L. Dewal, M.K. Rohit, A modified hybrid filter for echocardiographic image noise removal, Int. J. Signal Process., Image Process. Pattern Recogn. 5 (2) (2012) 61–72.

[49] B.C. Porter, D.J. Rubens, J.G. Strang, J. Smith, S. Totterman, K.J. Parker, Three-dimensional registration and fusion of ultrasound and MRI using major vessels as fiducial markers, IEEE Trans. Med. Imaging 20 (4) (2001) 354–359.

[50] K. Rajpoot, J.A. Noble, V. Grau, C. Szigielski, H. Becher, Multiview RT3D echocardigraphy image fusion, in: N. Ayache, H. Delingette, M. Sermesant (Eds.), Functional Imaging and Modeling of the Hear. FIMH, Lecture Notes in Computer Science, vol. 5528, Springer, Berlin, Heidelberg, 2009, pp. 134–143, https://doi.org/10.1007/978-3-642-01932-6_6_15.

[51] C. Wang, M. Chen, J.M. Zhao, Y. Liu, Fusion of color Doppler and magnetic resonance images of the heart, J. Digit. Imaging 24 (6) (2011) 1024–1030.

Index

Note: Page numbers followed by *f* indicate figures, and *t* indicate tables.

Cardiac magnetic resonance (CMR) imaging *(Continued)*
  multimodal cardiac image analysis, 43–46
    automatic anatomical landmark localization in, 45–46
    edge-maps for, 45
    imaging artifacts in cardiac 3D-US images, 44, 44*f*
    limited through-plane resolution and imaging artifacts in, 43, 44*f*
    multi-modal imaging data, 45
    semi-automatic segmentation methods, 45
    super-resolution with convolutional neural networks, 46
  multimodal cardiac image registration, 57–60
    evaluation of image registration algorithms, 60
    image similarity criteria in, 58–60, 59*f*
    transformation models and optimization techniques, 58
  planes, 41
  respiratory motion, 39–40
  super-resolution in, 54–56, 55*f*
    regression models for image super-resolution, 56, 57*f*
    variational inverse methods, 56
  and ultrasound image segmentation, 50–54, 50*f*
    anatomical priors in cardiac segmentation, 53–54, 54*f*
    energy minimization methods, 50–51
    Gaussian mixture modeling (GMM), 51–52, 51*f*
    multiatlas segmentation methods, 52–53, 52*f*
Cardiac output, 7, 41–42
Cardiac-resynchronization therapy (CRT), 140
Cardiac segmentation, anatomical priors in, 53–54, 54*f*
Cardiac simulation, challenges and recent advances in, 141
Cardiac systole, 37
Cardiac ultrasound imaging, 42, 42–43*f*
Cardiomyopathy, 5
Cardiovascular disease (CVD), 50, 134, 139–140
Chest X-ray, 7
Cine cardiac magnetic resonance imaging, 40–41, 40*f*
City block distance, 127
Classification, 102
  of images process, 106–107
CNN. *See* Convolutional neural networks (CNN)
Color Doppler echocardiography, 7, 16*f*
Color flow Doppler echocardiography, 13
Component-based analysis, 196
Computed tomography (CT), 22, 25, 195–196
Computer-aided detection (CAD) system, 101
Computer-aided diagnosis (CAD), 100
Computer-aided image analysis techniques, 54–55
Computer-based image retrieval (CBIR), 101
Computer-based medical image analysis, 100–101
Computer vision methods, 101
Confusion matrix, 180, 181*f*, 183–186*f*, 188–191*f*
Congenital heart abnormality, 6
Content-based image retrieval (CBIR), 117–118, 119*f*
Continuous methods, 58
Continuous wave (CW) Doppler, 13, 13*f*

Continuous wavelet transform (CWT), 121
Contourlet transform, 203–204
Contour recognition, 107
Conventional contour-based segmentation techniques, 158
Convolutional neural networks (CNN), 62–64, 63*f*, 71*f*
  anatomical priors in, 70
  cardiac MR image super-resolution with, 46
  for image registration methods, 25–27, 27*f*, 31
  learning anatomical shape priors with, 46
  in medical imaging, 66–68, 67*f*
Coronary artery disease (CAD), 4
Coronavirus. *See* COVID-19
Correlation, 102
Correlation coefficient (CC), 207
Covariance, 200
COVID-19
  cardiovascular disease and, 141–145
  cardiovascular manifestations of, 144–145
    organization implications, 145
    potential long-term consequences, 144
  investigation approaches for, 143–144
    contagious contemplation, 143–144
Cross-validation strategy, 111–112
CT. *See* Computed tomography (CT)
CT X-ray-based registration, 29, 30*f*
Curve evolution, 158, 160, 163, 164*f*
Curvelet transform fusion, 200–201, 202*f*
CVD. *See* Cardiovascular disease (CVD)

D

Daubechies wavelet transform, 118, 122–123
Decision forests (DF), 60–62
  in medical imaging, 65–66, 66*t*
Decision tree (DT)
  methods, 105
  model, 60–62, 61–62*f*
Deep learning (DL), 134–136
Deep learning neural networks (DNNs), 25–27
Deepmind applications, 106
Deformable model, 157–158
Denoising process, 78–79
Despeckling filters, 77–81
Detail preserving anisotropic diffusion (DPAD), 77–78
Diagnostic and Statistical Manual of Mental Disorders (DSM), 108–109
Dice coefficient, 166–167, 169*f*
Dice similarity coefficient (DSC), 181
Difference of Gaussian LTP (DoGLTP), 174–176
Digital Imaging and Communication (DICOM), 100–101
Directed gradient back-propagation technique, 70
Directional filter bank (DFB), 203–204
Discrete methods, 58
Discrete wavelet transform (DWT), 120–121, 121*f*, 200–203

Printed in the United States
by Baker & Taylor Publisher Services